TEN

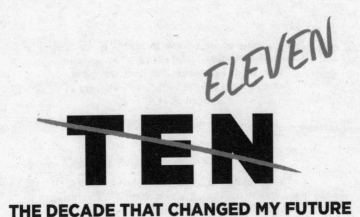

~~TEN~~ *ELEVEN*

THE DECADE THAT CHANGED MY FUTURE

RYLAN

SEVEN DIALS

First published in Great Britain in 2022 by Seven Dials,
this paperback edition published in 2023 by Seven Dials,
an imprint of The Orion Publishing Group Ltd
Carmelite House, 50 Victoria Embankment
London EC4Y 0DZ

An Hachette UK Company

1 3 5 7 9 10 8 6 4 2

A CIP catalogue record for this book is
available from the British Library.

ISBN (Mass Market Paperback) 978 1 3996 0392 8
ISBN (eBook) 978 1 3996 0393 5
ISBN (Audio) 978 1 3996 0394 2

Typeset by Born Group
Printed and bound in Great Britain by Clays Ltd, Elcograf S.p.A.

www.orionbooks.co.uk

This book is dedicated to my family, blood and chosen ones. I wouldn't be here today without you all. Genuinely. Love you all. Thank you, Ross x

Contents

I find re-reading this book is difficult. Especially the first chapter. Because it was a time in my life I don't *want* to remember. However, it's quite crazy, the difference a year can make. Today, looking back on everything that happened and where I was twelve months ago, it makes me so proud – of how far I've come; of how I deal with both life's challenges and opportunities. And it confirmed for me that, now, for the first time in eleven years, my main focus is looking after me. And that's no bad thing.

I feel like I'm in a really good place. During my darkest times in 2021, I remember everyone saying to me, you can never be truly comfortable with someone else until you're comfortable with yourself. Well, over the past year, I've definitely learned how to be at peace with myself. I feel very confident and content with who I am. It's my time now. I'm ready to get back out there and start my new life.

But to understand the significance of where I am today, you've got to appreciate the highs and the lows of the journey before.

INTRODUCTION

This book celebrates ten years of me being in this crazy industry. We all know I should have lasted ten minutes, so how I've lasted ten years, I'll never know.

I've learned so many lessons, especially in the last year, but it's been a helluva journey. That's the whole point of this book. It's about how the world has changed, what fame means today and how people deal with it. Is the idea of fame the same as it was back then? Is it what I expected it to be? Is it what I wanted? It's a different perspective on reality TV, modern celebrity and twenty-first-century *real* life for me, Rylan. And actually it's a lot of reflecting, looking back and thinking about what I said, thought, and felt when I first started out – and well, do I still stand by it? Recently, I got my first book out, *The Life of Rylan*, which I wrote eight years ago. As I flicked through it, I kept thinking, 'How and why on earth did I write *that*? Did I really think that? Does it still make sense? If I do feel differently about certain aspects of my life, then *why* do I feel different?'

This book goes some way to answering those questions. It's also about how *everything* can just change overnight. And it did. Things did change. Some for the better, some for the worse. Now, after a decade of being in your homes on TV and in your ears on the radio, it's time to share. This is the decade that changed my future.

1

1

THE MORNING
THAT CHANGED
EVERYTHING

I woke up and I knew I had to say it . . .

When some people wake up and have the urge for change, they maybe go and get their barnet all shaved off, or get it dyed blue. Or decide to get their bottom bits waxed. Others might bin the Corn Flakes and get into Special K, or Frosties – or fuck it, go the whole hog and start making their own granola. But, you know me, I've never exactly been one to do anything by halves. I mean, look what happened the first time I had my teeth done! What can I say? I just have to push things that little bit further. Genuinely, I don't know what made me do it, but in March 2021, three days before I was due to commentate on the first *Eurovision* semi-final, I woke up one morning and decided to tell my now ex that I had cheated on him, years ago. I'm not sure why it was that time, or that day I had to do it. But I did.

That morning he woke up and I just came out with it. Like word vomit. 'I cheated on you. But it was years ago. And I just have to tell you.'

There, I said it. And that was that. It was out.

It wasn't that there was a threat of it coming out in the press or that I was worried that he might find out, not in the slightest. There was none of that. And if I hadn't said anything to him, to this day I'd probably still be bobbing along in my married life. Something hit me. Guilt, I suppose. Just deep delayed guilt about what I had stupidly done. It had been on my mind, building inside me for days and was actually making me feel physically ill. As I say, I don't know why it was right then or how I'd managed to keep it in for all that time. But that morning, like a *Rentaghost* escapee, the thoughts took over and it was out, never to be forgotten or hidden.

I have no excuses for what I did way back then, but I had my reasons. I think for many years I had felt a bit like an imposter. That nothing I was doing was right or not quite good enough. There were times when people told me this, and so confirmed my own self-doubts. And you know, when it's those closest to you giving you this feedback, of course you take it to heart. Similarly, someone loving me this way was all I had ever wanted and now I'd found it.

Yet why did everyone around me seem to be less convinced?

The reality is that over the course of my relationship I had started to feel wrong: I felt I was wrong for being successful, wrong for being me. Everyone around me could see it, literally everyone.

'You shouldn't feel like that.'

'Why are you doing that?'

'You know that's not normal, right?'

But you know me, I know best. How could anyone tell me that the relationship wasn't right?

He was my partner. Someone I loved. They couldn't say anything, because I would have always taken his side. Like I had in the past.

He left. Told me it was over and that was that. You're not surprised? I get that. But I couldn't believe it. For some stupid reason I thought he would understand what had happened. Maybe see it as a wake-up call? A moment for reflection? I think I thought we could have it all out, talk it all through. Truth and reconciliation, tears and hugs, hearts on sleeves. This would be the part of the film where we got closer, not further apart. All that. But no. Naïve? Probably. I was devastated; so devastated, and I couldn't comprehend what was unfolding. Why had I told him? Why had I cheated in the first place? I loved him, always have done. But he left.

And I couldn't rewind, or even press pause.

A few days passed and I made the decision not to work as I was ill with worry. A few messages were exchanged; insults too. Understandably, maybe, but still deeply hurtful. He had made his mind up. After eight years, all of the good times and everything we had built together was over. He was adamant. It wasn't up for discussion. I couldn't see beyond the realisation that I was alone, and the feeling that I ALONE had single-handedly ruined my life, the world that I'd created around him, for him, for us. I'd completely destroyed all of it – for nothing. The feeling began to worsen and turn dark. I couldn't eat, couldn't sleep, couldn't talk, nothing. I couldn't watch TV or listen to music. I just couldn't do it. I felt like I was having a stroke, or worse. I stopped working completely. It's hard to go to work when everything is foggy and dark.

Mental health is a strange thing. I've always been so empathetic towards people who suffer badly from depression and anxiety. But like, shit, did people really feel that bad that they couldn't get out of bed? Don't get me wrong, I've had tough periods, especially in 2013 right after *The X Factor* and when I came out of the *Celebrity Big Brother* house. There were times when my agoraphobia overwhelmed me, and I physically just couldn't go anywhere on my own. But I kept going. Someone went with me in the cab, I got onto the stage, and I completed the *X Factor* live tour. And I'd kept going ever since. But now it was happening to me. And it was really, really hard to deal with. It literally hit me round the face like a baseball bat and left me fucked up. I was mentally unwell and completely unstable. I wasn't able to be reasonable any more. I was obsessive and unable to speak. I made stories in my head about what might and what could happen, and endless, looping 'if onlys' and 'maybes'.

I couldn't bear to be in the house we had lived in together. Everything reminded me of him. So I moved in with my mum – yes, old Linda. She's always been there for me. But it wasn't like we was curled up under a blanket together with a tub of Ben & Jerry's, watching *Steel Magnolias* and crying about how shit life and men are. The actual fact was that I was sitting in her dressing gown, alone, in the front room with the blinds down, refusing to talk. Well, not refusing to exactly, but incapable of it. If you've never felt like that, it's hard to describe, but it was almost as if I was just trying to shut down. I would go to bed and pray I wouldn't wake up. I know that sounds so awful. But I just thought if I die in my sleep, it won't be my fault. I was numb; as if my mouth had stopped working. And then when I did start talking, I talked with a slur, everything was slowed down, and I had a stammer, the words just weren't connecting in my brain and at the same time everything hurt. Like an ache in my head that was so, so bad, but not like a normal physical pain. It was like someone was holding my head in this numb grip. It was there the whole time, an endless, incessant, pure mental agony. There'd be a few blissful seconds when I first woke up in the morning and it wouldn't be there. Then BANG. I was gone again, a million dreadful things swirling about my head, but actually it was filled with emptiness, which makes zero sense. Even if I could logically see that something was a positive course of action, I could not find any route that would get me there. I remember racking my brain and I could not make any good connections. I shut my eyes and it was like a dot-to-dot map and I had to join the lines but I just couldn't do it. Because everything would always go back to the fact that my marriage was over.

This is not meant to be a WOE IS ME, POOR RYLAN! BOO HOO HOO story btw. This is just to explain about being caught completely off guard and not being able to cope – which happens to so many people. We can be walking along, and bang: there you are on the floor without the ability – or no, the *desire* – to stand up. Call that a lesson learned. (Hello publisher, see, I'm following a pattern here . . .)

With no further communication between me and my ex, no chance of apologies, no chance of explaining, I went into self-blame. I started spiralling down, down, down, majorly catastrophising. In my confused and upset mind, the bad outweighed everything. Maybe I deserved it? Maybe this was the right way for me to be treated? Maybe I was supposed to feel like this? I'd told him in order to punish myself. I'd told him because I didn't deserve to be happy. I was a useless lump of shit. This misery was all I was worth. Everyone would hate me. I'd never work again because I couldn't watch the telly or listen to music. Nothing made sense. It all just felt like the end. That was it. It was over. My life was over.

And repeat. Repeat. Repeat. For weeks.

I had to disappear. I couldn't bear the thought of seeing anyone. I hid in my mum's house and never left – I couldn't: my body wouldn't let me. Mum was worried and getting increasingly unwell, trying to feed me and look after me, but there was nothing she could do. All she and anyone around me could say was, 'Why did you tell him? Why the fuck would you tell him that?' And my only response was: because I just had to. I had too much respect for our relationship not to.

I sounded crazy, fucked in the head, who in their right mind does what I did and then TELLS their partner? It made no sense. And that one question is what turned my head into a ticking time bomb. I thought there was no recovery from this. I thought I would never get over the loss of him, that I would never get better and no one around me seemed to understand. They kept saying, 'We love you,' but in truth I didn't care because at that moment, I only wanted HIM to love me. The way he had, and the way I loved him. HE was my family. I knew the others would be there, but I didn't care about that. I know this will be hard for them to read, but the point is, I was not living in reality: I was living in the reality I had obsessively created in my head, and I'm not just talking about while I was in this state, but the reality I had created for years.

And for the first time in my THIRTY-TWO years, I felt I couldn't carry on no more. 'What's the point?' I thought. I'd lost what I thought was everything, the one thing I always wanted. A man I loved. A family of my own. And now it was gone. And so I tried to end it.

I won't go into detail as I don't think it's fair on my mum, but thank God I was unsuccessful. That's when I knew I had to go away. Mum has her own life – admittedly mainly spent down at Lakeside in the M&S café – but I wasn't safe to be on my own at her house. And more importantly, I knew she was getting increasingly ill from worrying about me. I could hear her outside the door, checking what I was doing, wondering whether it was OK to offer me tea or one of her trifles again, even though she had only just asked me five minutes before. I sat her down and told her I wasn't safe and I needed to be locked up. I said, 'I can't do it any more.' She didn't know what to say. I could see in her eyes that she couldn't believe what was happening to her baby. She called my big brother Jamie and my managers and they arranged for me to go to a mental health hospital where they knew I would be well looked after. I'm all too aware of how lucky I was that I could go to a private place, which is a privilege most don't have and I understand the pain it must cause to other families of loved ones who go through similar mental health crises and just can't get the help they so urgently need.

It was all such a blur. I remember getting in the car with my brother to go to the hospital and all I could think of was, 'I hope I'll have the opportunity there to finish it.' That way my mum wouldn't be the person to find me. That was the only thought running through my mind. I would receive nasty, insulting messages, and they all hit the right spots. Nothing anyone could say or do could be as hard as I was being on myself. I'd let this happen. That's how I felt, wrong, disgusting and dirty.

When we got to the hospital, I was taken to my room. A white, cell-like room, small with a shower room attached. The first thing I noticed was that every wall was curved, smooth, no edges. Even the shower head was a strange shape, and I know why, because I'd already thought of how I could end it. I was made to unpack my suitcase that Mum had got ready for me. The first thing to go was the belt from my dressing gown. I just remember sitting on the bed, sobbing while the suitcase inventory was completed. Then Jamie had to leave and I was left alone. I spent just over a week in there.

In the meantime, for my husband, life and work was business as usual. But for me, I was literally grieving, only he wasn't actually dead. And, again, I know that sounds awful. It would be easier if someone had died because you know it's finite. That's it. That's the end. And you have to deal with it in a certain way. But when he walked away from our marriage, I was left with the same feeling of grief, but he was walking up

11

and down the road twenty minutes away. How does someone just disappear like that out of your life? And then their whole family? And what has been your life for nearly ten years, all of a sudden it's like it never happened, but it *did*. I couldn't understand how he could just carry on, like our world hadn't just been blown to smithereens. It confused me. I was so ill. It hurt, but again in my head I felt I deserved it all, for what I had done. It was summer, apparently really hot. I didn't see any of it. For three months, I was back at my mum's house, laid up, hiding from the world. Cut off in my own head from everyone and everything. I had another spell of bad thoughts and had to go back to the hospital for another week. It was hell. I just laid there daily, thinking about how I'd ruined my life. I just wanted it all to end.

When I was let out again, I tried to slowly move back to my house, at first just for a few hours at a time during the day. I needed to try to make some steps towards feeling normal again. It still didn't feel right; I wasn't behaving normally, I still couldn't speak properly. I needed the pain to go away – it was killing me, literally. I started to drink. Heavily. I've NEVER in my life been a heavy drinker. Most times when I'm out, in the time it takes people to neck several vats, I'm still on my first. Now it was the only way I knew to stop the thoughts, stop the pain of my life falling down around me. It got bad. Really bad. It makes me feel sick just thinking about it.

One day, when I knew my husband was on holiday abroad, I was so intoxicated, I messaged him constantly, apologising, wishing he would come back. The following day when I sobered up I had a vague memory of him saying he would cut his holiday short and come back to see me and we could talk. Was I right? Was I making this up? I messaged him; he said he would see me at the house for an hour the following

Sunday afternoon. I couldn't believe it. I felt like I'd struck gold. I stopped drinking and prepared myself to see him. Sunday came and I waited. And waited. He turned up an hour late, with a car full of alcohol, snacks and England flags. It was the men's Euros final. I'd forgot. We spoke for a bit. He seemed disinterested and guarded but I'd expected that. Then he left with his snacks and beer to go and watch football with the rest of his family and friends, and no doubt party the night away. I felt sick: I should be there – this ain't right – but I understood why I wasn't. My mum came and picked me up and I went back to hers. To sit and think like I had done for months. But the sheer thought of knowing he was close by instantly made me feel better. Maybe he was the drug I needed and craved so much. The man I loved. That's how it felt. I couldn't wait to see him again.

I felt like a kid waiting for Santa to arrive and every time he replied to a message, I was elated. They were always cold and never loving but they were something. He agreed to see me again one evening at the house. I just sat in silence waiting for him, like a dog pining at the window wondering when he would eventually arrive. But when he came he was cold, distant. But again, I felt I deserved it. We saw each other sporadically after that, then for about two weeks we made a go of it and he moved back in. Some type of normality resumed. I say 'some type' because it still didn't feel normal, but it did feel the most normal I'd felt in months. Things were looking good; at least we were back together in the house and I thought we would try to work through our problems.

I went back to work. I presented my BBC Radio 2 show (on which MUCH more later, and I promise that's a MUCH JOLLIER story, trust me, guys). I tried to pretend everything was OK, but deep down I knew something wasn't right. My mind started working overdrive. I started to think of all the times I'd doubted in previous years. Then it came, the night when I knew for sure that things weren't going to work out. I confronted him about some of our issues. He got angry. I drank and drank until I fell asleep. Some hours later I woke up to find him walking out of the front door with his suitcases. No conversation. He just got into his car and drove off. I couldn't fucking believe it. I'd answered every fucking question, told him everything, and now he cuts and runs away and I'm the one who's left with questions? Bullshit, mate. I called him, no answer. I called his brothers but they wouldn't tell me where he was. I drove around looking for him. I couldn't find him. The following morning I messaged him. He replied saying, 'It's over.'

NO YOU FUCKING DON'T, I thought. I need clarity. I need my mind clear.

The tearful reconciliation never came, and that was the last time I saw him. I've never seen him since.

It still keeps playing on my mind why he didn't want to work to fix what we had. Well, unfortunately/fortunately, I found my answers. I won't go into any more detail about what happened. I can't bear to, and I don't want to. Even after all this, I'm not that person, but we both know the truth. And THAT is all that matters to me. I could be that person that writes it all down, that shows you all the dirty laundry, but over the last ten years I've never done that. And as awful as this time has been for me, and for the family, I'm not gonna start now. I know I did the right thing and I can live my life guilt free. I think a part of me can't live a lie. I mean, I can play up to the character that I am in the game that is work, if you like, but ultimately, when it comes to my personal life, I just can't do that.

It's only now, all these months on, that I can sit here and go, 'You know what? In a really fucked-up way I'm glad I've been through what I've been through because I know I will never let myself feel like that again.' I would never, ever let anyone else get as ill as I was either, especially if I could have stopped it before it got as bad as it did. But the best thing to come out of it? NOW I know why I told him. NOW I know why I decided that morning to wake up and (supposedly) ruin my entire perfect life with a bombshell. I didn't, in fact. Quite the opposite. In the end, in spite of all the darkness I went through in the aftermath, what I thought was a form of self-sabotage was actually a way of me *saving* myself. It was almost like a cursed blessing. I just didn't realise it at the time.

It was a wake-up call and it made me reassess everything. Literally my whole world and every single part of my life, which I think is something lots of people can relate to. It made me stop and reflect and really think about everything that's happened in the last ten years in a completely different way. And coming out of that darkness was like a new start. I'm glad I stayed in the world and had the chance to realise that. I don't regret it either. I genuinely hope he finds happiness. I hope I do, too.

So what did I learn? It's hard to say in one line so I've written a list:
- Don't put your life or your happiness in the hands of one person – it doesn't always go to plan
- Don't give ALL of yourself to someone too soon
- Next time, if there is a next time, I'll look after me, before I start to look after someone else – it's time for me to be a bit selfish
- It's OK to be successful – don't stick around in any relationship where you have to suppress your achievements

- The people who TRULY love you are proud of you, and will support you in EVERYTHING YOU ARE
- Have a look around – those annoying people you've been around all your life may actually be pretty important
- Ask for help – it sounds obvious but it's true. And let people help even if you don't think you need it
- Don't be frightened to make mistakes, but for fuck's sake own them. Because take it from me, the lies and guilt will ALWAYS catch up with you
- Be honest and make sure the people around you are honest too

But the biggest lesson I've learned is that wanting things to be a certain way doesn't mean that they *are*. Life is fucking complicated and that's a bastard, but it also means that there are things that we can't predict.

2

THE RESTART

When you've been at the lowest of lows, you learn not to sweat the small stuff . . .

Looking back, after I got out of hospital I should have given myself a bit more time before I went back to work in early September 2021. But even though I wasn't encouraged to do so, and I was terrified, I had to go back. My work is a massive part of my life and for the past however many weeks and months since my ex had walked out of my life, I hadn't been able to bring myself to do it. But once I'd regained my power of speech and I was discharged and back at home, I needed to go back to work because I felt that was the first step towards becoming me again.

Maybe it was also because I've never forgotten my darling, much-missed Nanny Rose's words: 'Work as hard as you can because there's always someone else who's waiting to jump in and take it away from you.' Or, maybe, I just didn't know who or what I was any more if I wasn't working, and I couldn't bear being on my own with myself and my thoughts in an empty house. Someone once asked me, cleverly I thought, if I ever worry that I use work to deal with deeper stuff. And 100 per cent, I know it's true. But also, most importantly, I now had my own Saturday afternoon BBC Radio 2 show, the slot Zoe Ball used to do, and I knew and still know what a huge privilege it was to be doing that job. I didn't want to let anyone down for one day longer if I could help it.

I've always grafted. Ever since I was sixteen, I've literally never stopped. For those of you cheeky bastards who haven't bothered to read my first magnum opus, the *Sunday Times*

NUMBER ONE BESTSELLER *The Life of Rylan*, or even if you have and have forgotten, here's my potted CV (skip the next couple of pages if you know all this already): At sixteen, I left the Coopers' Company and Coborn School (a school in Essex for really brainy kids, so fuck knows how I got in – but believe it or not, when I was younger I was actually quite clever), the proud owner of fourteen GCSEs (and I would have got one more, only I forgot when the English Literature exam was and decided to go shopping over Lakeside).

I lasted just three months in my first job, in a hair salon in Kensington. I started on work experience and earned about £1. It was nothing because I was a Saturday junior, but what I remember most is that my train ticket was more expensive than my wages. I got sacked for asking Geri Halliwell for her autograph – it wasn't Geri's fault, but the manager was an arsehole. I didn't even get the autograph, but after she left he sacked me, saying I was very unprofessional, so I told him where to go and I left. I was embarrassed and upset and skulked off quietly. But fast-forward nine years and Geri walked in and gave me a one-to-one masterclass on *The X Factor*, and afterwards she sent me a beautiful bunch of flowers with a lovely handwritten note, so it was well worth the wait. And now we're good friends.

So I got a job in the menswear department at River Island in Lakeside – that was in 2005, also the year I came out to Linda. When I left there, I worked on the Benefit cosmetics counter at Debenhams on a basic wage – I made a lot through commission, but it was hard. But then I got the sack there and all, for giving too many discounts on 'Mega Discounts Days'. Meanwhile, though, I was also fitting in a bit of modelling work, under the name Keelan Clark (sounded sexier, apparently, than plain old Ross), but I still fell on hard times every single week. In 2008, aged eighteen and working in a pub, I applied for *Big Brother*, but it was jinxed and I never made it into the house. That's when I got the job in an optician's, but it ended terribly when I reached through to grab some glasses and the sliding serving window cracked and smashed over me. It cut my arm open and I was rushed to hospital. A few weeks later people advised me to claim because it shouldn't have happened and it wasn't my fault – and well, obviously, 'Where there's blame there's a claim'. I was later awarded £10,000, which paid off my credit cards and bought me my first crappy car. But I've still got a massive 4-inch scar on the top of my arm today.

In 2009 I got my first proper boyfriend and was so besotted, I turned down an offer to join a boyband in Ibiza. He cheated, so I fucked off to the boyband and became the fourth member of 4bidden (a Westlife and Take That tribute band). The following January I was off to sunny San Antonio on the west coast of the island, to work a season in the clubs. I had a ball in Ibiza. But when I came back from my sunny popstar adventure, I had no big plan B. Wondering what on earth to do next, I was living with Mum and after my money ran out I got another job as a shop assistant, this time on the Benefit counter at Boots Chelmsford. And that's when I ended up entering a local competition, The EsseX Factor, more or less by accident; my mate was a judge so I went along to the auditions for a laugh, had a few drinks and got talked into performing to a backing track of 'Bad Romance' by Lady Gaga. Suddenly I'm on stage and everyone's screaming – I got through, and for five weeks of the 'live shows' in Chicago's in Basildon, I sang and danced my way to the finals. It was brilliant. I didn't win, I came second, but on the back of it, Lee the organiser got me some gigs in glamorous far-flung locations like Stirling,

Scotland. And that's what made me go, 'do you know what, that's what I want to do.'

Because of that, I had to quit my job at Benefit, but I also got part-time work doing airbrushing for my photographer mate Helen.

In 2011, I made it to the finals of Katie Price's ill-fated television show called *Signed by Katie Price* (more on that later). Then, in 2012, as most of you will know, I auditioned for the actual ITV *X Factor*, got through to week eight of the live shows, i.e. the quarter finals, and my life changed forever. Afterwards, I went straight into Channel 5's *Celebrity Big Brother* house – and walked out as the winner, so maybe that's the job that actually changed my life. That show changed people's perception of me. They realised I was normal.

That led to a presenter's gig on *Big Brother's Bit on the Side*, the spin-off Channel 5 show, then a stint as a showbiz reporter on ITV's *This Morning*, and the rest is history, as they say. I'm not sure I can actually remember all my TV presenting jobs over the last ten years, from *Ready Steady Cook*, *Supermarket Sweep* and *Strictly: It Takes Two*, to *The Wave*, *Babushka*, *Eurovision*, *The One Show* and Channel 4's *Alternative Election Night* special. I've also been a guest on practically everything from *Have I Got News for You* and Alan Carr's *Chatty Man* to *The Great Celebrity Bake Off for Stand up to Cancer*. No word of a lie, I have to pinch myself daily.

In the space of ten years, I'd gone from 'national joke' to 'national treasure' (not my words, someone else's, but I'll wholeheartedly repeat them) – and somehow, being a presenter on Radio 2 sort of proved it. So, I went to work.

Saturday 4 September, my first day back to present my show, came along. 'This I can do,' I thought. It's just three hours, between 3 and 6 p.m., and it wasn't like doing telly, no one needed to see my face and how thin and terrible I looked. I thought I could just sit there and speak and get through it. I was so nervous, though, which was such a strange feeling knowing I had been doing it most weekends for two years, but now stepping back into BBC Wogan House, I felt like it was my first time.

Five minutes before going on air, my boss Helen came in to see me and I completely broke down. I was so embarrassed. It wasn't even like a little cry, it was one of those embarrassing, snotty, sobbing hurt cries. How I managed to do that show I don't know, but as always, I did it. I knew I wasn't doing the best job I could be doing, but it's live radio and I knew I had no choice but to carry on. The show went well, people were lovely, my team were amazing and I got through it.

They were all worried about me, though, and I was offered a year off from work. I refused. In my mind, I had no choice but to try and piece my life back together. Strangely, going back into the BBC studio and getting back to being live on air on a Saturday, albeit without anyone having to see me, *that* was what I needed to wake up, to feel halfway back to being myself, and to try and get back on the straight and narrow after the worst five months of my life.

Three weeks later, I went back to presenting *Strictly: It Takes Two* with Janette Manrara and it was the best distraction I could have had. We're all like family on that show, and I had Bernice by my side, my close friend who is my makeup artist who had been there throughout it all, so I knew I could handle it. She would hold my hand the whole way. But, underneath the makeup, I didn't feel myself for quite some time at work. Don't get me wrong, I painted the smile on and tried to make light of everything, but deep down I was still really hurting.

TEN

As the weeks went on, I tried to start catching up with friends and family and ease myself into being alone in my house. That was a scary time. I'd never lived on my own. I'd moved out of my mum's straight into my new house with my ex. This was the first time in my life I'd had no one around me and I'm not ashamed to say that even as a thirty-two-year-old man, it really scared me.

The next milestone looming was my birthday in late October. I didn't want to celebrate and I certainly didn't want to see anyone. My friends and family told me I had to, I needed it and I should have a party in my home with my closest. I did, and it was one of the best decisions I made during those months. To have Mum, Jamie, my sister-in-law Jayne, my niece and nephew Olivia and Harvey, the people I love and really trust around me that day was exactly what I needed. But as crazy as it was, because I was hurting so much, I couldn't help thinking about my ex not being there. I couldn't *not* think about him. It was almost like the dark side of my head was constantly pushing him to the forefront of my mind. Then, two weeks after my birthday, it was my wedding anniversary. Great, throw me a fucking bone. Not only that, Christmas was just around the corner.

Christmas 2021 was a strange one for everyone. Covid was still very much in circulation and generally there wasn't much festive cheer. I was dreading it as it would be the first one on my own. Each year without fail in the past, we would always do Christmas at mine; I'd cook and everyone would be at the house. That year Jayne's sister invited me and my mum to her house with all of her family. It was really kind of her and I was grateful that I had people to be around. But then unfortunately Jamie and Jayne both got Covid, so couldn't be there. And as grateful as I was that me and my mum were with Jayne's beautiful extended family, it was a really hard day for me. I'd tried to make it all as normal as it could be, I put the tree up and the lights, but it hurt to wake up alone on Christmas morning. Usually, every year on Christmas Eve, I'd lay the presents out in the lounge, and like a kid, I couldn't wait to get up and exchange gifts. This time round I woke up to the empty house, went downstairs and sat in silence for an hour, just staring out the window into the garden. The whole day felt like that. Just a blur. I wanted it to be over. Nothing felt real or normal. I still felt like I was in some fucked-up dream that I couldn't wake up from. I could feel myself slipping again, but after how bad I had got during the summer, I knew I couldn't go there again.

The next and last hurdle of that horrible 2021 was New Year's Eve. The clock struck midnight and I knew that was it. The worst year of my life was over. There is always something about New Year's that does make you want that new start. Maybe I needed that symbolism, that impetus to start again and become a new me. Don't get me wrong, it wasn't easy, but embracing that whole fresh 'new year, new me' approach seemed to be the way forward. I didn't really have a choice.

First on my New Year's resolutions list, I decided to work on my fitness. When I was ill and stopped eating, I'd gone down to 9 stone and I'm 6 foot 4. I was grossly underweight for my height. I've never been a gym bunny by any means, but I've always wanted to have the dream body. I met Scott Harrison, a real decent bloke, who was willing to help me with my goals. That man has done more for my body and mental health than I ever could have asked for. When we did a session, we put the world to rights. It was like an hour of therapy. It was such a release for me; something to focus on and take my mind off all the shit. I remember one session when I completely broke down. I had weights in my hand, continuing to do bicep curls, while tears were streaming down my face. I was hurting, physically and emotionally. Scott looked me in the eye and told me I was gonna be OK. He taught me so much about how to look after myself.

Another person who made a big impact was my therapist, Amy. I'd always been against therapy. It wasn't really something I wanted to do, but as time went on I grew to trust her. You now know how low I got, as did she, and sitting there, talking to her, there often were times when I genuinely felt worthless. Amy taught me how to like myself again, and helped me to start to accept that just maybe, I was worth it. Not gonna lie, she did an amazing job of keeping me on the straight and narrow.

I also made the bold decision to get a new PR company to help me manage the stories that were being written about me. Since it had become public knowledge that I was single, I seemed to be followed almost every place I went. All of a sudden, I noticed that I was being written about most days, with endless press stories made up out of nothing. 'Rylan tweets something', 'Rylan goes to restaurant' – ridiculous nonsense. I've never been one of those people who sells every second of my life to every magazine for a tenner, and I never will be.

Instead, I decided to do an interview with Eva Wiseman from the *Observer* to talk about my return to work and the fact that I was looking for a new start. I didn't realise how emotional I would get during that interview. Eva was amazing and she was really accommodating, but for some reason I just opened up and it was the most unguarded interview I've ever done. It appeared on 16 January 2022; the reaction to the piece was really positive and a lot of other outlets picked up on the story. I suppose in a really strange way that article felt almost like validation that I was OK and I wasn't a horrible person. I felt good that I'd taken control of the narrative, and I was making tiny steps in my life to get my body and my mind back in good shape. Then, just a few weeks later, I was brought crashing back to earth.

I received a phone call from a *Sunday Mirror* journalist who told me that a video of me asking for drugs had come to their attention. I was really confused because I knew I hadn't asked anyone for any drugs. Being completely honest, I lived out in Ibiza for a year after all, so without giving too much detail, I think it's fair to say I've tried most things. However, on this occasion when I was informed about this video, I genuinely had no idea what the journalist was going on about. Me and my team received an email saying that the *Sunday Mirror* was going to run the story regardless. If I wanted to comment on the piece, they would listen with a sympathetic ear. Are you fucking joking me? How was I supposed to comment on something that a) never happened, and b) I had never seen? We asked to see this supposed video. The newspaper editor flat out refused and said that they wouldn't be sharing their 'evidence'. Evidence? Are you taking the piss? We weren't on an episode of *The Bill*!

I'd be lying if I told you I wasn't wound up, but I turned to my management team and said, 'Let them run the story. I don't give a fuck. I know I've done nothing wrong.' That next Sunday morning, I woke up to find my face covering most of the front page of the *Sunday Mirror*, with the headline, 'GIMME THE GEAR'. It was sickening. The picture was a screen-grab from a video in which I looked absolutely horrendous. The paper had also made the video available to view online, which along with everyone else I did for the first time. That's when I realised what this video of me supposedly trying to get drugs actually was.

After my time in hospital, I'd been out with my cousin and friends in Soho in central London, and we'd gone for drinks in a bar. Now, anyone who's ever frequented bars round there will know that late at night, a group of guys who are clearly selling drugs will usually be hanging about outside. Every time I go into any of those Soho bars, blokes will always recognise me and give me a shout, and I always wave and smile, because I'm not rude. When we left that night, believe me, I was VERY pissed, and one of them put his arms around me as I was walking towards my driver, waiting nearby in the car. In this video, you could see that I'd said something stupid like, 'Come on, mate. Get the gear out, then. Let's have a party.' This was in the middle of the street, in public, and clearly I was making a joke. I was so drunk, I didn't realise at first that the bloke was filming me on his phone, but when I did twig, you could see me laugh, then even in my drunken state, I said, 'I'm going to kill you.'

This is where it got interesting. The *Sunday Mirror* had splashed me all over its front page, making it look like I had been taking drugs. However, when you opened the paper, one of the first lines they had written was something like, 'the star was clearly joking'. But they knew what they were doing and the harm was already done. Most people would only have seen the front-page headline – hardly anyone actually reads the fucking story – and that was incredibly damaging. How fucking dare they do that to me? Especially since just a few weeks earlier, the very same paper had been so quick to capitalise on the *Observer* piece, commenting how 'brave' I was for speaking out about my mental health. Luckily for me, though, my employers all defended me, and people I didn't even know spoke out on social media to stick up for me, all saying exactly the same thing. In fact, the journalist ended up having to come off Twitter because of the abuse she was getting. Don't get me wrong, I wouldn't wish that on anyone, but it was a proper piece of gutter journalism.

I'm not stupid. I know how this industry works. I also know that the *Mirror* wasn't the first paper that the bloke tried to sell that video to. A friend who works at another outlet had already told me this video was doing the rounds and that they had declined to cover it because they could see that it was a non-story. Unfortunately for the *Mirror*, the powers that be there thought different, and decided that running that fake story while I wasn't feeling at my best was the right thing to do. Let me publicly say now that it really wasn't. It was disgusting. Sadly, with the job I do and the experiences I've been through, I just have to accept that some people will always be out to get me. But fortunately not all journalists or publications are like that and I've always had a good relationship with most of the media. Treat me right and I'll treat you right, it goes hand in hand, but don't ever lie about me or to me. That's when you'll see me angry.

Since then I've been working as much as ever, if not more. But I've also been trying to piece the rest of my life back together. I've been really trying to regain friends and the people I somehow lost along the way in the course of my marriage. I've started to have a social life again that doesn't revolve around my relationship. I've properly reconnected with my own family, much more so than I ever have before. I'm trying to enjoy myself and I've been trying to feel better.

Am I there yet? No, of course I'm not. Am I getting there? Absofuckinglutely.

People keep asking me what's next. Am I going to do a new show? Am I dating anyone? The honest truth is that I don't really know what's next, but read on and you can find out more about my relationship status. If I've learned anything over this past year, it's that you should never think you have a plan. You can have a goal. You can have a dream. But you can never really have a plan. As the old Yiddish proverb goes, 'If you want to make God laugh, tell Him about your plans.'

Lessons I've learned:

- A restart can be the best thing for you
- If you've lost people along the way, don't be frightened to reach out and try and get them back in your life
- When people talk bollocks about you, let them, if it makes them happy, because at the end of the day the truth will always come out
- In the words of the great RuPaul, unless they're paying your bills, pay them bitches no mind
- The biggest blessing about being so low is that I know I could never let myself get that bad again

LESSONS WE'VE LEARNED . . .

Claire Richards

Friend/Steps sister

On 2 January 2013, I was in my hotel room near Elstree studios the night before entering the Celebrity Big Brother house. I was with my assigned chaperone when there was a knock on my door. We answered it and the lady standing there simply said, 'Rylan is having a spray tan and he wanted to ask you if you wanted one too?'

Me being the stickler I am for the rules, I declined politely, saying, 'Please tell Rylan, "Thank you very much. I don't do fake tan, but I guess I'll see you tomorrow."'

That was my first encounter with the young man we'd all come to love on The X Factor but most had probably seen as a bit of a joke. I was excited about meeting him and hoped we'd become friends over the three and a half weeks in the house.

We were lucky with our group of housemates as everyone was lovely – with the exception of Speidi (the American reality TV couple Spencer Pratt and Heidi Montag) – and soon Rylan and I became inseparable. He protected me and tormented me in pretty much equal measure. I knew fairly early on that I would be friends for life with this kind, generous, incredibly funny and insanely intelligent boy that I was getting to know. We came out of that house not just friends but family! He was my annoying little brother.

Over the nearly ten years we've been friends, our relationship has shifted somewhat. While in the beginning he would try and call me for a chat quite often, I'd rarely answer. 'I don't like talking on the phone,' I'd say. 'It's not that I'm ignoring you, I just don't do it with anyone!'

Now, though, I probably call him two or three times a week and HE NEVER ANSWERS AND HE NEVER CALLS ME BACK! He's *turned me into a phone-chatting stalker that doesn't quite get the message. The process started in 2021: I was in Scotland recording a TV show, again in a hotel room. I was watching Lorraine interviewing Scott Mills talking about the upcoming Eurovision Song Contest. He said that Rylan was poorly and would no longer be co-presenting with him, so I immediately picked up the phone and texted Rylan:*

Hello

T's you ok

F's

Are you

Ok

Scott mills has just told everyone on lorraine that you're not well!

What's wrong?

Just going through some stuff I can't really talk I'll be ok . X

Talk to me

What's going on

I'm worried now

I love you. X

19 May 2021, 14:03

How you doing today ? X

21 May 2021, 18:06

Love you ♥ Hope you are ok xx

Eventually Rylan called me and told me what had happened. We ended the call with me saying I'd call him when I was on the train home.

Weeks followed of him not answering the phone, not replying to my text messages.

I'd beg him to just let me know he was OK, and in those cases he'd send me a short text to say he was. His sister-in-law Jayne eventually messaged me and we spoke on the phone. She told me everything that had been going on and how bad he was; we arranged for me

to visit him at Linda's to try and talk to him, but we didn't tell him so he couldn't stop me. I drove to Essex. I was really nervous on the way, cos I didn't know what was going to greet me when I got there. Linda answered and when Rylan saw me he freaked out a bit, but we sat and talked for hours. I tried to reassure him that his worst fears were never going to be a reality and that he was going to be OK, but he'd been overcome with insecurity and guilt and self-doubt. It was heartbreaking to see my self-assured, confident friend reduced to the broken, almost shell of a man sitting in front of me that day.

Eventually I left and as I drove out of sight of the house I pulled my car over and cried. I left there honestly not knowing if I'd ever see him again. He was in such a bad way, and I couldn't believe that he had been reduced to this state. I was angry, scared, worried and so, so sad.

As the months have passed he has gradually become more like the little brother I first knew, but there's still a way to go, I think. I just wish he would learn to take each day as a blessing and concentrate on the things he has, rather than the thing he doesn't right now. He has so much love to give and as long as I've known him all he's wanted is for someone to love him, truly, and madly, deeply. I just hope for now, for the time being, he can make do with the likes of Claire from Steps doing that. I love you so much – more than you know, little bro. But for God's sake ANSWER YOUR PHONE!!!

Your Steps sister, Claire

3

POTS, PANS AND A PANDEMIC

Stay home. Protect the NHS.
Save that box set for next week

What a crazy ten years it's been, but I have to tell you, the last two have most definitely been the weirdest. I mean, Covid. What the fuck was that all about? Was I having a nightmare or did we just go through the most horrible, surreal time of our lives? (And I'm not just talking about my marriage and breakdown!)

I have to be honest and say that also, at first, in January 2020, the pandemic was kind of exciting (yes, I know) in a really fucked-up way. 'Oh, what's going on in China? What's that you say, Huw? SARS-CoV-2? This is something new.' Then we were advised against all but essential travel to Wuhan and well, I wasn't planning on going there anyway. But then by the end of March, it was all Chris Whitty and Cobra meetings, and Boris with his serious face telling us to all stay at home. When we saw that first lockdown announcement, I think we were all thinking it would only be for a couple of weeks, but then the weeks, then months just rolled on and on and on. And, hang on, have we not found a solution to this yet? It was just fucking nuts.

Don't get me wrong, obviously some terrible things happened, but when I look back I just sit here and go, 'How the fuck did that happen?' When it first started there was all these videos coming out from China and people just collapsing in the street and stuff. Why do we not talk about that? Because that weren't Covid-19. What the fuck was all that about then? I'm not one of these massive conspiracy theorist people, but there is something weird about it all. Very, very weird. They may tell us that it was possibly some Chinese horseshoe bat that infected some other animal that then ended up on the meat counter in some food market or other in Wuhan province, but I genuinely think it was man-made, 100 per cent. But we're never gonna know, are we? No, we're bloody not.

In Ryland, I tried to keep it as light as possible. Obviously, because of her age and her pre-existing health condition, Crohn's, Mum was in the highly vulnerable category, so during the early months of lockdown, it was difficult, especially early on because we weren't allowed bubbles at that point. So she was self-isolating, all on her own in her house. I'd nip round there in the car and I'd just be stood at the end of her drive, waving at her, because I'd be frightened to go anywhere near her. Back then, you thought you could just look at someone and you were going to kill them, plus I was still going out to work as well, so I never knew if maybe I'd got it and just didn't know I had. I could have been a superspreader for all I knew. But even though she sometimes grumbles about her condition, she was weirdly lucky in that her nurses were still coming to her house every day, so it wasn't like she had no face-to-face human interaction whatsoever. Obviously she was on the phone to me every five minutes too, as per bloody usual, but it was really, really difficult and awful at first. Every time I thought about going and popping in for half an hour, I just couldn't do it because I was so scared about potentially being the one to finish her off.

To be honest, though, as the months went by and she was still on her own, I was that close to just being at the point where I didn't give a fuck. I thought, 'well she can move in here then. I don't care, it don't bother me.' Then thank fuck they announced the bubbles. Mum could actually come round here and not get arrested. It is slightly odd thinking back to how that all felt at the time, because obviously now that we've got the vaccine, thank God, most people, even the elderly and vulnerable, aren't dying when they catch it. But right at the beginning, in February, March 2020, when it first happened, and for that first five or six months before we had any hope of a vaccine, it was horrible. Awful.

So of course, me and the rest of the family stuck by all the social distancing rules. We all did – well, with a few notable exceptions as we now know; Barnard Castle and Partygate to mention just two. But even young kids, teenagers who could have been going out, seeing their mates, having a laugh; they didn't. They stayed at home, maintained social distancing, and got bored off their tits. Because they were responsible human beings, and they didn't want to be the ones giving it to their mum or their dad, or their grandparents. Or whoever.

Thankfully, Linda has still never had Covid. And I never got it either, which is crazy and surprising because my ex had it twice. And we were in the same bed and I still didn't get it, and I was testing all the time, so I definitely know I never had it. I don't know why. But my body's always been like that; I'll only get ill when I know I can get ill. When I was hosting *Big Brother's Bit on the Side*, for example, a day or two after the series had finished, without fail I would come down with the flu, or I'd have a cold at the very least. I think it's because I knew I could never get ill during the series, so I'd never get ill. But then the second I knew I could get ill because I had two days off, I'd be ill. My body somehow controls itself in that way. I wonder what Chris Whitty would make of that? Diagnose me as a fucking weirdo, maybe? Anyway, I realise that I'm not good when I stop. If I switch off, that's OK. I've not stopped, I'm just on standby. But whenever I stop, I'm fucked.

I was lucky during lockdown, because I got to keep working. Unlike most of the country, my life didn't have to stop, as we were classed as key workers because we were broadcast. I was doing my Saturday afternoon Radio 2 show, and even when I couldn't go into the studio because my ex got Covid and I had to self-isolate, I built a studio so I could pre-record it in the house. I could also do all my voiceovers from there, or my dubbing for the Cinch adverts – which I still do now to save me having to go all the way into London to do a two-second read. Now I can just literally walk in wearing my pants and do it myself. I do my podcast from here as well. Everything. So much easier. I was also hosting *The One Show* on BBC One and, obviously, I had to go into Broadcasting House for that. Lateral flow tests weren't a thing for a while, but when they did come in, we had to test every day and then as long as it was negative, I'd go with my negative test to the BBC.

I remember driving through London to get to Broadcasting House, which is just off Oxford Street on Portland Place, W1A. I drove halfway down Oxford Street all the way up to Tottenham Court Road and looking out, I didn't see one solitary person out on the streets. It was such a hauntingly lovely, empty landscape – in a fucking terrible way, like a scene from an apocalypse movie. Wow. As beautiful as it was to be able to see London like that, though, I hope to never see it again. But if the deserted streets of London felt surreal, actually being inside Broadcasting House during lockdown was an even stranger experience. I'd be walking around the BBC building and there was not another living soul in sight. A skeleton staff of one masked person on reception and all the office areas empty, when somewhere like that is usually a hive of activity. The makeup people were all in hazmat suits. Literally. Bernice, my makeup artist, looked like an astronaut. It was just so bizarre.

We'd filmed the first series of a new, rebooted *Ready Steady Cook* up in the BBC studios in Glasgow in early 2020, just before the lockdown measures came in. I felt so lucky to be asked to do that show. I mean, that was my childhood, first with Fern Britton and then with the legend that is Ainsley Harriott. The minute I got home from school, 4.30 p.m. every day, I'd switch it on to see what ingredients Ainsley's contestants had brought along in their plastic bags. When they told me I'd got the job, Fern and Ainsley were the first people I called. I rang Fern first and she was lovely – she was more excited for me than I was at that point, which was hilarious. To be honest, I was a bit more worried about calling Ainsley, because although I'd met him loads of times over the years on *This Morning*, you know to me, Ainsley *was Ready Steady Cook* when I was growing up, and everyone knows him so well for that show. But I rang him, I was up in Manchester, and he was so kind. He was just getting his MBE at the time, so that was a handy way in to the conversation: 'Well done on your MBE!' But he was so lovely; he said, 'You're going to love it. Just go and enjoy it and make it your own. Just put you into it because the show runs itself.'

A year later, during the second wave of Covid in early February 2021, when we'd just gone back into that really strict lockdown right after Christmas, I was back in Glasgow for a fortnight to record the second series. While I was there, it was snowing, and I remember looking out of the hotel window and, again, like London the year before, the city was ghostly quiet, empty. The sky was completely clear, but saturated in a strange greyish mauve light, and the whole city, everything, was just blanketed in snow. I could have been in Lapland, literally. No one there. It looked almost too perfect, like it was absolutely fake. It was the most beautiful thing I'd ever seen.

With a programme like *Ready Steady Cook*, we make the entire series in one go, over two weeks, filming three or four shows with different contestants each day. Each forty-five-minute television show took about two and a quarter hours in real time. So those were two intense weeks with long, long days in the studio. I'd be up at 7 a.m., in work for 8.45 a.m., and we wouldn't leave till about a quarter past or half past ten at night. Sometimes you'd get one day off or two days off in the week, and if I had two days off, I'd fly down home, then fly back to Glasgow the evening before, ready to be up and back at it on set the following morning. It was hard work. But I like doing it like that because I love routine, so it was great – but it was such a completely different experience from the year before, back in those uncomplicated pre-pandemic days.

On the first series it was all very sociable, with a big studio audience, and – you know me – I was constantly giving people a hug and a cuddle. The chefs used to get me involved with some of the menial cooking tasks too, if they were running out of time. You know, Rylan chop this, Rylan mash that, Rylan add a pinch of salt to that sauce. But in 2021, we obviously had to be Covid secure and maintain social distancing, and so, of course, there was also no studio audience. Again, the people working on makeup all looked like they'd just come out of surgery, head to toe in PPE, with big clear-plastic face visors and hazmat suits. No one was allowed to go out for lunch or in the evening, so for me and the contestants on the show, it was just hotel, studio, hotel, studio. To go from that touchy-feely vibe of series one, to no audience and everyone on the crew masked up to the eyeballs, was just a very odd feeling indeed.

For any of you who haven't watched it, the format and the food budgets hadn't changed much from the days when

Ainsley Harriott hosted the show. Quite simply, two contestants, family members or friends, one in the red kitchen, the other in the green one, have a budget of between £3.50 and £10.00 (that's the 'luxury' budget) to buy a bag of ingredients. They are each paired with a professional chef – Anna Haugh, Akis Petretzikis, Romy Gill, Ellis Barrie or Mike Reid, who was replaced by Jeremy Pang when he got stuck in Australia during the pandemic – who then has to dream up a main and a dessert dish from scratch using the ingredients, with the help of my well-stocked Rylan's pantry, chock full of all the usual things most of us would have to hand in our cupboards – oils, spices, herbs and some basic staples like biscuits or flour – and all in just twenty minutes. Then, in the second part of the show, we have the Ten-Minute Challenge. The audience holds up cards which spell out READY STEADY COOK, and contestants choose three cards, one letter from each word, on the back of which is a mystery ingredient. The catch is that behind the last four cards is an extremely random 'wild card' food item. For example, someone might end up with some chicken mini fillets, a head of fennel and a jar of kimchi, or some salmon, tinned lentils and a tin of baked beans, or the worst that I ever saw: a haggis, a pear . . . and some leftover birthday cake. At the end of the show, the audience then votes for the kitchen that has rustled up the best dishes of the day, by holding up a red tomato or a green pepper.

It was a lot of fun, with lots of jokes and banter with the contestants. We had very, very good chefs, so we got brilliant food, and I used to love getting a good taste of all the dishes – unless it was anything involving fish or seafood, which I would never eat (I'll explain why that is later). But obviously, with the Covid-19 social distancing rules, all that went out the window, and only the contestants were allowed to eat their own food. With no studio audience, we also had to change some of the show's traditions and format – but we still kept the red tomato and green pepper voting cards. We brought the three remaining chefs that weren't cooking onto set, and they sat at a chef's table watching everything going on, and then voted for their favourite dish to decide the winner. That was actually lovely for me because we got all of our chefs involved in every single show. It gave me a bit more time to have a laugh with them as well, because when they weren't actually cooking they'd be more at ease and able to have a bit of a banter. Don't get me wrong, even when they were cooking we did that, but they also had twenty-eight pans on the go, trying to make a soup out of a cardigan.

Ready Steady Cook was a bit different to other shows I've worked on, because it was a family-oriented tea-time show. It was all quite light-hearted and to be honest I found it fairly relaxing, unlike *Big Brother's Bit on the Side* where I was always worried I was gonna come into work and find someone had smacked someone and then tried to drown them in a hot tub. You knew you weren't going to get that on a show like *Ready Steady Cook*. We were just giving people ideas for bits and bobs that they could do at home. And it couldn't have come at a better time when we were all so bored of cooking the same old thing every week, especially when we were all living in our pyjamas 24/7. It all felt really clean-cut and wholesome, not my usual smut, and it was actually quite nice for me to feel a bit more grown up. The major thing I missed on that series was getting a free dinner every night because I was banned from sticking me fork in and sampling the teams' creations. I was just so annoyed I couldn't eat it. I also missed that buzz you get from a living and breathing studio audience. But I totally get it; you certainly wouldn't have wanted anyone to come on *Ready Steady Cook* and then contract Covid-19. I mean, imagine the headlines! 'Pensioner Dies After Attending *Ready Steady Cook*.' Still, I learned so much on that show just standing and watching, soaking up all the tips and tricks, everything from how to chop an onion to how to make flatbread in five minutes. Next thing you knew you'd got this beautiful flatbread or a gyro or whatever, and we're literally talking minutes to rustle it up. After the first series, I bought some sumac and some harissa paste. I hadn't even known what they were before that, and it changed my life completely. It's crazy, the stuff I learned.

I was just so happy to be working right through that whole mad pandemic time. Everything that was happening was so, so sad and we were very lucky to be doing it.

And it was such a people's programme. There's no airs and graces on that show. It doesn't matter what age you are, what background you come from, where you live or even how much money you've got, because all the food we did on *Ready Steady Cook* was on a REALLY tight budget. We weren't sitting there cooking a full lobster with a bottle of champagne. We were genuinely dealing with a tin of lentils we'd found in the back of the cupboard and a butternut squash. So, it was sad that the BBC decided not to recommission it, but not the major career blow some of the papers made it out to be.

I was already a pretty good cook, to be fair. I mean, I'd had a crash course in 2015 on BBC TV's *Celebrity MasterChef*, when I made it through to the finals alongside ex-Pussycat Doll Kimberly Wyatt and Sam Nixon. This was a massive personal achievement for me. That competition is actually on talent and I couldn't believe it because before I went on, I didn't really know how to cook. I mean, like I could cook, but not 'cook'. And the thing is, and I haven't told anyone this before, I didn't

47

want to do it, but my management were insistent: 'You really should do it. It's a really good show to do.' But I didn't want to embarrass myself. This was *MasterChef*; it was the BBC, and this was before I'd really worked on the BBC. But I ended up going on there and when you're in it, you really wanna do well. It's crazy. It just sort of gets under your skin. So it was a good journey – difficult but good. And I loved it and just sort of surprised myself. I'd come home after each heat and even my ex was confused as to how I'd got through to the next round. I remember him saying, 'I don't understand. How the fuck are you getting through?' Like, cheers for the fucking support, hubby dearest! Story of my life. But I kept on cooking and was kept in the kitchen.

It was only when I was faced with Angela Hartnett and a WHOLE HALIBUT and a bucket load of squid in the penultimate challenge that I had a bit of a wobble. Fish, and any other form of seafood, give me the absolute ick. I HATE fish. When I was younger, my brother pushed me into the fish counter at Sainsbury's Stepney. Have you ever seen a hake up close? Well, it looked like a person and I tell you it is the ugliest bastard I've ever seen in my life. And you think *my* teeth are bad? Anyway, I just remember the shock and the hideous sensation of that wet, cold fish in my face. It was just the worst thing ever. Call it a phobia if you will, but the only way I got through the squid prep on *MasterChef* was by telling myself, 'It's banana, it's banana, it's just fruit.' And my halibut, according to Gregg and John, was perfectly cooked, flaky and moist and done to a tee. I've no idea what it tasted like – I couldn't bear to look at it, never mind put it in my gob.

My thing on *MasterChef* was that my food always looked good and I just had to remember to make sure it tasted good. My final dish on the show was Wagyu beef done three ways with a truffle mash potato and Wagyu tea. Personally I can't stand truffle (we'll get to that later) but I'm told it tasted great. I tried loads of fancy techniques I'd picked up along the way but not used before, and my dessert involved crafting a mini replica of the Shard, with the Thames made out of a blueberry foam – it came out a Technicolor bright blue. It looked amazing, but John and Gregg weren't convinced. 'There's nothing wrong with a bit of blue, Gregg,' I explained. My other slip-up was undercooking my beef cheeks, so admittedly they were a bit of a tough chew.

In the end, Gregg and John crowned Kimberly the well-deserved winner. It didn't matter – I was proud I'd made it that far (bribery gets you anywhere, don't it, Gregg?). Seriously though, I was just genuinely shocked that I'd actually managed to cook things that didn't instantly make anyone vomit.

I loved taking part in that show and will be eternally grateful for that chance to learn what a foam actually is – and I'm still the only contestant that's made a McDonald's Happy Meal on the show. But it was fucking difficult, and when I was in the middle of doing it, and I came out of the *MasterChef* kitchen and came home, did I walk in and go, 'Babe, I hope you're hungry because it's Wagyu beef three ways tonight!'? No, if I'm perfectly honest. It was more a case of, 'Get me a fucking takeaway. I'm knackered. I've been cooking all day.' The last thing I wanted to do was cook a fucking bit of Wagyu beef. Anyway, I doubt you could pick up a piece of Wagyu down at Sainsbury's round here. I remember that they went to Harrods to get it for me that day. And Karim, who was one of the food tech boys, said he loved it when I told him my menu. 'Don't you worry, Rylan. I'll keep you in Wagyu beef, mate,' he said, because he's got a Harrods reward card, so he put his card down and got all the points. Very clever bloke.

I was also really chuffed to be invited back to be one of the judges and actually eat the food rather than sweating over it for a change. The first time was when actor Phil Daniels, conductor and singer Karen Gibson, TV presenter Dominic Littlewood and Olympic hockey player Sam Quek were wearing the famous aprons; the second time was just after my summer horribilis when I joined John's missus Lisa Faulkner and Greg Rutherford at the judges' table. Unfortunately, that time, former *Newsnight* presenter Gavin Esler's scallops were practically raw (or so I was told – what with my fish phobia, I didn't go anywhere near them), and his pear sorbet and plum compote was like eating a bowl of cold soup. On a happier note, we were very impressed by *Love Island*'s Kem Cetinay and his various family-favourite Turkish delights.

Once I'd recovered from filming *Celebrity MasterChef* – because I tell ya, that was intense – cooking played a hell of a big part in my life. I got a bit more creative in the kitchen than I ever had been and then, doing *Ready Steady Cook*, I learned a lot more on there with the chefs. It's not like I used to do all the cooking in my marriage, we definitely used to split doing dinner. But I'd say I used to do more of the 'cooking' cooking, as in making something from scratch. Thanks to that run-in with the hake I NEVER go near fish or any form of seafood – I will go to a Japanese restaurant, but I won't eat sashimi. I'll only eat chicken or vegetarian sushi. Or I'll order a chicken katsu roll because there's no fish in there. Or cucumber sushi. But if it's come out of the sea, I don't want it. Any friend of the fish is my sworn enemy and will never pass my lips – not even a fish finger.

I once accidentally ate a prawn ball and I thought it was all over. I thought I was probably gonna die because now I've convinced myself that maybe I've got an allergy to fish that

I don't even know about. And then old Linda fucking makes it worse. On a Saturday, there's a very good fish stall up the road at Smith's of Ongar; and there's one in Wapping and all. My mum loves it, so then she comes around before I leave to go to Radio 2. I'll be upstairs getting ready and I'll hear the door going, and it's her saying, 'Don't mind me. Let me just put this in your fridge. Otherwise it'll go off.' We're talking cockles, fucking winkles, the worst fucking things you could ever put in front of me, and old Molly Malone there only goes and stinks my whole fridge up with it. YUCK.

And mushrooms, don't get me started on them. Nothing traumatic happened with a mushroom, but it's fungus, innit? And I'm not eating fungus. There's just something dodgy about mushrooms. I don't trust them. I think they're up to something, I think they're judging us. You know when you go to fancy restaurants and they're all, 'A touch of truffle oil on your entrée, sir?' Or a shaving of truffle this, a knob of truffle butter that? No thank you very much. I mean, that's growing among all the mud and shit on the ground and all. I'm not having any of that.

That's fish and mushrooms dealt with then. But would I say I had a signature dish? My go-to would always be a pesto pasta, with maybe a bit of nice grilled chicken and warm focaccia. I've always loved cooking Italian food, anything to do with pasta and different pasta sauces, I love doing all of that. But then I also like doing a 'fancy meal', so if I do a fillet steak with mash, it won't just be mash. It'll be a potato puree with Dijon mustard, and I'll be putting it through a sieve and all of that.

I'm not gonna lie. I might sound like I know what I'm talking about with me purees and all that, but I've had my fair share of kitchen disasters. I woke up one Sunday morning with a bit of a hangover, turned on the telly and it was Nigellissima in her boudoir. So I thought, 'I wonder what Nige is showing us today.' It was Nigella's 'Meatzza' – a pizza, she told us, but with a mincemeat base. Basically a giant burger, which I thought sounded really nice. So I made that, but it tasted like foot. Really not a winner-winner-Meatzza-dinner at all.

It's weird, I used to love getting in there and rustling up something different, but if I'm honest, it's also something I gave up when my marriage ended. The truth is that since then, I can count on one hand how many times I've cooked. I don't wanna cook for myself. I wanna cook for some*one*. I feel like cooking is such a social thing for me. And even if it weren't social, it could just be a case of chucking something in the oven for a weeknight dinner, but I'll hardly even do that now. I just find it really pointless – what am I gonna do? Stand there for three hours making a meal and then sit and eat it on my own? If I'd a son or a daughter or someone, then fine, but when you literally sit and cook for yourself, then sit by yourself eating it, it's just a bit sad. That doesn't feel right to me and for some reason I can't bring myself to do it. So I've fallen into the habit of ordering in, or going out to a restaurant.

And I know that nurturing myself and looking after myself is just as important as being in any relationship. I remember my therapist talking to me about it, and I remember the exact words: you need to cook yourself a meal. And I said, 'Why?' She said, 'You've got to feed yourself.' But I kept saying, 'Nah, I can just get all the takeaway.' And she said, 'That's not feeding yourself, that's being *given food*.' She said it was the act of doing it, the actual act of cooking for myself, that was important. It's not even about the food, it's about the activity, or the ritual side of cooking, if you like. That's also another form of self-care, self-love. And also, she said, in some ways it's like a meditation. So, maybe I need to get more Zen about that too.

People, and by that mainly I mean my mum, are always telling me that I need to make myself breakfast. But I rarely eat breakfast. I'm a terrible breakfast person. Always have been. I'd like to say I rustle up eggs and bacon, but it's more likely to be a bag of Monster Munch, at best. When I'm working out, I'll have a shake. But other than that, no. I never wanna eat in the mornings. Never. All I want is coffee and fags. It takes me six coffees to get up. Literally, a nicotine macchiato, that's me. But now, I've decided I'd *like* to be a breakfast person, so as part of my new me, new start, I'm going to try to change up my morning routine.

I don't really do dinner parties, but again, I'd like to. Sometimes when I was with the ex, we'd invite people over for dinner, but we'd always end up going, 'Fuck it. Let's just get a takeaway, all of us.' My fantasy dinner party guests? All five Spice Girls. And I'd tell them to sort it the fuck out. That is what my fancy dinner party would be. 'Vicky, stop mucking about. Get back with the girls. We want all five of you. Four is great, but we need five for the Power of Spice.'

Now that I'm single again, I'd also love to do a *Come Dine with Me* week with four friends, where we'd all go round each other's houses and cook for each other. I'd like to do that. I think I might, actually. I'd probably have to do it as a whole week, and be really bossy about it: 'Right. This is what's happening.' You know me, I love a bit of structure. For my version of *Celebrity Come Dine with Me*, for a laugh, I think if I wanted to just have a brilliant week, it would be Alan Carr, Adele, Gok Wan, me, obviously, and Alison Hammond. I think that would be a ber-illi-ant week, and every single night I would piss myself laughing. Yeah, and get hammered. None of us would eat. Well, maybe at Gok's we would. Gok's a fantastic cook. I've eaten round Gok's before and it was lovely food. And obviously, he's written a couple of his own cookbooks too, so I'm sure we'd eat well on his night.

Lessons I've learned:

- During the pandemic, the world might have been turning to shit, but I realised that taking time out is something I need to remember to do
- Make time for the people that are important to you, because you never know when you'll be forced to just talk to them through a window, while it's pissing down outside
- Never boil broccoli, grill it. Trust me, it's fucking better
- Have a look in your cupboards because genuinely you can make a three-course meal out of a can of soup, a bag of crisps and an old cardigan
- Never trust a prawn – or a mushroom

4

A WORD ON THE WIRELESS

How old do you think I fucking am?

Every Saturday, tune in to BBC Radio 2 at three o'clock, and you'll hear me. That's 88–91 FM, and it's *Rylan on Saturday*. My show goes out live, just after Gambo with his *Pick of the Pops* and the news. And that's been a major thing for me. I got given that job when I was thirty and I've made no secret about it, I didn't want to do it. I turned the job down. I didn't even listen to radio.

Obviously growing up, it was different. I remember I used to love the charts, just listening to the Top 40 on Radio 1 on a Sunday night, because until that came on you didn't know what was number one. It was a genuine surprise every time. And it was such a massive thing because that was the only time you used to get to listen to what you liked. But over the last ten years, I had streamed all my music. I just listened to Apple Music. I didn't even know that people still listened to the radio. Genuinely.

'Radio 2 want to talk to you about maybe taking over the Saturday afternoon show from Zoe Ball,' my management said. And the first thing I said was, 'No.' I'd covered a few slots for Matt Edmondson and Scott Mills on Radio 1 back in 2017, and it was all right, I enjoyed it. But I didn't think, 'Oh my God, *this* is what I want to do' – radio was never that. And like I said, I really didn't think anyone still listened. How wrong was I? But my management were very adamant that this was a really good thing for me to do. I just didn't get it.

For a start, did I wanna give up my Saturdays to sit in Wogan House all afternoon? And secondly, I thought, 'Why

Radio 2? I'm too young to be at Radio 2! Why not Radio 1? Am I not Radio 1? What the fuck?' I was only thirty – surely I was too young for Radio 2. I'd always had this perception of Radio 2 just being very old-school BBC with quite an older audience. Don't get me wrong, I love all the Radio 2 presenters – Elaine Paige, Tony Blackburn, Steve Wright, Gambo, Ken Bruce, Whispering Bob Harris, Vanessa Feltz, they are all broadcasting legends. But well, I just thought that wouldn't be the audience for me. I mean, you couldn't have more trad-sounding shows than Tony Blackburn's *Golden Hour*, or old Gambo's *Pick of the Pops*. It just didn't compute in my mind.

I'm so incredibly fucking grateful now to have had that opportunity, genuinely I am, but at the time I didn't get it.

Anyway, my management told me to just go and have the meeting. So I went to meet Helen Thomas, the boss of Radio 2. She said that Zoe Ball was gonna be moving to the *Breakfast Show* and they wanted me to take over on a Saturday afternoon, 3 till 6 p.m. She explained that she was changing some things up on the station. 'We think that you're what we need,' she said. And then, when they explained that I was basically being given a three-hour slot to do what I wanted and play what I wanted, it did make me think again. They weren't trying to fit me into someone else's mould. They wanted me to bring *me*.

So, it took some persuading from my management, as I wasn't 100 per cent sure that I wanted to go into radio, but the truth is doing my *Rylan on Saturday* show on Radio 2 was the best decision I ever made, because I now know what it means. I think it brought me to an audience that a) didn't necessarily know who I was or b) thought that they knew who I was and then realised very quickly that they didn't. And I love that show now. I finally get it. I understand why they wanted me to take on that slot. I'm thirty-three, and like loads of radio listeners, definitely loads of my listeners, I'm around that age now where I will hear the music they play on Radio 1 and I might be like, 'I don't have a fucking clue what this is.' But then I listen to Radio 2 and a bit of Spice Girls comes on, and I'm in. It took this new gig for me to realise it, but I guess it eventually dawned on me: 'I'm a Radio 2 listener now. What the fuck!' But it's got that mix of old and new that I love.

That's what's crazy about Radio 2. I mean, Paul Gambaccini, Gambo, is on before me, with his *Pick of the Pops*, and then I come on and smash out a bit of Chicane. Listeners must wonder what the fuck is going on. Then straight after my show it's two hours of Liza Tarbuck, who I fucking adore. So, I go out with 'Insomnia' by Faithless and then it goes seamlessly into 'The White Cliffs of Dover'. Liza's show and her playlist is very varied, very eclectic. She played the full version of the *Thunderbirds* theme tune the other day. I love it. And now I realise that my job at Radio 2 is to help listeners make that shift. Because it's happening, and that's why Radio 2 wanted me. So I'll be playing a bit of nineties pop – S Club 7, Steps, or a real house-influenced club anthem by Michael Gray, or whatever – and then 'Buffalo Stance' by Neneh Cherry, which everyone knows and loves from back in the day, followed by Dua Lipa's new single. So, there is that crossover now on Radio 2 because people do grow up, just like me.

I did my first ever *Rylan on Saturday* on 19 January 2019. I'd already sat in for Zoe the previous summer, but I was still nervous doing that first show. I was worried when I took over because I thought, 'What if people hate me?'

The week before, I had a test day when I had a little bit of training about how to use everything, a couple of hours doing some links and feeling it out. And then I just went straight in there. I remember that first show and I remember that the first two tracks I chose were Ultra Naté's 'Free', and 'It Feels So Good' by Sonique. The songs played in after the three o'clock news bulletin with Nikki Cardwell, and then my opening line was: 'Right, here we are, brand-new show, *Rylan on Saturday*. I'm free to do what I want to do and it feels so good!' And that was it. That just set me up. I thought, 'Here we go.'

For the first few shows I was always a little bit nervous. Because finally it had hit me that fuck, this was quite important. And there was quite a big backlash in the press and on social media. Obviously I couldn't stop myself from looking at some of the comments on Twitter, and naturally, some people were complaining: 'Why the fuck has Rylan got a show on Radio 2?' 'Thanks for the heads-up *switches radio off*' and 'Switched off after Gambo [winking face emoji]'. They had already decided that they hated me and were going to switch off before they'd even heard my show. I was used to it. I thought, 'Here we go! Your usual stuffy arseholes up in arms.' But of course I cared. I didn't want listeners to start switching off in droves after that first week and send the listening figures plummeting.

It was only as the weeks went on, you know, that something happened and I just thought, 'Fuck it. Fuck them all and just enjoy it. All you're doing is talking for three hours and playing some tunes you like. Well, all right. Let's just take it for exactly what it is.'

The hardest part of radio is not the buttons you need to press, though. It's the fact that you're not on TV. Radio is so different to telly, because obviously on TV you can use your face, your expression, your body language and movement. You can't do that on the radio. On radio, obviously, it's just your voice. People can't see you, so your voice is EVERYTHING. And that's so much more difficult than being on telly because you need to be happy, sad, shocked, bored and excited, but everything has to be conveyed just through your voice. You have to dial it up a lot. And for some people it's really hard. But I'm not gonna lie, once I got going, I realised it was like second nature for me. I mean, I talk all the time anyway. You can't shut me up. I loved it. When people listen to me, they tell me that it's as if I'm in the room with them. My show is on at that perfect time when people might be coming home from doing the shopping or just chilling, and we just have a laugh and get away with it.

Do you know what? I think the reason I find it so much fun is that I don't overthink it or try to plan anything in advance. I've got my brother Jamie as my full-time driver now, so he picks me up around one o'clock and I can just chill out in the back; I sometimes even have a snooze. When I turn up at Wogan House, though, it's like a switch being flipped on. I walk into the studio and either I just run with the planned playlist and go with the flow, because I like it and it's easier, or, if something really doesn't sit right with me, I'll say, 'I'm not playing that. Put the Spice Girls on.' And then we go.

Sometimes, either because there's been traffic or I've left Jamie waiting and cut it a bit too fine, I've been coming up in the lift during the three o'clock news beforehand. Literally. I can hear it's the sport, which is usually at the end of the bulletin, so then I have to sprint to the studio, then as the doors open, I hear Nikki say, 'BBC news on Radio 2 . . . more in an hour,' and I've got just about enough time to sit down and say, 'Thank you, Nikki Cardwell . . . This is *Rylan on Saturday*.' The rest of them are all in the producer's pod, just looking at me, nearly having a nervous breakdown.

And I know the reason why I'm able to do that is because I've got a fucking great team. From that very first Saturday in 2019, I have had the same producer, Simon Ward, and assistant producer, Lottie Uttley, all the way through. And obviously I also have Sally Boazman on travel, who I've had with me since day one. But I just call them Warwick Davis, Luscious Lottie and Sally Traffic.

Don't get me wrong, if I'm going to do any job, I'm going to do it properly. I'm always professional and I do what's right on my show, but I'm not gonna lie, I've turned up to Radio 2 on an hour's sleep from a really bad night out. The second I walk in, the team all know if it's THAT type of day or if it's a normal day. But I'm always honest about it. I tell the listeners that I'm feeling a bit rough because I went out on the Friday night. I'll have the mic on when I ask Lottie to go out and get me half of the Greggs pastry counter. That's if it's a full-on hangover. If it's a normal day, she just gets me a couple of sausage rolls. We did try the famous vegetarian or vegan sausage roll, but I like a bit of meat. You know me. It's not like work. We take the piss and have a lovely time doing it, but I think listeners like that because it probably just seems like real life. But even if I sometimes cut it a bit fine, apart from when I was ill last year with the breakdown, I've never missed my show. I'm always there. That's why the show works: because I'm not there three hours before thinking about it. I just walk in and do it. And go with the flow.

They always tell me if we have a guest and I'm interviewing someone, but I always forget. So I have to ask, 'Who's in today?'

They say, 'You're interviewing so and so about so and so.'

'Lovely.'

And then I let it happen.

A lot of radio shows are very promotion-oriented. Not mine. I like having people that I know on the show, because it's that type of show. So I'll get Rustie Lee in and why not? She's not promoting anything but she's just fucking classic and she kills me, so she's always good to have in. Or Claire from Steps has come in a couple of times, but rather than do an interview, she'll just sit there for two hours and do the show with me and we let it happen.

Simon and Lottie work together during the show, sourcing callers and, as I said, getting me my Greggs. Lottie is just hilarious. She's a trained carpenter, a singer, dark luscious locks, looks sort of Irish. And actually, I think she went to a convent school as well. She's brilliant. Me and her have got such a sick sense of humour. We have this thing that we do for some reason when we see each other: I'll go, 'Hello, darling,' then she says, 'Hello, sweetheart,' and then suddenly it's like we've just become two Victorian women from the East End and then we break out in song. We start singing shit like 'Roll Out the Barrel', 'Sling Your Hook' and 'Get Your Ankle Out', but it goes on and on, and I don't know why. Sally Traffic just sits there crying, probably thinking 'What the fuck is wrong with you two?' I've got such a good team.

We call Simon 'Warwick Davis' because he looks like the character in *Willow* where he plays a Hobbit, or Griphook in *Harry Potter*. He's lovely, just amazing. He's a really nice guy but he's got the facial features of a goblin, so we take the piss out of him. We wind him up all the time (he knows we're only joking!).

Sally does the traffic on the weekend on Radio 2, but my show's her last one on a Saturday. She's great. She's been delivering the traffic updates on Radio 2 since 1998. She sits with a little screen in front of her with a map of Britain covered in flashing lights, showing all the traffic jams. She gets calls from listeners telling her about snarl-ups and then she'll check the info with the traffic police, but there are a few trusted listeners who have been keeping her updated for so long that she knows their reports will be spot on. She looks like a British Stevie Nicks-esque rock chick. She's gorgeous. Mid- to late-fifties I want to say, but I'm sure I'll hear about it if I'm wrong. Single. And she's a fucking goer, in the best possible way, always up for a laugh and always up for a night out. Sally lives her life, and that's what I love. She sits there talking about the traffic all day and then she gets a train home! She's like, 'Fuck that. I'm not getting stuck on the A13.' She's just gorgeous inside and out, and she's hilarious.

The playlist for the show is prepared by my team, but then I sit down at the desk at three o'clock and change it all. 'No, I'm not having that. Put this in.' I'm cheeky like that. We like to put on big pop songs, stuff from the nineties and a lot of dance. Every now and then, me and Simon will come across an artist or song that we like to call a 'moment'. It's a song that makes you stop what you're doing and just lose yourself in the sound. The other day I had this song in my head that I hadn't heard for years and it was a *Pop Idol* runner-up track from 2003 that no one remembered, but I got Simon to google it and then I played it on the radio and everyone went, 'Oh my God, this was a tune.' So that's what I do. We have one or two playlist songs an hour, then the rest is what I feel like in that moment. All the stuff I want to hear. I know what my listeners love – the chaos – and so I just try to deliver what they want. And, luckily, that's exactly the same thing I want – to play some banging tunes, be a bit cheeky, and always have a laugh. Me and Simon come up with the ideas for the features and the different themes for the call-ins. We all just work together. There's no hierarchy on my show. Obviously we have to run stuff by the Radio 2 bosses, but sometimes we don't. We just do it and don't tell them.

Also, because it's on a Saturday and there's no one there in Wogan House, we get away with murder. At Radio 2 there's three main studios. Gambo's in another studio next door, so when I turn up there's no one in my studio. The last person in there would have been Claudia Winkleman in the morning after Dermot. Gambo leaves at three when I get in. Once he's finished his show he always comes in and gives me a cuddle and says, 'Have a good show.' Then that's it, the place is basically empty. The only people left in the building literally is me, Simon, Luscious Lottie and Sally Traffic, and whoever is my sound engineer for the day. And then at four or five o'clock, Liza Tarbuck's team turn up and they go into the studio that Gambo was in earlier. But Liza always gets in around four o'clock, because she's a swot and gets in really early and goes through her whole show. So it's just us, that's it – apart from the ghosts, that is. It can sometimes feel a bit spooky in there, especially when I'm there on a Saturday. Earlier this year we had a technical hitch and I swear my studio is haunted. I'm not the only one who thinks so, either. I'm not frightened but something always catches my eye. I'm telling you now, the spirit of something or someone is poltergeisting away in there! I shit you not – I have seen people walk behind me before. But apart from that, it's great. It's like you get the run of the building, which is why we take the piss because no one is there to tell us to be good.

I mean, it sounds terrible, and Sal does sound drunk some of the time but that's just Sally – though I did manage to get it out of her one week that Dermot had slipped some Cointreau into her tea. She's so good at her job, but I think when she's with me, she just relaxes. I bully Sal every week about what she's getting up to later on that night. I'm just trying to wind her up because I'm just waiting for the day that she cracks. That's what I'm waiting for. One day I'll get her.

I always take the mick with her. I mean, I can't help myself. Even when she's trying her best to do her serious voice, telling everyone about the problems coming up to such and such a roundabout, I'll be in the background, giving my own little running commentary. Then she'll start stumbling over her junctions and I'll point it out: 'That's it Sal, spit it out, love. Bring it all up.' Then she'll tell me off, because she gets embarrassed. But I love it. I always take the piss, but it comes from the biggest place of love, because I literally adore her. And yes, she does get annoyed with me – all the time – but in the best way. That's why it works. She's constantly saying to me, 'Will you shush?' and I just say, 'No. It's not *Sally on Saturday*. It's *Rylan on Saturday*.'

And sometimes I don't know how she keeps it together, but that's the funniest part, because sometimes she doesn't. And then, when Sally loses it, she's gone. That's it – bye bye, Sally Traffic. The other week, I don't know why, maybe it was something to do with my hay fever, but I started showing them all my party trick where I can click my nose really loudly. It nearly made Sally throw up, and then she had to go straight into travel. I don't know how she managed to do it without cracking up, because I either make her laugh or feel sick. She loses it all the time and then she snorts, literally. So she'll snort, and I'll say, 'Oh, here we go.' I think she makes up half the names on her traffic updates, too. Genuinely. She comes out with random areas, like Towcester, pronounced 'toaster', and I just say, 'You've made that one up. You're taking the piss, that ain't even a place.' And then you get 400 emails from people saying, 'Excuse me! I live there.' But honestly, the shit she comes out with. She's great.

It's not all one-sided either. Make no mistake, Simon, Lottie and Sal give as good as they get. They all take the mickey out of me too. Once they played a big trick on me. They told me they'd got this doctor calling in and made me believe that this bloke could tell what you'd eaten just by the sound of your voice. And he basically got everything right. He said, 'I feel like by the sound of your vocal cords, you had a meat feast pizza last night.'

'Oh my God, I fucking did.' And I was like, 'Where are you based?'

'Harley Street,' he said.

'Oh my God, that's literally just around the corner. Why don't you come in and we can do this with our callers?'

And I was like, 'This is fucking crazy. Let's get him in the studio.' I was all over it. But it turned out that it was Matt fucking Baker from *The One Show*. I believed it though. Like a prick. Why wouldn't I? Simon had rung up my ex and said, 'What did he eat last night? We're gonna fucking wind him up.'

I know. What a prick. That's what happened.

We just make it up as we go along. Every single week, Sally Traffic says to me, 'I just don't know how we get away with it on your show.' But I always know where the line is. I'm more than happy to go up to that line; as long as I don't step over it, I'm all right. And I think that's why people listen, because a lot of people like the fact that I go very near it.

Obviously we have certain features that we do every week that bring a bit of structure to the three hours, but the rest of the time we just wing it. In terms of the phone-ins, when we have our theme, I don't decide which callers we have on. Simon will just pass me a note or say in my ear, 'We've got a caller on the line. Great story.' And we put them on. We always get callers, but Simon's a worrier for that because he'll message me an hour before the show and be like, 'Can you please tweet this? I haven't got anyone to do Rybiza.' (More about that in a moment.) And I'll be like, 'Wait until I get in. You're gonna have callers for Rybiza, stop worrying.' And then we do, they just come through; there's a few million people listening, so someone always gets in touch. And that's why it's fun, because you don't know what they're gonna say or do. Well, somebody vets them beforehand – but it's Lottie. And is she trustworthy? Probably not. Because she's got the same sense of humour as me. And that's the worry.

I love all the features on my show. We do 'Couch Potatoes', which is the TV and film quiz which I inherited from Zoe's old show. People absolutely love it and will actually tune in just for that. The loyalty to that quiz is amazing, because the contestants get nothing, other than the glory. Not even a mug, not even a car sticker. Listen, we're not 'PopMaster' – if you want a prize, call Ken Bruce. But I develop such a good relationship with the people who take part in 'Couch Potatoes'. We've had some great contestants that we're genuinely gutted to see go. I like a little flirt with all the male callers, too. And I don't even know what they look like. Recently, I developed a very good relationship with someone called Lewis, who was our 'Couch Potatoes' champion for four or five weeks. It's just surreal. Radio is different, a weird world where people genuinely feel connected and you can have a relationship with people you've never even met. It's odd, but amazing.

Then we came up with 'Rybiza Rocks' at five o'clock, because obviously I lived out there in San Antonio with 4bidden back in 2009, and it's always been one of my favourite places in the world. I get callers on and whoever gets through is getting on Rylanair flight 88291 to Rybiza, and they get to pick their favourite track to drop on Rybiza Rocks. We have a chat and then I'll play whatever dance tune they love. I love all the bad puns. We had the 'We're Going to Rybiza' jingle done by one of Simon's friends and I always take the piss out of it because it sounds like something from a children's television show recorded on someone's phone. It's based on the 1999 smash hit by Dutch Eurodance group the Vengaboys, and I want to get them to do it properly for us, but Simon won't let me.

Then, there's my chat with my mum. I call it 'Looking out for Linda', inspired by the Hue and Cry number. I literally just call her up and ask her what she's doing, and it's hilarious. She obviously knows roughly what time I'm ringing her – it's normally about 4.50 or 5 p.m., and she knows she's live on the radio, otherwise every other word would be fucking this or fucking that. She's got a mouth like a sewer. But half the time I phone her, and she'll have let herself into my house, had a couple of doughnuts, broken my gate, and robbed me. She's always taking something. She somehow manages to never leave empty-handed, though to be fair, she does usually bring me a litre of fresh milk and a family bag of Walkers.

And of course, there are also my chats with Old Tarbuck. Liza's the best. We just get each other. One Saturday, we were just chatting and she shouted out the word 'pork' for absolutely no reason, and I didn't stop laughing for ten minutes live on air. I don't know how I've still got a show on there, I really don't.

I always think that if I was a little bit older and straight, me and Liza Tarbuck would probably have ended up getting married. 100 per cent, easily, we could have been Mr and Mrs Clark-Tarbuck – or Ryliza, maybe? – because she's so gorgeous and she's lovely as well. I adore her but we've never really discussed her romantic life. Liza is just a law unto herself. She's very much just, 'I don't need a man'. One of them. It's her who always asks me what I've been fucking up to. The shit she's got on me . . . But when you get us together, the gossip we've got, we could probably sink an entire fleet of ships. We know everything.

On the way home after my show, I now keep the radio on in the car. (Sometimes I'll have a bit of Capital Dance on, but don't tell them that.) But sometimes I'll put my earphones in and I'll put Liza on. And she just talks bollocks. She can't stand bullshit either. She really is one of the good ones.

Together, me and Liza are terrible. We're always complaining about the coffee machines, or the fact that we don't even have a work canteen, but it's all in jest, obviously. It's fine. We don't need a canteen – that's what Lottie's for. I just shout, 'Go and get me some Greggs.' We just like pushing our luck. I've been campaigning for years to open up the roof as a smoking area and a bar, but they won't let me go up there and do it. So I just say it on air. And I hope to God that I can grind them down and they just let me in the end. It worked with my whingeing on about getting a locker installed. I sometimes go out after work and I'd been campaigning to have a big locker put in like a wardrobe, so I can hang clothes in it and have my makeup in it and shit – and a couple of weeks ago, the Radio 2 facilities department actually came up with the goods. It turned up during the week, and obviously, I'm usually only there on a Saturday, so when I got in and finally saw it, Gary Davis had left me a massive signed framed photo of him in there. What a prick – a lovely one though. We're still campaigning for a minibar, like the good old days. I'm sure there used to be a minibar in the seventies. Are you joking? The things that fucking went on. But first I'm gonna get a locker for Liza as well because she's been seriously jealous of mine. She definitely wants one. I'm gonna start a trend, I know I am. They're gonna have to build a separate annex for all the lockers – we'll call it 'The Clark Annex'. That's what me and Liza are like – want, want, want.

When I'm chatting with Liza, though, we do forget sometimes that we're on the radio. Towards the end of my show one week, I nearly said, 'Fucking hell, Liza!' Luckily I didn't, but that's one massively difficult thing about being live on air for that amount of time – remembering not to swear. It's hard, especially having my mum on the show, and because my relationship with Lottie, Simon, Sally and Liza is hilarious. We always say that if you could hear us talking to each other during the tracks, we'd be taken off air. It would be an instant sacking. Fuck knows how, but nothing has ever slipped out – yet. Touch wood. I don't know how it hasn't because every other word with me is 'fuck'. It's funny. I am a potty mouth, but I can turn it on and turn it off; I've got the censor button in me and I think that's because I've only ever really done live telly. That's what I was brought up on, so not swearing on air was drilled into me right from the start. And I somehow manage to do it. There are the odd moments where I almost forget, and I go to do it, but luckily enough I don't because there's no delay on Radio 2, I'm fully live. So what happens, happens. And you know what? I'm sure the day will come where I accidentally say something I shouldn't. We're all human. But if and when that day comes, I'll apologise. After all, it's not life or death. I'm not doing open-heart surgery.

Another tricky one for me is not being able to have a smoke when I feel like it. That's a fucking nightmare. All I'll say is: I get through it. I used to run down during the two songs at the top of the hour, all the way down the stairs from the sixth floor, smoke really quickly and then run all the way back up. Let's just say I still do that.

We've had our disasters, but nobody's died. Although one day while I was on air, Lottie told me that someone was stuck in the lift. My radio show was playing in the lift, so while I was on air I was calling out to them, asking, 'Are you OK in there? Still breathing?' I mean, they were in there for hours. We still don't know who it was – but they're not there now, so at least we know they were rescued in the end. And still breathing, thank fuck. We've had phone lines going down. Pressing the wrong button at times, but I like the mistakes. Don't get me wrong, I love having a slick show. But I think people like hearing a mistake. People hate it when you try and cover up a mistake. Fuck it. I'll put my mic up and tell the listeners that I've pressed the wrong button, and put it down again. Simon, my producer, is the worst fucking person in the world because sometimes a text will come through from a listener, and he'll just have it printed out and bring it in to me. And he won't have read it. Or he might have read it and think, 'Yeah, that'll be all right,' but he's not really, *really* read it. I'll start reading it out and have to stop mid-sentence and say, 'I can't read this out on air!' But I'm doing it live so that's why it's funny. And he always talks to me in my ear when I'm talking on the radio, so I'll be having a conversation with him live on air but no one can hear the other side of the conversation. I don't care. I genuinely have so much fun and so much freedom to do what I want on that show and I think all the mistakes are funny. I mean, that's life, right?

During the first lockdown, when I had to self-isolate for a couple of weeks and couldn't physically go into the studio, I really missed seeing everyone. We had to pre-record the show as live, so as I said, I taught myself how to set up a studio in a garden outhouse. We were very honest about the fact that we weren't live because there was no other way around it. My team did such a good job, though, that if I hadn't said it was pre-recorded, you would never have known.

That's when we introduced a new feature called 'Desert Ryland Discs'. Basically, after I got the job at Radio 2, I started to get requests to do DJ sets. See on the radio, I'm not physically DJing. It's not like I'm mixing and scratching, as you would in a club, I'm running a desk. And I didn't realise, but quite a lot of celebrity names, who are paid a million pounds to come and do a DJ set, will just turn up and literally press play on a computer. I refused to do that. I wanted to learn to do it properly. I've always loved music, of course, and I just thought I'd love to have a go at it. I met a lovely guy called Dan at Pioneer and he taught me how to DJ. It's literally changed my life because even though you don't need to be a physical DJ to be a radio presenter, by any means, I just feel it backs me up a bit more now. And I love it. I love going out to do club nights and I love doing the festivals.

Anyway, during the Covid-19 pandemic and the endless lockdowns, for 'Desert Ryland Discs', I got my decks out, took three of my favourite tracks and did a continuous mix which I'd play at the end of every show so everyone could escape for fifteen minutes. I just fucking loved it and the listeners really enjoyed it too.

As soon as it was safe to be in the studio, I came back in, but it was like Covid Central. Somebody obviously came in and wiped everything down with disinfectant between shows, but my team weren't allowed in the studio with me. Sally was on a different floor so I couldn't even see her. I wasn't allowed to be handed paper. It was so fucking strange. The one thing

I do miss from the pandemic is Radio 2 Zoom meetings on a Tuesday afternoon. It was just fucking crazy because everyone was on there, Tony Blackburn, Gambo, Michael Ball, Elaine Paige, Gary Davis, Cerys from Catatonia, Zoe and Claudia, even Ana Matronic joined the meeting from New York – the whole fucking crew. It was the best thing ever just looking at that grid. You know me, I never shut up, but I just sat gawping at Michael Ball's lovely garden and Elaine Paige's bathroom. What is my life? Tony Blackburn sat there in his conservatory. What a collection of faces. Just so bizarre.

I feel like I'm now part of this funny big extended Radio 2 family and it feels good. I know they've all got my back and I've got theirs too. We've all got such a good relationship on air and off air, and I'm really looked after there. When I was ill after everything that happened in 2021, they gave me as much time as I needed to get better and I'll never forget the love and support I received. I've got a great team and it's turned into something that I actually love doing. It's crazy for me to think that I nearly turned the job down. I'm so grateful that Helen Thomas and my management talked me into it. I just didn't realise what Radio 2 could do for me, as much as what I can do for them. My show now gets 2.5 million listeners each week – and that's not including catch-up or listeners on Sounds, that's actual people, listening live. I've gained just over a million listeners in two years. And I never expected that. It's crazy. I just can't believe it. Three years on, it's turned into the thing that most people come up and want to talk to me about.

I feel like doing Radio 2 has made people look at me and think, 'Oh, you grew up.' Or, 'You *are* actually a presenter.' It's like a seal of approval, I suppose. And actually it's so prestigious. And that just really hadn't sunk in when I first started. I've always been so in awe of the people that have come before me, like Wogan, Jimmy Young, real legends, and of course some of them are still there: Tony Blackburn, Ken Bruce, Vanessa Feltz. It's the biggest radio station in the world and it's an honour to have a show on there. These people are institutions of radio, as are all of the other DJs – Zoe Ball, Sara Cox, Steve Wright . . . all of them are just amazing. I'm now the baby of the station that came in at thirty, and all of them have welcomed me with open arms like the little brother.

And radio is really fucking powerful as well. It was only when I joined Radio 2 that I realised the reach it's got and how much of a lifeline it genuinely is to people, especially during the last three years and the lockdowns. The amount of people who've told me that I got them through the pandemic. Or the other day, I got this letter from the sister of this woman who was losing her sight, and in fact, I think she is nearly completely blind now, so she doesn't watch telly any more. She only listens to the radio. Her sister posted a photo of her on the show's WhatsApp page, saying, 'Rylan, you're the highlight of her week because when you do your show, she literally feels she can see it.' I was really taken aback, because I hadn't properly thought about the fact that on radio it is just listening, but a voice can paint such a vivid picture. I didn't realise how important live radio still was in this digital age of streaming and listening to what you want, when you want. I didn't realise how enjoyable it is to listen to. Doing this job has really helped me fall in love with it. And between you and me . . . I think it's made a few more people fall in love with me too.

Lessons I've learned:

- Never underestimate the power of radio. We can stream what we want, when we want, but there really is something so special about sharing live moments with each other just using our voices
- Liza Tarbuck is the best and worst person to be around. Best because she's a decent woman. And worst because she'll definitely get you in trouble
- Don't be frightened to make silly mistakes. Doing a job like this, people love it. It reminds them that you're human as well
- You are never too young for a bit of Radio 2

5

MUMMY

For fuck's sake, Ross!

What can I tell you about my mum Linda that you don't know already? I mean, the whole world and his uncle know her now since we started doing Channel 4's *Celebrity Gogglebox* together – but more on that later. The best way I can describe her is that she's like the perfect mix of the nan from *The Catherine Tate Show* and Pam from *Gavin and Stacey*.

I grew up in a beautiful council house in Stepney Green, east London, with my mum, my late nanny Rose, who really was like my second mum, and my big brother Jamie, who is fourteen years older than me. So I was the baby. Mum never married; me and Jamie had different dads, but neither of us really knew them. And I never knew my granddad. I never met him because Nanny Rose wasn't with him when I came along. She'd divorced him after she had Mum and her older sister, Auntie Susan; then there was another husband and with him she had my Auntie Pat.

I don't know what happened to either of Nanny Rose's husbands to be honest. I just never really asked. I just knew my granddad was never there. And I suppose because I'd never had a granddad, I didn't know what I was missing, so it wasn't something that I felt was lacking. Growing up, it was always just my mum, my nan and my big brother Jamie.

Jamie left school at sixteen and from what I remember he went into building work. That's what everybody did back then in east London. I was just a little kid when he started working, and that's how he became more like a dad figure in many ways. I was probably a proper Little Lord Fauntleroy in my family, in a way. I used to get what I wanted, put it that way, or I'd just have a tantrum. Nothing's changed.

Actually, when I was growing up, everyone around me in my home life was much older. It's not like I had a brother or sister of a similar age so that we could just do our own thing. The only time I was ever with people the same age was at school. That was it. But I think that was quite a good thing for me because it was almost like I grew up early. I just got exposed to things earlier, conversationally, everything, which is why I think I was quite advanced early on. But I had the best upbringing. I really did.

Mum suffers from Crohn's disease. It's one of those things that can go undetected for quite a long time, but she got diagnosed before I was born, so she's had it all my life. She's had three major bowel operations, her first when I was really young. She couldn't work, so I got to be with her at home when I was little, which was amazing. Most of the time when I was a kid, if my mum was ill you wouldn't have known. She just got on with it. But when you knew that my mum was ill, then you knew she was REALLY ill, because otherwise she just kept going. Sometimes, she would be in so much pain and so unwell that she had to stay in bed all day. She's told me that she used to be crying all the time, and sometimes it got so bad that she felt like she wanted to get a knife and punch her stomach open to make the pain go away.

Technically Nanny Rose was my mum's carer when the Crohn's attacks were bad, then in later years that all switched around because my nan got dementia. That was really sad but, really, right up until the last few months she was always the life and soul of the party. She was amazing, my nan. She was the proper matriarch of the family. Years and years ago, before I was born, she used to sing, then she worked in the rag trade in the East End, for a Turkish-Cypriot family-run company called Wearwells, and then for years she worked for the social.

Friday evenings, without fail, my aunt and her friends would come down from Essex to our house in London and my nan would cook dinner, which was pretty much always the same thing: pasta and Batchelors packet sauce, or sometimes it was boiled bacon with a can of potato salad, always buffet-style. I've never known Mum to be a big drinker, but Friday nights she'd always have a little Bacardi and coke. That's her drink. (I detest the stuff, the taste of it just makes me feel sick.) Then they would go to the Mecca bingo up the Troxy on Commercial Road – sometimes my nan would go, sometimes Mum would go, then when I was old enough to be left home alone, sometimes they'd both go. So I used to always look forward to Friday night: 'Everyone's coming round.' But they literally weren't – it was just three women down from Ockendon.

Mum always wanted the very best for me, and though we didn't always have money, she made sure that I had every opportunity she could get her hands on for me. She even became a Catholic to make sure I got into the best local Catholic primary school. I actually used to be an altar server at school, I would literally carry the cross and I had my communion and things like that. It was normal because it was the school I went to, but I wouldn't say Mum and Nan were majorly religious. We would always have Sunday lunch, with a traditional roast and all that, but it was never a religious day. Not with my mum, anyway. DEFINITELY not. Every other word is 'fuck' with her. Then I'll be with people and if I say 'fucking', for example, she's got the cheek to hit me on the arm and tut and say, 'Oooh, Ross. Don't swear.' Are you fucking joking, Linda? The reason I swear is because of you. You taught me all those words.

But seriously, my mum's always been the best. I know it was hard for her sometimes because she couldn't always afford to pay for things like the after-school drama classes at Pineapple in Covent Garden – I know, I sound like a demanding brat, right? – but she and Nanny Rose and Jamie somehow made ends meet and were always so supportive of everything I wanted to do. Mum was always making sure that I had treats, cooking me the things I wanted for tea. She was never much of a baker, though. Actually, for my thirteenth birthday, I was having a fancy-dress party and I was dressed as H from Steps, and she got me a football cake. I just thought, 'How fucking stupid have you gotta be to get me a football birthday cake when I'm at my party dressed as H from Steps?' It's like the woman was blind.

The second time she had to have bowel surgery was very worrying. I remember I was out with my friends James and Katy and it was really uncanny because I was sitting there and I just knew something was wrong. They said, 'You're acting really strange,' and I kept saying, 'Something's not right.' Then James's dad rang him, and I just knew straight away that it was something bad. He passed the phone to me and his dad said, 'Your mum's in hospital. You've got to go there now.' I've always been weird like that – a bit like that kid in *The Sixth Sense*.

I do worry about my mum, of course I do. I've watched her suffer from this disease all my life. Two to three years ago I had a brand-new house built for her round the corner from mine, and now I've installed cameras in there too, so I can always see her and make sure she's OK. And if anything's not all right I can be there in a jiffy. Mum's always been treated at the Royal London in Whitechapel, east London, and God forbid anything happened to my mum, and she was out cold in her house out here in Essex, because she would not go to any other hospital. She would rather spend the night at home seriously unwell, then get someone to take her into the Royal London in the morning, than risk getting an ambulance, because they might take her somewhere else. It wouldn't matter if it was the most beautiful private hospital in the world, she wouldn't do it. She's got to go down the Royal London because that's where her doctors are. She had the same lovely consultant, Professor Rampton, since she was thirty, but he just retired, so we sent him a huge Fortnum's hamper to thank him for everything he's done for her. She was under his care for all those years and he was brilliant. Mum will miss him, I know, but she's got Dr Mezzo now, who is equally good. I know he'll look after her.

A few years back she had to go in for a third operation because she wasn't too well. The doctors told her they were giving her a temporary stoma, then afterwards they said, 'Actually, we're not going back in and it's not going to be temporary. This is it.' The honest truth is that there's been a couple of times when I've nearly lost her – she got sepsis twice – but she's fine now, thank God. She's not in pain any more since she got the stoma bag. Also, because she's got so little bowel left now, just 70cm, she has to be hooked up to a feed tube five nights a week because everything just goes straight through her. Her body isn't absorbing all the nutrition and vitamins she needs. That's the only downside, really, but I think she agrees it's a small price to pay. She's fine with the colostomy bag too. To be honest, me and my brother take the piss, but that's what we're like. We call it her handbag.

The feed line is more of a problem really, because when she's on it, she's obviously quite restricted in what she can and can't do – she can drive if she's on her water line, but she can't when she's on her food line. But she just gets on with it. And actually, more so than ever, she's trying to be a lot more outgoing than she used to be. When I was a kid, she would never go out because she'd pre-empt being unwell. Frankly, she's always been a bit of a fucking hypochondriac. But now nothing stops her. She'll go out for lunch with her mates and she's never out of fucking Lakeside shopping centre. She goes there every Wednesday and always has a cheeky little cheese toastie in Marksy's café. She loves it. She's got a nice little life.

But the stories I've heard about my mum pre-me are brilliant. Mum says she was a bit of a tomboy at school, always the one to have a fight with the boys, like 'Don't you touch her! That's how I was. One of them.' Obviously, mine and Jamie's dads were never around, and before she got ill she was always a grafter. She left school at sixteen and got a job in a printers in Dyer's Buildings, off Chancery Lane. They used to do all the transcripts for the big courts, the Old Bailey and that. This was the height of the Swinging Sixties so she used to love it because in her lunch break she'd go up to Gamages, the famous department store at Holborn, and Leather Lane. And she used to love going up Tottenham Court Road to Anello & Davide. She used to have the Dolly shoes from there, they looked like tap shoes but they're not. They were all the fashion then and she had a gold pair and a black pair and she loved them. She used to wear them with miniskirts and Poodle socks from America – mid-calf, slightly bobbled cotton socks. They were all the rage, apparently. She always says that London was so lovely then. No traffic like there is now. They used to just get the bus or get the train up to Chancery Lane, and then into Carnaby Street. She loved it, all that sixties fashion and everything. She was into that Mary Quant look – she'd go to Biba in Chelsea, and the Chelsea Drugstore, because her best mate Pat used to work there on the weekends. And she's still her best mate. Mum and Pat and all their other school friends still FaceTime each other, every Monday.

But Mum never lasted in a job. She must have worked, worked, worked but never worked in the same place for long. After the print shop, when she was about sixteen and a half, she got a job as an overlocker at Ellis's in Stepney, a Jewish company that made beautiful wedding dresses. According to Mum, 'I used to jaw all the time and when you overlock a dress – you know, round the hems and that when it's near enough finished – there were times I was talking so much, I just cut right through the cloth and ruined it.' They sacked her in the end, which Mum found baffling, for some reason: 'Don't know why. They said I was talking too much. I was always talking.' It's true, the woman never shuts up.

Anyway, after that she had quite a lot more jobs, mainly machining, and then my nan got her a job as a nanny in Wanstead for the daughter of her boss at Wearwells. But then, when she was eighteen, before she had Jamie, she started working in the pubs all around east London as a DJ, places like the Carpenters Arms on Ben Jonson Road and Kate Hodders in Duckett Street, Stepney, which was also known as the Prince of Wales.

When I asked her about it, she said, 'I loved it. We used to have parties and I'd play Tina Turner, "Nutbush City Limits" and things like that. It was just brilliant. The pub used to get packed, they'd be outside on the kerb dancing. It was just the best atmosphere. And I never jawed, I didn't never talk, I just played the records, but I was always drunk. Because they used to say, "Oh, that's for Linda, someone's just bought her a Bacardi."' I never knew, but now I realise she was a right little goer, our Linda. So yeah, pretty much most of east London knows my mum. She used to see all sorts of celebs out and about on the scene, like she'd bump into Kenney Jones a lot, the drummer with the Small Faces, because his dad used to come in the Carpenters Arms.

Thursday nights, her and her best mate, Pat, used to go to the Room at the Top, a nightclub in the penthouse of Harrison Gibson's furniture showroom in Ilford. That's when Bobby Moore was alive and all the West Ham squad used to be up there. Friday nights she'd be at The Lotus. And then she used to go up the West End to Studio Valbonne on Kingly Street, just off Carnaby Street. That's where she met the actor Kenneth More, star of *Doctor in the House* and *The 39 Steps*. This bloke who looked after him come over to Mum and said, 'I've got a friend over there, Kenneth More, would you like to buy him a drink?' Mum said, 'Buy him a drink? Is he taking the piss? Tell him to go and piss off, buy a drink. Tell him to buy his own drink!' That was Linda. She was out partying all the time, and she saw loads of celebrities up there, but she'd never take any shit.

Mum says that's why Nanny Rose always used to say to her, 'I bet I'll get a copper knocking. They'll find you dead in a gutter.' Pat always tells me what Mum used to be like when she was younger; she says that my mum would go out and if someone looked at her funny, she'd end up having a row. I asked Mum about it, and she says it was never like a real fisticuffs: 'I wasn't really a hard nut. I mean, I wasn't like *hard* hard. I wouldn't cause a row, but if anyone gives me any trouble, I'll tell 'em what's what. Too right I would.' But she was a proper girl, my mum.

Now, my mum's like my rock, but she's also like an annoying sister. We fight like cats and dogs, but that's the relationship we like to have. She'll either be in a huff because we've had a shouting match over something stupid and not talk to me for a week, or she's never off the phone. No word of a lie, she literally does not give me five minutes' peace. Even though she's in the new house, and everything is brand new and top-notch perfect, even though I did all that so everything is easy for her, still week in week out, she will call me twenty times a day – at the very least. Seriously, I go to the toilet, come back – seventeen missed calls! All in the space of a tinkle, just to tell me to put the bins out! Or she'll be fretting about something not being right: 'Ross, something's wrong with the windowsill.' 'Ross, the kitchen tap's dripping . . .' 'Ross, the toilet ain't flushing proper!' 'Ross, the oven timer's going off. I can't shut it up!' She just can't do it. It always has to fall back to me. I thought building her the house would sort it, and I might get a break, but no. And literally the biggest mistake I ever made was giving her a fob for my front gates because now she just turns up whenever she fancies. And then she took a key as well. She normally strolls in, says, 'I'll just get the ironing board out,' but then she always makes everything she irons a hundred times worse. And then she always walks out with something. She robbed a pair of sunglasses off me the other day. She just walked out with them, and then she had the cheek to say to me, 'You know them sunglasses you gave me?' I'm like, 'No?' Now she's round at mine all the time. I mean, don't get me wrong, I wouldn't have it any other way. But sometimes, especially now I'm single – well, that's a bit risky. Um, yeah. So that's my mum for you. (There goes my front door. One guess who it is?)

She had her eyebrows done yesterday, apparently, so now she's complaining they are a bit dark. That's what I have to put up with. But that's what we're like, always having a go, as you will probably have twigged if you have ever watched the two of us on the sofa on *Gogglebox*. We started doing it together a couple of years ago and everyone immediately fell in love with her, which wasn't exactly surprising as I think most people would like her. But the response was still sort of unexpected.

We couldn't do it for a couple of years, first because Mum got ill with her Crohn's, and then obviously 2021 was a write-off for me in terms of work, but we started again in June '22. We agreed to do it originally because it's at my house and my mum feels comfortable being on camera with me beside her, just behaving like we always do when we're together. She can stop and start when she wants to if she needs to go and deal with her 'handbag', and she's not physically doing anything, she's just sat on my sofa. And because we're literally in my kitchen, we do forget the cameras are there sometimes, which is a bit of a worry. I mean, I love doing it with her; it's the easiest job in the world for me because I can literally sit there and do fuck all and she just gives great telly. And she has no idea she's even doing it, she doesn't realise how hilarious she actually is. But just like when I ring her on a Saturday on the radio, it's also the most worrying job because I never know what's going to come out of her mouth. She comes out with things and I'm like, 'Why would you say that? Why would you? What's wrong with you?' She sat there the other week, and Omid Djalili came on, competing on *Who Wants to Be a Millionaire? for Soccer Aid*, and she says, 'Oh, I'd just want to go up and rub his bald head.' But my favourite moment was when I offered her some of those mixed vegetable crisps, and she turned her nose up because she thought I was offering her a bowl of pot-pourri. But she couldn't even pronounce it right, she called it 'pot purrrrrrrry', to rhyme with 'curry'. She's got no filter. Let's put it this way, it's lucky the editors like us, because some of the things she's come out with are career-ending. But really, the unpredictability of what Mum says is what makes it so funny to work with her.

The *Gogglebox* team have always been great with Mum so it's lovely to be a part of it. Bernice comes over to do her makeup and then she can never make up her mind about what she's going to wear. She does worry about things like that. She'll bring four outfits round, then there's the whole rigmarole: 'What the fuck should I wear, Ross? Oh, I don't know about me hair. I don't know about this. Oh, I want this done and I want that done.' She'll change four times and I'll tell her she looks great in all of them, then she'll just go back to what she was wearing originally. And she does exactly the same every single time she's on *Gogglebox*. It does my head in because she always looks great in whatever she wears. I'm not gonna lie, sometimes I tell her, 'Oh, fuck off, Lin. Give me a day off, will ya?' But I've said it before and I'll say it again, I really wouldn't have it any other way. No, I really wouldn't.

Honestly, the amount of people that just want to talk about my mum now. I think there would be a national uproar if we decided to axe our 'Looking out for Linda' chats on my Radio 2 show. I mean, we just talk bollocks for five minutes, but everywhere I go people are always asking me things like, 'What's she eating tonight? What's she been doing? Has she been over Lakeside today?' My brother Jamie just doesn't get it at all. He finds it so bloody weird that she's 'famous' from being on the radio and stuff. And Mum doesn't really get it either. She honestly still can't understand it when people she doesn't know come up to her on the high street or down

Lakeside and say, 'Hello, Linda!' She's like, 'Do I know you?' That's my mum, though. She hasn't changed whatsoever. Not at all. She's just off somewhere on her own little Planet Linda.

The other week when I rang her on the show she was with her mate Geraldine. We're live on air, on the biggest radio station in the world, and she goes, 'Oh, hang on a minute. Gel, Gel!' (That's what she calls Geraldine.) 'Them ones. Them ones, Gel.' She couldn't hear me, because she was talking to Geraldine, but I thought, 'I'm gonna let it happen.' Then she pretty much forgot she was on the radio and was just having this full-blown conversation with Gel, for about five minutes, then all of a sudden she must have remembered she was still on the radio, because all I heard was, 'Oh gawd, I forgot. I'm on the phone to you!' She's a fucking nightmare.

She came on *This Morning* with me recently to talk about *Gogglebox* coming back and she did really well, but she was so nervous, bless her. She doesn't like anything like that. I just kept telling her to breathe and she would be fine. The whole makeup department and production team were so lovely with her, though, and made her feel at ease. They gave her a pair of gold shoes and a load of makeup to take home. Honestly, they treated her like the Queen. It was Dermot O'Leary and Alison Hammond that day and they were lovely with her. I was so touched when they asked her if she was proud of me, and she said, 'Well, I'm proud of both my sons.' That's Mum all over. She must have relaxed a bit after that, though, because then she started flirting with old twinkly blue eyes Paul Hollywood. He offered to give her some of his freshly baked focaccia, but given half a chance I think she would have taken him home with her and all.

Seriously, everyone loves her. I think they like the fact that me and my mum are just very normal together – and my mum is a Very Normal Mum. I've treated her to get her teeth done though – veneers, like me. And yes, she still believes that she's got my recycled old ones (see TEETH, p291). She doesn't mind that – waste not want not, as she says. But she HATES me telling everyone she's had them done – it makes her self-conscious, so she won't smile, which is a bit bloody ridiculous because I tell her that's the whole point of having a nice new (well, nearly new, as far as she's concerned) set of teeth. I don't know. The woman, honestly. She's got the top set all in now, and they look great, but she's taking a while to get used to them. There's certain words she always pronounces in a real East End accent, like instead of trousers, it's 'Where's your trahzes?' Or anything in another language like 'pot purrrrrrry' she always gets wrong – she calls Pret a Manger 'Pret Manager'. And there's some words she's never been able to say, so for 'statue', she says something like 'stashel'. Genuinely. And 'chewing gum' comes out as 'Tring gum'. But it seems to have got worse now with her new teeth in. She was asking me something about Swiss Cottage on *Gogglebox* the other day, and it came out as 'Swish Cottage'. What is she like? It cracks me up every single time. She's a fucking character. She's a liability, she really is. But I think that's why people love her.

I've got so much to thank my mum for. It's hard to know where to start because she's really given me everything and more. Don't get me wrong, she drives me up the wall sometimes and she knows exactly which buttons to push to wind me up – if she mentions the bins one more time, I'll fucking throttle her for a start. But I wouldn't change her or our relationship for all the world. I'd do anything, absolutely anything to make sure Mum's happy and as healthy as she can be. I'll even let her put her stinking cockles and winkles in my nice clean fridge when she wants. Because, you know, I couldn't have got through the last year without my mum – she was there for me majorly. She was my entire support. If I was a puppet, she was the strings. I'll never forget that.

Lessons I've learned:

- You're tougher than you think
- After what Mum's been through I can handle anything
- My mum is my world, my number one
- ALWAYS look after your mum!

LESSONS WE'VE LEARNED . . .

Linda Clark

Mummy

I'd say that I am and I ain't strict as a mum. When Ross was young, I never let him get away with anything. I never hit him, but I shouted. And I will still shout at him to this day. My mum, his Nanny Rose, wouldn't. She'd just say, 'Come 'ere.' My mum loved the grandkids, and they all loved her. She died eight years ago, in the July of 2014. When we had her laying in the coffin, it was only her in this big room in the funeral place. We were all sitting there and Ross got his chair and sat beside her. We were in there for an hour and a half. The woman even brought us in a cup of tea. And Ross said, 'Nan, sorry, I'm drinking it. You can't have one.'

We buried her in Corbets Tey, Upminster. We go up there every two weeks, do her flowers, me and my sisters, but we've all got a bit of her in a paperweight as well. And I know that's Ross's most treasured possession. I know he misses his nan. He loved her, he really did. She loved her perfume, Thierry Mugler, the blue bottle, Angel, so he'd always get her a new gift set every year. And he kept her last bottle of it, he's got it in his drawer. He don't never hardly wear it, just probably sprays it and smells it.

Ross has always been kind, always a very loving, giving soul. And very funny and so bright. I mean even when Countdown *used to be on when he was only little, he'd sit there and you know the conundrum thing? He'd make the word out nearly every time. He was brilliant. He was good at everything. He would have been a little Einstein, I reckon. He's always done well at anything he sets his mind to – even at primary school his piano teacher said, 'You know what, Linda? He's so gifted. He's going to do so well, he is.'*

Well, to me he was just my little ginger boy, so I said, 'What you mean?' And he said, 'How he is. He's very musical, and he'll just pick it up. You tell him something and he don't forget it.' And it's true, he remembers everything. It's like he's got a machine in his head.

Of course, because Ross was bright, they gave him a place at the Coopers' Company Secondary School in Upminster. Well, the first couple of years he didn't have a good time there, because he loved being with the girls. The girls he hung about with were so beautiful and he used to sing all the Spice Girls songs with them. He adored the Spice Girls, that was him. A friend's daughter took him to see them when they were performing, and he was on her shoulders, he loved it. But he had a hard time there at school because people used to call him names like 'little gay boy', and when he was with all his mates, they'd say, 'What a crowd of gays.' That's what they said to him for two years. Especially at night coming home on the train, because he had to come all the way back from Upminster to Stepney Green.

It wasn't Ross that told me. He'd tell me nothing. It was a girl I know, Caroline, her son Thomas said, 'Mum, tell Linda what they're doing, because they're starting on him when he's just standing at the station and I'm worried someone's gonna push him on the lines.' He had that every night coming home, so Thomas got Caroline to ring my house. But I knew something was wrong because my mum had met him one night and he'd collapsed on the traffic island near the house. I don't know if the boy had hit him, or something. My mum wouldn't take no shit, and I'm like her, the way I express myself. I just don't let anyone walk over me. She was very protective of us. And she wouldn't let anyone say anything bad about us, and that's me. I would always row for Ross and Jamie.

I weren't having it no more and that's when I walked to meet him off the train, and then I clocked it. Ross just stared as I was walking along but I could see this chubby boy, the bully, and his little sidekick mate, right in front of him. I used to see the little sidekick a lot,

*he was from a nice family that lived further up in Whitechapel, so
he probably come home with the chubby boy and thought he'd get
off early just to have a go at Ross. I was walking towards them, the
little one would have known it was me, but he never said nothing. I
said, 'You all right Ross? What's the matter? You got a problem with
him?' Then I said, 'See you, you little fat bastard, I've had enough.
He ain't told me. Someone from school's told me and I'd advise you
not to start on him no more because he's got a brother who's older.
You leave him alone. You don't live here, so in future you get off
at Whitechapel, and if you ever open your fucking mouth to him or
poke my son again, his brother will see to you.' I phoned the school
the next day, but he never touched him no more after that.*

*I said to Ross, 'Anyone else starts, you fucking retaliate. I've had
enough of you being the quiet boy.' But then he did, didn't he? And
that's why I was up the school at meetings about him all the time
because he'd had a row with someone. I'd say to them, 'Well, what
did that someone say to my Ross? I'm fed up with yous lot saying it
was him. He's took it and been quiet for three years. And now he's
retaliating, you don't like it?' I said, 'I've told him, no one hits my
kids. I've always said, "Stand up for yourself. The kids start on you,
you start back."' Well, they said, 'We don't do that in this school.' I
just took no notice and said what I had to say: 'I know that ain't
your motto, but that's my motto now. I've had enough. I'm not gonna
take no more bullying.' I said, 'It's up to yous what you want to do,
but he thinks for himself now. And you tell the kids that have been
starting on him and all. I'll give you their names.' But the school
didn't deal with it. It was Ross, and that's why I was up the school
in meetings every six months. I used to say, 'I've been up this school
more than he's been in it.'*

*And it wasn't just the rowing. When he was fifteen or sixteen, his
last years at the school, he started fucking about. He was me to a tee.
He always had an answer back to the teachers when he shouldn't*

have, but he did. And you know, they wanted to expel him at the end. But I think he knew what he was doing. I always said to him, 'Just do your best.' Then he did everything himself. I never knew when he was going in for something like the Katie Price thing or The X Factor, *because he went to all the auditions on his own. He used to come home and tell me things after, and I'd say, 'Why didn't you tell me you were going there?' And he said, 'I don't tell you nothing when I go through these auditions and that, because I know you'll worry.' He just did it all by himself.*

I've never known anyone with so much confidence as him. Even when he meets people, he's never starstruck. He just goes, 'Hello, how are you?' and talks to people. I mean, he does get on with a lot of people, but I do speak my mind. I say to him, 'Please don't get smart-arsed. Don't get big-headed. Don't start thinking you're too good for these. Just stay as you are. And honestly, people will like you and respect you.' I've always been down to earth, and I think it's important to tell him to keep his feet on the ground.

I am proud of Ross, and Jamie too. I'm proud of both of my boys. They're both grafters, just like me and my mum. And Ross works so hard – of course I'm proud of him for that. And he helps everyone. He helps so many people. But you never see me going to his shows. I don't like all that. I mean when he was on The X Factor, *I never went until six weeks in. They took me mum the first night for the auditions. Well, her dementia had started then and she wanted to go and hit Gary Barlow because he kept having a go at Ross. She started shouting in the audience, yelling, 'Who the fuck is he talking to? I'll go down and fucking punch him right on the nose. That's my grandson down there.' Well, my sister had to take her out of there because she wanted to get up and have a row with him. But that was just me mum, she wanted to protect him.*

Of all the things he does, I liked him doing Big Brother's Bit on the Side *because he was like his own little boss on that show. I loved him doing his* Ready Steady Cook. The Wave, *that's when he went to Portugal, that was good but that was a one-off, and* Supermarket Sweep *he enjoyed, but then he seems to have a good time on every other thing he's been on. He enjoys himself in his work.*

I thought he was brilliant when he did MasterChef. *You know what? I never in the world thought he would do so well. That's what I mean – if he sets his mind to something, whatever someone's teaching him and all, he keeps it all there in his head. I was so proud of the way he done everything there, I couldn't believe he got that far. On the* Bake Off *as well. Michelle Keegan won that but I think he was near it. He done so well.*

It was hard during Covid because I didn't go out, but thank God I had moved over here, close to Ross's new house. The hospital rang me all the time and I had nurses morning and night, and Ross ordered me shopping online which I've never done. He'd say, 'So, what else do you want?' and then if I forgot something, he'd say, 'Mum, the order's gone. I can't add it now.' But I was all right, you know. As long as I had milk, bread, something to go on me sandwich and stuff in me freezer, I was fine. I would walk round me garden, do me gardening, because it was hot that first year. It was a lovely summer. And I'd read my books because I was into Kimberley Chambers' books. As long as I've got a book to read, I'm happy to sit there.

I'm not sure about what lessons we've learned together, me and Ross, but there are plenty of things I'm still trying to teach him. If I'm not happy with something with either him or Jamie, or I think they should do something different, I just tell them. And then they'll tell me to mind my own business. So I do advise Ross but he don't listen to me all the time. I talked to him about writing this and I said, 'OK. We won't bring the bins up again.' But I am going to, because every Friday I message him to remind him to take his bins out. The brown garden bins are every two weeks – they've got to go out this week, as it happens. I have to tell him because when the gardener comes to cut the lawn, he fills them up. When I bring that up, he goes, 'You keep telling me about the bins.' He gets all annoyed, but sometimes I remind him, and he ain't pulled them out. And there's a lot of rubbish from all the grass cuttings and the hedges and all that, and then when the gardener comes he's got nowhere to put the rubbish, has he? That's what happens. He can't be told anything.

So we've covered the bins. Then I've told him I think he smokes too much, for a start. He's terrible. I wish he'd get on something like nicotine patches or the chewing gum. But he just ignores me. I say to him you need to eat breakfast. And I know he orders stuff in. But I do ring up even now and I'll go to him, 'Have you eaten? You got milk and stuff?' And he goes, 'Yes, Mum. What do you think? That I'm gonna starve meself? I've done a shop.' But I bring him milk anyway and maybe some fresh doughnuts when I go round to his. And every time if I'm going Lakeside or anything, I'll go, 'You need anything picked up?' That's me. He goes, 'No, Mum, I'm all right.' Unless sometimes he says, 'Oh, can you get me a nice birthday card for Jamie?' Or something like that. So I got him a nice one for his brother Jamie that said, 'Happy Birthday, Brother'. I gave it to him for him to write in it, and he said, 'What's this? I ain't giving him that. It's like something you'd give your granddad!' I thought, 'You ungrateful sod.' It probably cost me £4.50 out of Clintons and all.

He does all his own washing, he does all of it now. He can cook. He'll clean. He's like me, he don't like mess. I mean, I'm always cleaning, unfortunately. Because I've got the stoma bag, I have to go to the toilet all the time, and I have to clean everything. But he's always been clean and tidy, and his brother Jamie's like that and all.

If I go round his house on the weekend, I like to do some ironing for him when I feel right, but I won't do his skinny jeans. I asked his cleaner to take them and iron them for him because he puts them in the tumble dryer and there's nothing worse. I don't know how he gets them on after that, honestly. He's got skinny legs anyway, *but I say, 'How on earth can you tumble dry jeans?' I've told him so many times. I say, 'Ross, stop tumbling your jeans. When you wash them, hang them up to dry and then they're easier to iron. I don't need to do a lot then with the steam iron. But when you tumble them I can't get the creases out.' The thing is, the tumble dryer dries the creases into them and then I'm there forever blasting ironing them.*

Then he'll say, 'Leave 'em.' But I say, 'What is wrong with you? You can't go out like that, without your trousers ironed.' He'll say, 'You won't notice.' But I say, 'You will, because you put them in that poxy tumble dryer and now they're all creased. Just wash them, and let them air dry on your lines.' I don't know why he don't put a rope up and hang all his washing outside to dry. That way, they don't shrink and they get all the fresh air round them. 'I ain't having no washing line over my grass,' he says. But I tell him you won't notice, nobody would see it because you take it down afterwards.

I've told him: there's nothing like washing that's been left to dry in the fresh air, especially your bedding. I love my bedding all dried outside. When we were kids my mum used to have flannelette sheets in the house and every Sunday, she'd send them to the bag wash. They didn't go to a laundrette, it was a proper laundry and we called it 'the bag wash', and all our navy-blue school knickers used to go in there and all. Oh my God, the smell of those clean sheets when you got into the freshly made bed. And that was bath night, Sunday night. Two of us slept in a double bed, the other in a single, and you'd get in and the smell of the pillows, you know, was just so lovely. It was so fresh, that smell. When I smell that smell, it takes me right back to my childhood.

Anyway, with Ross, I like to iron his shirts and tops and that and hang them up in his room. But he's very organised. He'll have all his whites together hanging up, his jeans and then his black jeans, then his white jeans, all colour coordinated. He's like that, all Mr Perfect.

*I go to him, 'You got any suits that need taking to the cleaners?'
'No, Mum. They're all right. I can do it in there if I want to.' He's
got like a wardrobe thing in his dressing room that cleans them,
apparently. I don't know what it is, but it's got all buttons on it and
a mirror at the front, and it presses them and it must steam them
and all. But I said, 'Surely you need to take your suits and get them
cleaned?' because of his sweat and that. I don't understand it, but
he must know what he's doing, so I've stopped asking him.*

*But his shirts are the worst, because of his fake tan. I say, 'Give me
them shirts and I'll take 'em home.' I get the Vanish and soak them
in that first, then I rub 'em so it all comes out, then I wash them in
the machine. But I use Ariel soap powder for them; I don't use the
liquid because that's no good. It doesn't get it out. And you've got to
leave it to soak. Otherwise, he'll put them in the washing machine
and they'll come out and they've still got the fake tan all over them.*

*And his sheets. Oh God, they take some soaking. About six years
ago we went to Tenerife for four days, so of course he's got the fake
tan all over him because, well, he's white as a sheet normally and
if he sunbathes his freckles all come up, what with his auburn hair.
That's what he's like. We were staying in a villa and he had cleaners
coming in to make it nice every day. I said, 'Look at these sheets. The
cleaners must think you've shit yourself in the bed.' 'Well, Mum, it's
the tan,' he said. 'But we're on holiday,' I said. And he said, 'Well,
it's not that fucking hot!' And it wasn't, because it was November
we were there.*

*When he puts the fake tan on sometimes, I'm sorry but he looks
like he's been up the chimney. And the tan is a nightmare. I don't
know why it comes off him, but it gets everywhere, including his nice
new velvet dining chairs. When he comes round here to my house, I
say, 'Don't go on me chairs.' Terrible. I mean, can you imagine if he
went round someone's house and they've got all white furniture? He
couldn't sit down, he'd have to sit on the balcony or out in the garden.*

He does keep his house tidy, though if I go over there, I'll say, 'Why did you move that picture? I liked that one where it was. Why don't you move it back?' And he says, 'Do you live in my house? You come round here, you tell me to move this, move that. It's my house, it's not your house. Why don't you go home and move something around in your own house? Go and do your own moving about.' That's all I get out of him. I say, 'You should do this or that.' He says, 'Mum, I should do a lot of things, but I don't.'

But I've learned that he can stand on his own two feet. And he doesn't need me, because he's very clued up. I ask him questions, and he knows everything, honestly. When I think about the brain in his head, he is so clever, and he's always acted older. He's quite quiet, often, but he can be loud, when he's having a laugh and that when he's had a drink. And he's ever so funny; he is so comical, honestly, you could fall over. When you're with him, the answers just come as quick as that. You say something, and he's always got the funny comebacks, just like that. And he's so funny on the radio with Lottie, Simon, Liza and Sally and that. When him and Lottie get going, they're terrible.

I went in with him to the Radio 2 Saturday show and I said, 'Yous two, honestly.' And Lottie said, 'Linda, I love him.' She said, 'He's such good company.' I said, 'He is.' And she's got such a dirty laugh, hasn't she, Lottie? He always has been such good company. But then when you think these days he comes home, sits here on his own . . . but he'll potter about, always doing something, and he's always on the phone. That's the thing now with kids, the phone. And that does annoy me. I'll go to him, 'You're on that phone the whole time and you don't answer me.' And he goes, 'I don't answer you because I know what you're gonna say: "Have you put the bins out?" Sod the bins,' he'll go. But I do. I'll phone him in the morning and I'll say, 'Don't forget to put all them bins out.'

I mean, it's not always about the bins. I ring him to see if he's all right, especially after all he went through after his marriage broke down . . . But he never answers and he never rings me back. Then in the end, I won't talk to him for two days. I'll let him stew a bit, then he rings and says, 'Why ain't you rung me?' And I say, 'Because you don't fucking answer me, so what's the use of me ringing you? Half the time I could be murdered in me bed.' He goes, 'Oh, Mum. I'm sure they'd run out when they seen the fucking state of you.' He's always got a little smart answer.

Swearing. That's another thing I'll talk to him about. But he'll say he gets it from me. But he doesn't get it from me because my Jamie, he's like me, he might have a little swear, but not a lot. I swear being nice, if you know what I mean. If I'm having a laugh, I'll say, 'Fuck's sake,' but just in a sentence. It's normal, it's just like I'm talking. But I'm always telling him off about it. 'Stop swearing,' I'll say, cos he's in a position where he should stop swearing. I don't know how he don't swear when he's on the radio. I mean, when I do Gogglebox, *I know I slip up sometimes; I'll say, 'For fuck's sake, stop mucking about,' but if my mum could hear me, she'd say, 'Stop swearing.' I know she would. But then I think Ross is his own person now. He's grown up. He's been married. He ain't got to answer to me. He answers to himself now.*

I baby him, though, I suppose. I worry, cos he's the youngest. Plus cos he's gay, I've always worried about what if someone hurts him? I don't want no one to hurt him, you know. Like I said, right from when they were little, anyone hurts my kids, I'm there, but I know Jamie can maybe handle it more. And Ross still gets jibbed. They all do, gay people. You hear it. But why don't people just leave them alone? Let them live their lives. They're normal people. They're not aliens. I mean, it's a day-to-day thing now. It doesn't bother you. It's like getting on a bus or riding a bike. That's it. But you always get nasty people in this world, and that's where I've got to keep an eye on Ross, because you always get that nasty one.

I'm not overly protective, but I do worry about him getting hurt. I always have, ever since he was that little fat ginger boy getting bullied at school. I advised him about getting married when he did, but he didn't listen to me then. I said, 'You know, it's a bit quick.' I thought it was too soon and he should wait, but he wouldn't be told. And I thought they were happy. Well, I did and I didn't think they were happy. Because I could see a change in him, for a long while. In the back of my mind, I could tell something weren't right. When I asked him, he'd say, 'Mum, mind your own. It's my married life. It's me. I'm all right. Everything's fine.' But it wasn't all right. I said, 'Ross. I can see when you're miserable.'

And last year was terrible. Awful. It was really hard. I moved up round here two years ago, in August 2020, and thank God I did, because I was just round the corner. Thank God I was there for him. He's got this beautiful home, but he was here with me for three months and all he was doing was just staring. He wouldn't eat nothing, and he's not very big, is he? He'd lost so much weight. I was crying all day with him, and I was forcing him to eat. I kept telling him, 'You've got to eat little bits.' He couldn't sleep so I said, 'Get in my bed with me.' I was so frightened because he was in a bad place, a dark place. I didn't know what he was thinking of doing so I had to have him in with me, in my bed, so at least I knew he was there beside me. If I'd left him, I would have been awake all night listening to see if he'd got up and gone somewhere. It's a mother's worry when they're like that. You think they're going to die on you, that's your fear, and I think every mother's instinct is you don't want to let them out of your sight.

I couldn't see him like that. I said, 'You can't be like this, Ross. I can't lose you.' I said, 'I'm not having this. I can't have it. It's hurting me.' That pain, it's like a knot and you can't untie it. You just want to cuddle them and wrap them up in cotton wool. And God knows how he was feeling. I said to him, 'You can't live like this. You've got everything to live for. Everything. You've got to be you. Because you are you. It's took you how long to get where you've got? You've done everything on your own, and you can fucking do it all again on your own. I know it's hard. It hurts now, but you'll look back and think, "fucking hell, why did I waste all that time?" Eight years of your life. And when was the last time you were really happy? That ain't how you want to live.' I just didn't want to see him hurting no more, so I said, 'You'll get through it. People break up. They get through it. And I'm telling you, if you come through this, Ross, you'll come through anything.'

And he has. He's a bit like me, I know he is. He's proved it to me. He's got it in him to stand up now and be himself again. And in terms of lessons he's taught me, this last year I've learned that he can stand on his own two feet. He works his bollocks off. He always has, all his life. He's a good boy. They both are, him and Jamie. I love my boys dearly, and I'm proud of them both. Jamie's got a lovely wife and family, Olivia and Harvey. And of course I'd like Ross to give me more grandkids, cos I know that's what he wants. Though I don't think I could handle them – I'm too old now to look after 'em, aren't I? But I love babies, always have loved babies.

So, one last piece of wisdom from your old mummy. I'll know you'll be all right, Ross. Your time will come around soon, and you'll meet someone who's gonna appreciate you for who you are and how you are. But I wouldn't date for a while. Just get yourself together, get yourself right. You've been hurting, you still are hurting. Just let things take their time. Go out with your friends and have a nice time. Don't go too wild, though. Just go easy and enjoy yourself. You're single again. But every time you go on some programme or when you do your radio, you don't have to keep saying you're single now, because people know you're single. Just carry on with your life. You're holding all your cards now.

You work so hard for everything you've got and I'm proud of you. You've got a lovely family and a load of friends round you that love *you and have been there for you. Everyone who needs to be there anyway, let's put it that way. And that's a good thing – in fact, that's the best thing. Ruth and Eamonn have been there for you. Claire, Bernice, Nads. All the family – my Jamie, and Jayne, my daughter-in-law, has always been there for you. She loves you. But you know your own mind now. I'm just glad you're out of that dark place and getting back to the Ross we know. Just do me a favour. Answer your fucking phone. Stop swearing. And put the fucking bins out.*

Love you always, Mummy xxx

6

THE 'SOCIAL' LIFE

I wouldn't mind sliding into your DMs, babe

I remember the very first time I trended on Twitter. It was a Saturday night, 25 August 2012, and I was about to fly to Dubai for Judges' Houses on *The X Factor*. I knew that my audition was being aired that evening on ITV, so while I was queueing at the airport to get onto the plane, I looked at my phone. Millions of messages were coming through on my Twitter feed, and I saw that my name was the top trend. That's when the show's producers took my phone off me; while we were in Judges' Houses we weren't meant to know anything about the public reaction and what was happening with the show. I didn't get my mobile back until we were home in the UK, so for the next three days, I didn't know what the fuck was going on. It was only when I landed at Heathrow that I realised that quite a lot had happened in my absence. I mean, it was crazy. Just from that first audition appearance, my Twitter followers shot up to 9,000 overnight. By then, I was in my twenties, and no wide-eyed novice to the ups and downs of the fickle world of social media. Still, I was fairly new to Twitter and that was a pretty thrilling moment.

I guess you could call me a social media native. Like many millennials, I grew up with it and it grew up with me. My brother took me to get my first computer when I was at primary school. Back then, those were the MSN years, the popular chat-room platform that came with your Hotmail account. I'd be with my friends at school all day, then we'd all rush home to go and talk to each other all night on MSN on our home computers. It seems completely fucking pointless now, because these days obviously everyone just texts each other, but back then not everyone had a mobile phone. Most of the kids I hung out with had access to a home computer though, so MSN was like the best thing in the world. We were able to have webcam chats with each other, so we'd all be watching each other in each other's bedrooms on our computers, even though we'd only just said goodbye and we'd be seeing each other again the very next day. God, I miss those days of MSN Messenger. That was when life was simple.

By the time I hit adolescence I was on things like Plenty of Fish – remember that? But that was for dating. That was also the era of Myspace and Bebo, where you would message friends and post blogs, photographs, music, videos, and stuff, and questionnaires for other friends and users to answer. I had Myspace too, because that was mostly music pages and obviously that was my dream – to make it as a pop star. That's where people like Adele, Calvin Harris and Lily Allen got discovered. Everyone's Myspace page looked completely different; you could choose your background, change your font, and you could put a song up there, to put across a bit of you and what you liked, so if anyone visited your page it would immediately start playing. I used to put up videos of me singing and stuff. I remember you used to have your top ten friend profiles showing, and, honestly, the fucking arguments you would have with people about it. 'Why aren't I in your top ten friend list? Because you're in mine.' Then they'd take you out, or you'd have to put them in just to keep them happy. It was such an important status thing if you were in someone's top ten friends on Myspace. But yeah, gone are the days when my biggest concern was who my top ten friends on Myspace were. It was brilliant, though.

In the early noughties, I was also on Faceparty, which was basically an early Facebook – I had a profile and could message people – but it was a bit more . . . not exactly creepy, but I don't know, it just became more of a slightly seedy hookup site and very much NOT like Facebook.

Then, of course, Facebook went public in 2006, when I was eighteen, and I was on there like a shot – what can I say? I was an early adopter. At that point all my friends had Facebook. It was pre-Insta, so I used my profile page for putting up photos – holiday pictures, nights out, parties happening, or literally just a picture of me in my mirror. Just shit, like a picture of a pair of shoes. I'd spend hours organising all my photos and creating albums because every photo I took would just go into my uploaded photos on my page. When I think back at the amount of random pics that were on there, it was so fucking dangerous. I mean, if you were a burglar you could probably have cut and pasted all my photos together and had the whole blueprint of our house – not that we had anything to rob, but still.

I posted a load of old shit on Facebook, basically. That's what we all did. Then you'd always get that one mate that would write something dramatic on their status, like, 'Oh my God, can't believe what's just happened . . . but can't really talk about it.' Then you'd get everyone posting their replies, like: 'U OK, hon?' and 'Sending love, xxxx'. And basically they'd been getting a corn removed or had a stomach ache. Or something like that. But they were desperate for a bit of clout on Facebook; they just had to reel everyone in. And then I remember with all the girls in my year, it just used to be photos of them really dressed up with their tits out in their little vest tops and ra-ra skirts, and you'd see all the boys liking them, in the hope of maybe getting off with them at the next club night. I loved it. It was all so innocent back then.

I got Twitter pretty soon after it launched, too, when I was in the boyband I think, in 2009. I was just starting to do a bit of modelling and The EsseX Factor and stuff, and I worked out that I could use Twitter to try to make showbiz connections and further my glittering career. When I was with 4bidden in Ibiza we were talking about what we were going to do when the job ended and we went back home. I remember tweeting a woman called Jane, who was involved with The Saturdays, to say that I'd really love to meet her. I don't think she even replied, but then, weirdly enough, a couple of years later when I was on *The X Factor*, she was one of the advisors for rehearsals. But obviously, I would also tweet shit – absolute shit.

When I first started using Twitter, I didn't really understand how to use it. On the screen as you were typing, the Twitter caption used to be: 'What's happening?' Once, I tweeted, 'Not a lot', but I didn't realise that the 'What's happening?' bit isn't actually shown in the tweet. I thought it was like having a conversation, but it's not – it's just a statement you're making. 'Not a lot'! Jesus. What a prick. Another time I posted, 'Just had a lemonade.' That's the kind of riveting content of my first few years of tweets.

Obviously, back then you could only fit in about four words, but now everyone can write a fucking essay and say what they want. I remember when Twitter was still a little bird and it was very, very harmless. You could pretty much tweet any old shit and people would like it for the sake of liking each other's tweets. Now you could sit there and tweet, 'The sky is blue,' and some arsehole will argue with you and say, 'The sky is red. You're a fucking liar. You shouldn't

be a broadcaster. You should be sacked from all your jobs.'
Literally. I think Twitter makes people crazy. It's the platform
for arguing now, isn't it?

But back then, there were a couple of comedy sites that
I loved to follow, like the Grumpy Cat website, or Faces in
Things, or the one with pictures of pugs in hats. I love shit
like that. Often the original images popped up on Reddit, but
Twitter really was the disseminator of those 'viral' accounts
and moments. Before that I don't think we'd heard of that
term. Along with Instagram a bit later, it created a new breed
of celebrity as well, as in the influencer phenomenon. Even
though early vlogger stars like Zoella, Thatcher Joe (AKA her
younger brother Joe Sugg), and Sprinkleofglitter were big on
YouTube, it was only when social platforms like Instagram and
Twitter appeared that they broke out beyond their YouTube
notoriety and became public knowledge.

I remember when I first reached 1,000 followers on Twitter.
Honestly, I thought I'd hit the jackpot, like, 'Oh my God, I'm
an influencer now!' Then I went on *The X Factor*, and it was
just fucking bizarre. Over the course of the live shows, my
followers kept rocketing week on week – 100k, 200k, 300k,
and up and up and up. It was crazy. I think I was one of the
first contestants to reach a million followers that year. That
just doesn't happen now, maybe sometimes on Instagram,
but not on Twitter – that was back when people still used to
watch these shows religiously as they went out, live, because
Netflix and catch-up didn't exist for most people and there
was nothing else on telly on a Saturday night.

But you know, ten years ago was also when I experienced
the dark side of social media with all its full fucking force. I'm
not gonna lie, the online abuse nearly crushed me. There was
one guy that had been tweeting me saying something like:

'When I see you I'm going to cut your throat, I want you dead, blah blah blah.' It was full-on. I was really scared. Why would someone send me messages like that? Then the turning point came two days later when I met someone standing outside my hotel asking for a picture with me. 'Do I know you?' I asked. I knew I'd seen him somewhere. But he was like, 'What? No, I just love you on the show, can I have a picture?' He looked at me and his face dropped, like he was really shocked. I kept staring at him. I knew I recognised his face from somewhere, but I just couldn't place him. Then I went back to my room and looked at Twitter. And that's when it clicked. There he was, and that's when I knew for sure it'd been him outside the hotel. I just started laughing. And I thought, 'Oh my God, I've been letting this get to me so much. But these are people who'll say anything as long as they're hidden behind a keyboard – and then in real life they want their photo with you.' That's when I was able to put everything into some perspective. I realised: I can handle this. I can carry on. Since then, I've tried my best to just treat it like someone booing and hissing at me in a pantomime.

I didn't get Instagram until 2013. That was the year Kim Kardashian posed in her white swimsuit with her bum pointing at the camera, creating one of the most popular hashtags of the year: #belfie (bum selfie). I remember exactly when and where I made my very first post, but thankfully it didn't go viral. It was a picture of me on *The X Factor* live tour holding a piece of paper saying: 'My first Instagram post' and then my @username. If you go on my Instagram, you will find it. But Jesus, it's gonna take you a while. You'll probably be scrolling back for about two days. Ditto with Twitter. But yeah. It's all still there somewhere, lurking in the mists of time. Then, as now, I loved all the funny stuff, things like 'Terrible Family

Photos'. And, oh my God, the amount of funny cat pictures I used to see on Instagram. Mind you, people still love a funny picture of a cat, I'm surprised it's not called Pussygram. That was when it was all so innocent.

I was so busy looking at cats and absorbing the blows from the trolls back then that it took me quite a while to consider how powerful and how potentially damaging Twitter, and social media in general, actually can be. I'd like to think that even when I was young and stupid I would never have posted anything truly offensive or future-career threatening. And I don't believe, even in today's 'cancel culture', that any of my random thoughts or opinions might have offended anyone, but who knows? Now, though, as a BBC employee, I'm very much in the public eye so in that sense I do have a reputation, of sorts, to keep. Holly and Nads, my managers at the firm, have a go at me about my social media activity ALL THE TIME, especially about my Instagram posts. I'll be on a night out and I'll put up a story, captioned: 'Hey! Look at me having a crazy time.' They hate that. When you're in my position, you can't do that, apparently. But I'm not very obedient. My response to being told what I can and can't post on MY Instagram account is, 'I can do what I fucking want!' The management line? 'Yeah, but we don't want you to look like you're pissed all the time.' But why not? I'm thirty-three years old. I've just gone through a shitty break-up. Of course I'm gonna be going out with my friends and enjoying myself, having a few drinks and a fag, and so what if sometimes a few drinks might occasionally turn into a small off-licence's worth. But they say, 'You know, best stay off Instagram if you're pissed. You've got an image to keep up.'

I understand their point of view, of course I do. I'm not an idiot. I'm not gonna post a dick pic. But actually, as far as I'm concerned, the only image I've ever tried to protect for the last ten years is the fact that I'm just me. I've not changed, I'm still the same person – a very normal, down-to-earth person at that. Like everyone else, I'm only too human; I just don't want to pretend that I never make any mistakes in order to make out that I'm not. I love my team for it though; they're only there to look out for me, and to be honest I wouldn't want it any other way.

Don't get me wrong, these days I keep a lot of stuff back on my social media profiles. And there's a reason Linda isn't on social media. No way! She's got her group chat with her friends on WhatsApp and I put her on Facebook for her mates last year during Covid. But that's it. There is no fucking way I would let Linda go public on social media. She would start fucking people off. I'd lose my job. Everyone keeps asking me, 'Is your mum on Instagram? Is your mum on Twitter?' And the answer is 'No' – and she won't be. I just couldn't trust her. I'd be shitting myself daily about what she'd liked by accident, or said to someone, or posted thinking it's private and it's not.

Joking aside though, on Twitter even I still find myself going, 'Should I, or should I not press the button?' I start to second-guess myself and if I'm going to write something, I'll start it about fifty times, because now I realise A LOT of fucking people are actually going to see it. It's not like before, when it was just my mates and a few randoms; I'm not exactly just shouting into nothingness any more. And yes, there are times when I think I maybe shouldn't have said this or that. I would never stoop so low as to troll someone or say anything personal or really nasty to anyone, because believe me, I know what that feels like. But I used to fucking love a good row on Twitter. When anyone used to tweet me and say something shitty,

I'd go back and shout something at them twice as loud in a tweet. It was always in a take-down, witty way, though. And I quite liked that. Actually, I don't know why I've written that in the past tense because I still do it sometimes, but you've got to pick your battles wisely. I remember one time someone tweeted about me doing the Cinch adverts on telly. They were obviously not a fan of the ad campaign, or of me. And that's putting it mildly. What they actually wrote was: 'I will never buy a car from you while that complete bucktooth ignoramus @Rylan is advertising your company! Illiterate, talentless, council nobody! @CazooUK please learn from this!'

So I just tweeted: 'Then walk mate.'

Though some of the responses from other followers were even funnier. Paddy McGuinness tweeted: 'Clearly one of big Phil [Schofield]'s undercover agents from We Buy Any Car.' Someone else adopted a more mindful tone: 'I would strongly suggest that these people explore journaling as a more positive outlet for such negative thoughts.' And Grayson Perry's wife, Philippa, added: 'I didn't even need a new car but I bought one from @cinchuk to feel closer to Rylan. Great car and a fabulously relaxed and entertaining TV presenter.' Aww. Wasn't that lovely. I love you too @Philippa_Perry.

Then there was someone else who tweeted something shitty like, 'The ugly cunt. Who the fuck would want to be with him?' and I just responded saying: 'Well, your dad left with a smile on his face last night!' My manager Nads called me, screaming, 'You can't do that!' I said, 'I've done it. And what?' Sometimes, I just don't care. What? Just because I'm on the telly or I work for the BBC, I've just gotta take it? Fuck off! No way!

Sometimes, I'll get someone tweeting something like: 'Oh, that Rylan, he's a fucking toothy cunt.' Those are my favourite sort of trolls because, to wind them up even more, I'll just add an asterisk and reply: '*rich, toothy cunt'. There are some sad people on Twitter, but I don't really care any more because I know they'd never say it to my face. Now, I just think, 'All right, you wanna do it like that? Well, I'll give it back to you then.'

And actually, I've learned that they quite like that. I can't tell you the amount of times that I've replied to someone with a witty comment and then they've come back saying: 'Actually, you know what, Rylan? You're well all right. My missus loves you.' I enjoy that kind of Twitter spat, in a weird way. James Blunt does it really well. He takes the piss out of himself a lot and when anyone tweets that he's a cunt, or whatever, he tweets back: 'Yeah, but I'm a rich cunt and I live in Ibiza.'

Sometimes, the social media abusers do wear me down though. Even now, I still get people threatening me or making homophobic slurs on Twitter. I remember the barrage of abuse I was treated to in May 2017 when I hosted a new game show called *Babushka*, which replaced *The Chase* in its regular 5 p.m. time slot for a month when Bradley and the chasers took a well-deserved early summer holiday. I was getting tweets saying: 'I can't believe *The Chase* has been axed for you. Bradley Walsh is amazing – but Rylan, you're a total faggot cunt' or words to that effect. Then I had people writing: 'I can't believe you're the new presenter of *The Chase*.' I mean, it was so crazy and also people can be so stupid, but rather than rise to it I decided to come off Twitter for a while. It wasn't because I couldn't handle it, but the show wasn't about me in the slightest. I was just the fucking host. The show hadn't even gone on air and it was already being slated. I just thought I should take a step back, let people actually watch it and make their minds up, because then the show could speak for itself. But yeah, I'm not gonna lie, it also really affected me on a personal level. I felt like I had gone back five years, and I didn't, and don't, need or deserve that level of abuse in my life. No one does. And I don't need homophobia either.

So when I hear of two gay women being beaten up on a London bus, for example, which is what happened only three years ago, sadly it doesn't surprise me. I saw all the statuses saying: 'I can't believe this is happening in 2019,' but then every day on my Twitter feed I'll get messages like: 'You're gay, you're a cunt, people like you should be killed because you're gay.' It's exhausting. Sometimes I just despair. I have to trust that where homophobia is concerned, finally, things are slowly changing, but some days it's harder to believe than others.

A few of my mates have anonymous Twitter accounts and I have to admit I have sometimes thought about setting up another secret profile, but I've never done it. Part of me worries I might fall into a trap of using it. But, more importantly, I think that the world is already full of enough liars and people not being who they are. I do all my socials myself because I want to be authentic. If people are following my social accounts, they're doing it to follow *me*. I don't think it's fair if I allow someone else to post on my behalf, or make out to be me. I am the only person using my social media accounts and I see everything – everyone's messages, everyone's comments – it's not someone else looking at them or vetting anything for me, because I post everything myself and I want to see everything. As I said, I quite like knowing that not everyone likes me. I like the fact that it keeps it real, in a really fake world, which I know is quite rare. I get why people don't do it – I mean, social media is a full-time job. My screen time this week? Well, my daily average of social media is four hours twenty minutes.

And that's down 62 per cent from last week. The highest is Instagram, then Twitter and WhatsApp. Crazy.

I don't know, I just find it really, really strange that there's so much shit and so many evil people on socials, or people pretending to be someone they're not. Is anyone who they say they are unless they've got an official blue tick next to their name? I genuinely think you should only be allowed to have a profile if you're tweeting for yourself, as yourself.

I would love to see a world of social media where everyone was verified to some extent, to the point where you may need some form of ID verification to have an account. It won't affect most normal, decent people but it would stop a lot of the shit. You could still be anonymous in the public domain; the only place that you would be able to be traced is through your server. And actually, the people that are sending death threats, or harassing someone, or stalking someone, if you made a complaint through the platform, well then they could be traced and prosecuted more easily. I think that would really change social media for the better.

I'm not saying we should stop people having an opinion, absolutely not, that's what the whole platform is for – if you don't like someone, you don't like someone – but hopefully it would make people think about what they say. People could still tweet: 'Ugh, he's so talentless'. That's fine, I can take that. But when people are saying: 'I'm going to come for you and cut your throat' and things like that, would they still be saying that if they knew they were completely traceable? No, I don't think they would. And if they did, they would have to face the legal consequences. I don't think it eliminates free speech – it eliminates arseholes. We live in a world where it's very easy to be traceable. Big Brother is a reality now, so I think social media accounts should be accounted for.

I've had a few people say to me, 'Well, how would you feel if you were a young gay person who's not come out and wants to remain anonymous? So, what, they shouldn't use social media then?' But sorry, no. That's not what we're talking about here. I'm not saying anyone's name and address should be on their profile, absolutely not. You can still be anonymous in the public domain. And if people don't want anyone to know their sexual preferences, well maybe they just shouldn't 'like' someone having a wank on social media. I just think everyone should be verified. I get the whole blue ticks thing. That totally makes sense. So let's do a green tick for everyone else. Social media would be all the better for it. It would clean up the fucking sewer.

I'd also love to see how many followers everyone drops. I mean, Instagram did a big cull not long ago and my followers dipped below a million. WTF? But it was actually a blip in the Instagram system and then they went back up to their pre-cull numbers, more or less, minus 3,000 or something like that, which is nothing. Apparently, Instagram were looking at the biggest profiles on the platform and it turned out that Kim Kardashian and people like that had millions of robots following them, rather than actual real human users. I totally believe that. I mean, I get that sort of thing sometimes on my Instagram comments. It's always these 'women' – clearly not, it's lady bots – posting things like: 'I had a lovely time in the bathroom. Come and look at me!' Or: 'Hi there! I'm selling some crypto.' It really pisses me off. To be honest, I don't really understand how it works, but you can block them. Spending hours blocking bloody bots, though, is such a waste of time.

My main accounts are Twitter and Instagram. I follow one account on Twitter called 'Chaotic Nightclub Photos',

@ClubPhotos_, with photos and videos of people on nights out that are just horrendous, with people looking wrecked, being sick and shit. I just love it, because, believe me, I've been there. It's just so good. And I love things like @loveofhuns or @glenn_kitson, who posts weird celebrity lookalike pictures with mock-serious captions. He put a picture up the other day of a little girl looking terrified beside someone dressed up as Ronald McDonald, and the caption below was a mini-bio of successful sixties recording artist and *Blind Date* presenter Cilla Black. And I don't know why I found it so funny, but it's the way the caption works with the image that means you just can't help but laugh, because obviously Cilla Black looks nothing like Ronald McDonald – well, maybe a little bit. But it's the weird mismatch between image and caption which is hilarious. I love shit like that. That's when social media is brilliant.

I used to have Snapchat, when that was a thing. In showbiz-world we all got paid to use it at one point when Facebook were really pushing it. I remember there was a thing called Snap glasses where you could post stories through your eyes and shit. But now it's just for pictures of dicks and tits, basically. I also have TikTok and I keep getting pressured to use it more. I don't. Because hello? I'm thirty-fucking-three. But yeah, according to the management (them again, fuck my life . . .) I've got to have a getting-my-head-round-TikTok day – because it's something that I 'neglect' but shouldn't, because I need to 'get with the times' and, actually, it's very 'influential' (but I don't care!).

The social media world is a fucking weird place, I tell ya. But actually, in spite of all the shit, I still love Twitter because it keeps things in perspective. Trolling is wrong, but as I said I do quite like knowing that not everyone likes me and I like knowing that I can change people's opinions as well. It's the best tool for my job, and the best tool for clearing something up if I need to, especially with the traditional media. I really like that social media is a way of talking honestly and addressing issues myself, and that I can use it to make some really important statements. There doesn't need to be an intermediary any more. I can tell people my opinion, or my side of any story.

If the papers print that my hair is blond, whereas in the past people like me would have a meltdown, like 'You fucking liars. Why are you doing this to me?', and then have to arrange some weird photo op or something, now I can simply post a tweet or a selfie on Instagram, captioned: 'No. Actually my hair is black.' And that's where it's a brilliant tool.

There's the flip side to that, though (isn't there always?). And that is: it only takes one Twitter comment to make a story. On my way home, I might drunkenly tweet something like: 'I fancy a cuddle'. Then the next morning I'll wake up to twenty news stories headlined: 'RYLAN MAKES EMOTIONAL TWEET AT 2 A.M'. No. The simple truth is that I was pissed. And yes, I'm absolutely fine. Or, like the whole *Babushka* saga, my new telly job is announced and one person on Twitter comments: 'Oh, I hate this man. He can't pronounce his 'T's.' And instantly the press version reads: 'Twitter storm as Rylan takes on new presenting role. Viewers switch off.' But that's not really true, is it? No, that's after just ONE harmless enough tweet from ONE single person. That's what's mad. Anything goes. Anything makes a story.

Last year, in 2021, when I disappeared to look after my mental health, I also disappeared from social media for five months. But did I miss it? More importantly, did I miss anything? When I went back on Twitter – at 9.14 p.m. on 16 September, FYI – to be precise, that's exactly what I posted:

'So . . . What did I miss?' The honest truth, I suppose, is that I missed fuck all of any importance. But much as I loathe the shit on there, I think I would miss some aspects of social media if I was blocked forever.

Social media is the best and worst thing to happen to us. As long as we all remember that so much of that world isn't real, that's fine. I mean, hardly anyone ever posts a photo on Instagram, especially not a selfie, without sliding to the right and giving it a bit of a glow-up. You just don't, because it's so easy to do. All that editing functionality wasn't available when Instagram first launched. You couldn't do any of that shit, so in the beginning it felt more real. Filters, exposure, brightness, and all that – well, that was a revelation. Now everyone's a fucking professional photographer. I mean, not gonna lie, I like a bit of a filter. It's usually the 'Paris' one I go for on Instagram, because I just think it makes everything a little bit more smooth. I like a classic black and white too. Only when I've got tan on though, because otherwise I look like Casper the Ghost. So, yeah, sometimes I get lost in this fake world, of course I do. But actually, I like living in the real one.

Lessons I've learned:

- Don't get caught up in the fake world. Try to remember that not everything you see on social media is real
- Try not to interact with trolls, although sometimes it's quite funny to play them at their own game
- It's always good to have a break from the world of social to remember the important things in life
- Don't give anyone your logins cos they will definitely go through your DMs

7

EUR' 'AVIN A LAUGH

That one week of your life where you can disappear into a different world and leave all your cares behind

In 2018, I was asked to join Scott Mills on the commentating team for the 63rd Eurovision Song Contest. I nearly died when the call came through. I FUCKING LOVE EUROVISION.

Ever since I was a young boy, every single year without fail I have always made sure that watching the Eurovision Song Contest is on the cards. It's like gay Christmas, but in May. All the acts vying for the spotlight, the crazy outfits, the even more bonkers songs, the razzmatazz of the staging, the OTT enthusiasm of presenters in the various different host nations, and the drama of the voting system – who's getting *douze* and who's getting the dreaded *nul points* – I love everything about it. All-time favourites? Genuinely, I have a hard time choosing: I loved Sertab Erener with 'Everyway That I Can' – that was an absolute tune. I think Sweden's Måns Zelmerlöw and Loreen were also amazing. There are so many that I could list off!

My earliest Eurovision memory is watching Dana International win back in 1998. I was nine years old and the UK hosted that year in Birmingham, following the country's victory at the previous year's song contest with 'Love Shine a Light' by Katrina and the Waves. It was a record eighth time that the United Kingdom had hosted the contest – a record we hold to this day, btw – so it seemed like a really big deal because it was taking place so close to home. Terry Wogan presented the show along with Ulrika Jonsson, and even though I was proud of our song, 'Where Are You?' performed by Imaani,

I remember that I really wanted Dana International to win it for Israel, because her song 'Diva' was such a tune – still is, in fact. Her outfit was pretty eye-catching too, with a feathered bolero-type jacket that looked like a giant tropical parrot. It was a really close-run thing right up to the last votes from the Former Yugoslav Republic of Macedonia, but in the end she did it: Israel came first with 172 points, just pipping the United Kingdom, with 166 points, to the post.

As she took to the stage to perform her winning song one more time, I'll never forget my mum telling me that Dana International used to be a man. I didn't really understand what she meant, and it really stuck with me. Mum wasn't being nasty in the slightest, but there was so much news coverage around this trans woman competing and she was explaining it all to me. It's strange, I was only young, but I vividly remember feeling really happy for this woman I had never met, almost *because* she was trans. I suppose I understood that she was different and so it was somehow special and important that she had won.

Fast-forward twenty years and twenty-nine-year-old me had been asked to be part of the BBC team to cover the annual spectacle, that year being hosted by Portugal for the first time, in its capital city Lisbon. Being invited to host the semi-finals was a dream come true; I basically did it on Twitter anyway, so I might as well go there, I thought! Scott Mills and me had never really worked together before but we'd met a few times and I knew he was decent. Within seconds of getting off the plane in Lisbon, I knew we'd get on like a house on fire. We had the same sense of humour and could both take the piss out of ourselves.

We were taken straight to our hotel to meet the rest of the team and again, within seconds, I knew Scott and I were going to have an absolute fucking ball because everyone was so lovely. At this first team meeting, that's when we were given the BBC 'Eurovision Bible', basically this huge folder containing the low-down on the performers from each of the forty-three competing countries, and all the info about their songs. Honestly, it was literally every single detail that you might want to know about every single contestant and their song: photographs, who wrote the music, who wrote the lyrics and what they 'meant' – come on, I'm not that stupid. I mean, I could read the words to the songs myself. Either they were sung in English in the first place, or they'd been translated for us if not. Anyway, you name it, it was in that bible! I understood that to present this show properly, I needed to read and use what was in that folder, so I could add a bit of knowledgeable commentary along with the banter and laughs.

The second thing we were given was our Eurovision accreditation. We were told that we had to be really careful not to lose or damage this vital bit of kit, because it was a personal biometric-based lanyard that you had to wear around your neck to get into the arena and certain 'off-limits' areas.

I remember proudly flashing my precious lanyard, casual as a cucumber, and sashaying into the Altice Arena, one of Europe's largest indoor venues, built right on the edge of Lisbon's Atlantic seashore. The glamour! It was exactly everything I wanted it to be, and more. Scott and I found our way to what's called the 'delegation bubble', the area where all of the dressing rooms are and where the delegations from every country hang out with each other. No word of a lie, it was like walking into *Fame Academy* on crack. Netta, Israel's twenty-five-year-old Eurovision hopeful, was parading around with a twenty-strong entourage. Benji from Sweden was being the cool kid with all the girls wrapped around him. And then there was us – Team UK with fellow Essex girl, the lovely SuRie.

Now, for those of you that have never really followed Eurovision over the decades, you probably don't really understand how big a production it actually is. Having competed on *The X Factor* and performed on the live national tour, I thought I'd seen what a big production looks like, but this was next level, and even as a fan I hadn't properly realised how much of a big deal Eurovision was. Thousands of people work on that show. It is the biggest music contest in the entire world. Don't quote me on exact numbers but I'm sure it costs about £30 million to put together just the three final televised shows. But having seen it up close, the money spent really shows in the production values of the sets, props, lighting and all-round staging extravaganza. I was filming with the BBC, so with my special 'access all areas' lanyard I could get backstage to do VTs with selected acts, which meant I could see how the show really worked. Excitement. That's where you really get to see all the secret tricks and what each country has spent on its performances and, believe me, we're talking some serious amounts of money. I shit you not, one country had shipped in a piano coffin, Israel had brought along several truckloads of Chinese cats with bobbing hands, and then casually in one corner of the vast space was what I can only describe as your basic Toys "R" Us robot, which was the prize property of little San Marino, bless 'em.

The other eye-opener was all the rules and regulations behind the running of this international event. There were so many that without my Eurovision Bible to hand, I can't tell you them all, but, for example, the songs can't be any longer than exactly three minutes, no live animals are allowed on stage, and countries can only put six people on stage – and that includes backing singers and dancers. That might sound quite simple, however the Eurovision referees go to full lengths to make sure that no one manages to creep onto the stage or hide under someone's dirndl as a sneaky seventh performer. Before each act goes on, one of the production team tapes six square boxes out on the floor at the required starting positions for each of the performers, and it's actually someone's job to make sure that all people that are going to be on stage stand in those boxes, then someone counts them off to prove that there is not one extra. For real.

It is this crazy whole fantastical world within a world. For that whole week, Eurovision is the only thing that matters. What's really amazing about Eurovision is the energy within the host city. That year in Lisbon the whole city was swept up in Eurovision fever. It's like having the Olympics in your hometown with fans from across the world all gathering in this one place for that one point of the year. Both inside and outside the arena, morning, noon, and in the middle of the night, the only songs you hear are the Eurovision entries. In every bar, club, restaurant you walk into, it's all you hear and see. That year, I really liked Benjamin from Sweden with 'Dance You Off' and Equinox from Bulgaria with 'Bones'. And honestly, I fucking loved every second of it. Lisbon was an amazing experience, but it was my first year, so I was quite new to the drama. I couldn't wait to see the acts in action and seeing what people brought to the stage, as well as looking forward to having a laugh and some fun with Scott and being a bit cheeky with the commentary. And I wasn't disappointed, though I couldn't help but feel for the acts that didn't qualify from the semis. It's got to be awful to get that far and then not get through.

While some of the other semi-final commentators had to travel back home to see the final on television, I had the opportunity to stay in Lisbon. I couldn't go all the way to Eurovision in Lisbon and not stay for the grand final! However, when it came to it, my ex wasn't too well so I narrowly missed out on my first ever final – and I'd been so looking forward to cheering SuRie on from the front. But family comes first. We were hoping for a really strong result but it was not to be. It was a very disappointing night for the British delegation – 'Storm' by SuRie came twenty-fourth, third from bottom, with a miserable 48 points. Still, it could have been worse: poor old Portugal, the host nation, came last on just 39 points. With her belting performance of 'Toy', complete with funky chicken noises and moves, and the Chinese waving cats, Israel's Netta stormed to victory, with a whopping 529 points.

After Netta's resounding win, in 2019 it was Tel Aviv's turn to host the competition. I was a little bit apprehensive about going because of the political situation in Palestine and we were informed that we would have to have twenty-four-hour security with us wherever we went. The idea of walking into a potential war zone did concern me, but there was no way I was missing it. From the second we touched down at Ben Gurion Airport, you could see how much the Israelis wanted to host the competition. The moment we stepped off the plane, all you could see was Eurovision branding across the entire airport and into the city beyond. This was the ultimate tourist postcard for Tel Aviv.

The drama really began when myself and my manager Nads got into the arrivals terminal. As we made our way to border control, the atmosphere felt quite tense and my nerves only grew worse because everywhere I looked, there were these proper military-looking armed Israeli border police. Nads is a British-born Persian and on the plane I'd made a joke to him that even though he was travelling on a British passport he'd get stopped by the Israeli security services before they'd checked his ID – and he was. The seriously scary-looking guards held him for about an hour and I was fucking fuming. I understand why searches and questions need to be asked, especially in a conflict zone like Israel, and even more so at a time of increased security when the whole world is watching your country, but why should Nads be stopped and not me? We couldn't help but wonder if it was based purely on the colour of his skin. I tried every trick in the book to get him out of there. I flashed my BBC pass, my Eurovision Bible, but those guys mean business and they're not the kind of people you can fool about with. For the first time in my life I think I used the words, 'Do you know who I am?' Maybe not the most sensible choice of words, looking back. They had no fucking clue who I was.

They finally let him out after a full-on interrogation as to why he was coming into the country. We can laugh about it now, but actually at the time I was seriously upset because I thought they weren't going to let him in. But thank fuck, he came out the other side and we could collect our bags and get out of there.

Our delegation hotel was absolutely gorgeous. Really everything out there in Tel Aviv was next level. Call me shallow, but because everything looked so beautiful, I almost forgot about the nastiness at the airport and the wider ongoing conflict. That was until one of the hotel receptionists took us on a tour to show us all the amenities. You had the gorgeous swimming pool, the luxury spa, a beautiful bar and, last but not least . . . the bunker room in case of a rocket attack on the hotel. Yep. The bomb-proof bunker room. If I'm being honest, it looked more like a cleaning cupboard than a high-security facility, but thankfully we never had to use it.

I had invited Nads to come with me to that year's Eurovision as he hadn't been before. He had been my friend and manager for years and I just knew that we were going to have such an amazing time. The 2019 competition had so many banging Eurovision songs. Our clear favourite that year was definitely Norway's catchy foot-tapping and occasional fist-pumping anthem, 'Spirit in the Sky', performed by supergroup KEiiNO. Nads and me both had it on repeat in our hotel rooms and we learned every word.

The next day, we went to check out the arena in Tel Aviv. I could hardly believe what I was seeing – this was a whole other level of spectacular. I'm even going to go so far as to say it was probably twice the size of the Lisbon arena in 2018. Again, the first place we checked out was the delegation bubble, but this time the size of the bubble was humongous.

Second time round, hosting the semis felt really comfortable for me because I was a lot more relaxed. I knew what to expect and I knew what I was doing. What's more, I'd got to know Scott much better. We had built a relationship and were getting on really well. We really were onto a winner. The more time we spent together, the more we realised just how much we found the same things funny and, mostly, had the same taste in the tunes, too. There was this one entrant from San Marino called Serhat whose song 'Say Na Na Na', was not necessarily a UK number one hit, but a classic Eurovision track that will get you bopping. Check it out. Everyone thought Serhat wouldn't make it through the semi-finals but Scott and I were really championing him. On the night of the first semi, we had our fingers crossed for him and during the results, when they announced that he'd made it to the final, we felt like children whose own football side had got through to the FA Cup Final.

And so it begins . . .

The woman who changed it all for me.

I nearly died when Geri walked into rehearsals.

Spice up your life!

Fear for my life . . .

Walking into the *Celebrity Big Brother* house a joke . . .

. . . walking out a winner.

My gorgeous Nanny Rose. Miss her every day.

Behind the scenes at #BBBOTS.

With my telly mum and dad.

Lock up your ovens – he's only gone on *Celebrity MasterChef*.

The final three: me, Sammy and Kimbo.

Launch day for my first book, couldn't believe it!

My number one – Mummy.

Sweetie, darlings. On set of *Ab Fab: The Movie*.

My loneliness is killing me . . . but it's fine because I've got Britney.

When 2012 Rylan meets his future in the hall of fame at *X Factor*.

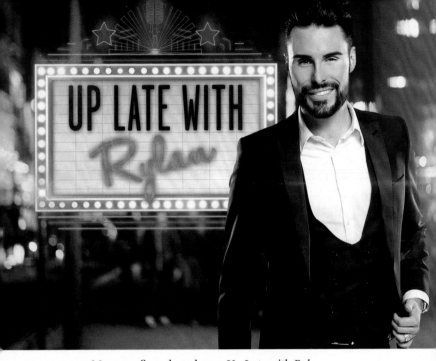

My very first chat show: *Up Late with Rylan*.

I always knew I'd grow up and still be playing with dolls.

Me and Ruth hosting *This Morning*.

My very first Eurovision – Lisbon 2018.

Every year at Eurovision, the organisation takes over a nightclub in the host city and turns it into Euro Club for that week. On a 'Say Na Na Na' high, that evening we decided to go out to Euro Club. This year it was in a massive aircraft hangar in Tel Aviv and they had done it so well, with a massive stage, delegation areas, VIP tables, indoor and outdoor bars, the lot. That night Serhat performed his 'Say Na Na Na' but he also decided to give us a rendition of his new single, 'Chocolate Flavour'. The less said about that the better. But that's what's so wonderful about Euro Club. Eurovision acts, past and present, perform there live every single evening. All of the music played is Eurovision, live, remixes, new mixes, and everyone is just there to have a good time. There's never any drama.

Once again, I was not able to go to the final, but this time for more exciting reasons: I had to fly back to London on the Friday evening because I'd been asked to be the UK spokesperson to give out the jury votes. Casual, not. It was actually me saying those iconic words, 'Good evening, Europe. This is London calling. Our 12 points go to . . .' Truly, hand on heart, that was a massive honour for me, not only to host the semi-finals and commentate alongside Scott, but to actually be on the show itself, doing that iconic job of announcing our votes that so many 'somebodies' had done before me. Our entry that year was 'Bigger Than Us' by Michael Rice. He is such a sweet boy; he was just twenty-one at the time, and it was a pleasure to spend the week with him. Michael's voice is amazing, it was a fantastic performance and a beautiful song, but sadly we didn't do too great. In fact this time, unbelievably, we came LAST, with only 11 points. Serhat and San Marino did a bit better – 'Say Na Na Na' came nineteenth, with 77 points. But it was Duncan Laurence with 'Arcade' for the Netherlands who came out top, narrowly beating the Italians, and the gorgeous Mahmood singing 'Soldi'.

In 2020, the global pandemic struck, with especially devastating results in Italy, and obviously as the world ground to a halt, so did the Eurovision Song Contest. It was the first time since the very beginning of the show in 1956 that it couldn't take place. So in 2021, Eurovision 2020 was carried over to be hosted in Rotterdam. However, new Covid variants were still a threat and travel restrictions remained in place, so it was decided that myself and Scott wouldn't be travelling to the Netherlands and would be commentating live on the semis from London instead.

As you now know, three days before I was supposed to join Scott in a BBC studio in London, my life changed dramatically. And I didn't end up commentating in 2021. I couldn't watch it either. That was the first year that I've ever missed Eurovision.

Fast-forward to 2022 and I was back, bigger, better and more ready than fucking ever for Eurovision, and that year we would be travelling, along with the United Kingdom delegation, to Turin in Italy, no less. Neither myself nor Scott had ever been there before, so we were really looking forward to visiting the city. I truly felt like I needed that week. Even though I was working and even though there would be people that knew me, it couldn't have come at a better time, because a short break away in a foreign country would allow me to be a little bit more anonymous and just enjoy myself. That's the beauty of Eurovision. As I said, when you're there nothing else in the world exists and that is exactly what I needed. And I had the best time EVER. From start to finish, the whole week felt amazing. Yee-haaaaa!

Luscious locks Sam Ryder, our UK entrant, was the nicest, most talented guy I've had the pleasure to meet. For the first time in over a decade, other delegations were looking at the UK like real competition. On the Sunday when we arrived, first up was the opening ceremony, where all of the acts get to meet each other and the press for the first time. In Turin, it was held in probably the most beautiful palace I'd ever seen. It was like something straight out of *Bridgerton*. This occasion is the ultimate show-and-tell, and so this is when the games really begin. In that way, strangely, Eurovision reminds me of *The Hunger Games* except that thankfully, no one actually dies. All the acts are paraded around in front of the press from all over the world, so everyone can place their bets and see who they're gonna back. It really is such a spectacle.

Now, for me this was also the first time I'd been at Eurovision as a single man, so anytime anyone looked at me, I felt like I was allowed to look right back. And there was so many nice people there this year. None more so than the Swiss delegation. The Swiss guys were staying at our hotel and we were the only two delegations there. Their entrant was Marius Bear, a proper sweet boy with a fantastic voice who was definitely always up for a laugh and a drink. Him and his whole team were legends and we would stay up drinking with them till three in the morning, just laughing about anything and everything. It is so much fun to have friends from other delegations because it brings a new aspect to the whole experience. I'd met so many great people previously in Lisbon and Tel Aviv, and now I had a chance to see them again in Turin. It's like it's now become my once-a-year friendship group where for that one week I get to catch up with all my mates. And I've also become friends with some seriously die-hard Eurovision fans who are there every single year and at every single Eurovision event without fail. Now, I'm sure a lot of people will think, 'Fucking hell. What sad fuckers!' But actually, I get it. I understand why so many people spend so much money to have that one week of their life where they can just escape their normal lives and forget about everything. I also know that for years, the popular perception of Eurovision has been that it's a bit of a joke competition, but I'd say that over the past decade the competition has really changed into a fantastic music contest. Don't get me wrong, you still get the odd entry that's there for a bit of a wind-up and a laugh, but that's what makes it Eurovision. Most of the music is totally amazing and that's the core of the competition: great music, immense performances, and an important message . . . everyone coming together from across the world to share in the love of music. As part of the team, that's what has really stood out for me over the years.

Commentating on the first semi-final in 2022 was the first time that I'd felt back to my old self in a very long while. Andrew, our head of delegation, and our producer, Adam, sat in the commentary box with me and Scott. And I don't know what was different this year, but for some reason they just let me and Scott roll with it, and it really worked. From a personal point of view, even though I knew I was technically working, and that I had to make sure I'd swotted up on my Eurovision Bible to be able to drop in the odd fascinating snippet about the acts here and there, I felt free to do or say what I wanted. It just felt like a really relaxed and uninhibited experience. At the end of that first semi-final, we all looked at each other and we were really proud of the job we'd just done. Watching it on TV, you might not think it's difficult, but when you're working to the on-stage Eurovision hosts' timings – with presenters from all over the world – you know that those timings aren't going to stick, and it's the world's biggest live show. So with the best will in the world, sometimes things don't go to plan. You've got to be on your A game, so at the end of that first semi, knowing that Scott and I had only gone and smashed it, I felt like the old Rylan again. And that's when I knew I could relax. I'd done it. I was back with a bang. And I thought, 'Fuck it, I'm really going to enjoy myself this year and let go.' Simple as that. I was not going to be frightened to speak to people, not give another thought about giving anyone a cheeky look, and I was NOT going to feel like I was doing something wrong by enjoying myself for a change. And believe me, I enjoyed myself. Go on, Dolly! Oh my God, I had the best week of my life.

As my first single Eurovision, the whole joke for the week was that the UK delegation gave me my own scorecard. They'd say to me at breakfast, 'So, where did we go last night?' And I'd say, 'Albania.' And I'd be there, ticking off my scorecard, like the cat who'd got all the cream. Anyway, enough about me and my extra-curricular exploits – back to Turin and the actual song competition. The second semi-final came along and it was amazing. And then we were finally off the clock with hosting and it was time to just enjoy ourselves. Scott is such an amazing co-host and I'm so proud to call him not only a colleague but a friend. We really had the best time in 2022, more so than ever before. Don't get me wrong, there were times when I was out there in Turin, having the best experience, and a slight darkness would creep in, just to remind me that I was going back home to an empty house. We all have our moments. But I wasn't going to let it ruin my Eurovision week and it honestly didn't.

This was the first time I'd been to Eurovision and felt like I didn't have to worry about anything; I could just do my job and enjoy the ride. It was also the first time I managed to actually stay the whole week and get the full-on live final experience. Being at the final was better than I could ever have imagined. It was the perfect end to the perfect week. And to top it all off, our boy Sam came second, giving us our highest placing in years. I couldn't have been prouder of him. I mean, let's be honest, I've been lucky my entire career with the shows that I've worked on, but I know that I am so, SO lucky to work on that show. There's something about Eurovision that takes me away, and I don't mean literally. It takes me to this carefree place of happiness. I just love the fact that it's the world coming together. Even though it's a competition and it's got competitive elements to it, everyone that I've met who's performing seems more bothered about taking part in the competition than winning. That's really nice because even though I'm sure deep down they all want to win, it doesn't feel as though people are against each other. It feels like everyone is together having the same experience. For that one week a year, I am part of one massive family. It doesn't matter who you are, what country you come from, who you're supporting, we all become one in that arena. I know that sounds cheesy as fuck. But it's the truth. If you ever get the chance to go, do it. It's one of the most liberating, enjoyable experiences any of us could ever ask for. All that's left to say is: may the Eurovision Song Contest long continue!

Lessons I've learned:

- Eurovision is everything you want it to be and more
- Stop trying to sound foreign when you're saying words of a different language to people of that nationality, because they'll look at you like you're not well
- They say never to mix business with pleasure – but Eurovision is the exception
- And finally, for those people that don't get Eurovision and message complaining that their licence fee is going on us having a jolly, you've paid for the 7.30 a.m. Ryanair flight from Stansted – £27.99. I've paid for the rest!

8

A WHOLE
DIFFERENT REALITY

Yeah course, let's go to the Big Brother *house
and shout over the wall*

If watching reality TV was an Olympic sport, there's no doubt about it – I would be a five-times gold medallist by now. I just love it. Always have done. I don't get to watch as much telly as I used to – because my ugly mug's always on it – but it's still my absolute favourite kind. I just love watching people, I suppose.

In the year 2000, I was twelve years old. That summer we went on holiday to Spain and everyone was talking about this new TV show called *Big Brother*. I hadn't heard of it, but when I came home, it was in all the papers that I'd see on a Sunday morning – the *News of the World*, that was what my mum would get. It was all I kept hearing about, but I still didn't really get what it was. Then I remember turning on the TV one night and seeing these people plastering themselves in body paint then pressing their wet, naked, multi-coloured bodies up against a wall. I knew I shouldn't be watching it, it was late for a school night and Nanny Rose would have had a fit if she'd caught me ogling the bare-cheeked shenanigans, but for some reason, from that moment on I was completely fascinated.

It wasn't until 2001, though, that I really got into *Big Brother*. That was the second series, which Brian Dowling won. Of course, his whole storyline was that he was a young lad from Ireland who went into the house as a gay man, but he hadn't 'come out'. He hadn't told his family, so they were all going to find out at the same time as the rest of us. Obviously, as a young gay kid, I now know why I was so interested in his story; he was living the dream that I wanted to live, but at the same time he was struggling with his sexuality. I became obsessed, to the point where – along with probably half the rest of the country – I would watch the housemates sleeping while listening to bird noises and the train going past at Bromley by Bow at four o'clock in the morning. There was something mesmerising about this programme. The show itself was so real, yet set in a fake environment. I was mesmerised by the world-within-a-world format. Having no contact with the rest of society outside, not even seeing a camera person. Being disconnected from reality in the most reality-esque show on TV.

For me, I loved the fact that the housemates weren't big TV stars. They were ordinary young people, with very ordinary jobs, families and backgrounds. And even though it was just a TV show featuring a bunch of very ordinary people, there was something so extraordinary about watching them carry out even the most banal tasks in that bubble – smoking a fag, having a bath, fighting about doing the washing-up. And, of course, as soon as they were on TV, they weren't really that ordinary and some of them were total weirdos. But they quickly managed to capture the hearts and minds of the nation.

The *Big Brother* house was just down the road from our house, at 3 Mills Studio in Bow. One day when I was on my way back from school, me and my friend actually got off the train to go and walk its perimeter. On the way from Bow station, we nipped into a Tesco superstore and bought some clothes pegs. We wrote 'Brian to win' on them, threw them over the wall into the garden, then ran away. I wrote about this in my last book so I don't want to repeat myself, but looking back on it now there really is something very,

very strange about a child going to the lengths of walking all the way to the *Big Brother* house to shout and scream over the garden wall to the housemates. I don't know what it was about the show, something just enveloped me. I think it's that it's almost like you're perving; you're sitting there, watching, from your sofa and you become a peeping Tom. But it's OK, it's allowed – it must be, because it's on TV.

All those years ago, *Big Brother* started originally in the Netherlands, dreamed up by someone called John de Mol (hence the name of the production company, Endemol). When the British *Big Brother* house first opened its doors in 2000, it was a completely new television experience, the first studio reality competition show and the most original thing to hit our screens in decades. No one had seen anything like it. It was all anyone could talk about. There had obviously been other reality documentary-style shows in the nineties and even earlier, but I remember watching things like *The Cruise*, which launched Jane McDonald, or *Driving School* when Maureen Rees – remember her? – failed spectacularly to pass her driving test six times and ran over her husband's foot in the process. Then there was *Castaway*, also in 2000, which launched the television career of Ben Fogle. You could argue that *Castaway* was of a similar ilk to *Big Brother*, but it was somehow different. Firstly, it wasn't in a house – instead, the thirty-six men, women and children went to live for a year on Taransay, a remote Hebridean island. Secondly, it wasn't a competition – there was no cash prize at the end; rather, the experiment was to see if they could build a community. And lastly, there was no supporting camera crew, so the islanders filmed themselves. After that, in 2001, we had *Survivor*, which was a ramped-up, exotic version of *Castaway*, but this time with individual members of two tribes competing for an end prize, a whopping 1 million pounds, and set on an island in the middle of the South China Sea rather than the Outer Hebrides. I watched and enjoyed them both. They weren't without their own individual senses of drama, shenanigans and personal conflict, but I mean, call me a sadist, it somehow just wasn't the same thrill as seeing people locked inside the small, claustrophobic *Big Brother* house.

I also preferred fly-on-the-wall reality shows where you got to see people in their usually closed private or professional environments. There was *Airport* and *Airline* that started in the late nineties, featuring the staff at Heathrow and the crews on the EasyJet and Britannia Airlines respectively. The Great British telly viewing public became obsessed with this kind of show, so that spawned things like *The Salon*, which was more like *Big Brother* but in a hair salon. I fucking loved *The Salon*. It was great because you had real hair stylists and real clients and real arguments. I still watch episodes from years ago now on YouTube. But the big difference on that show was that the staff and salon visitors weren't cut off from the outside world, so they knew what was being shown on TV and what wasn't. Actually, in the early days, that didn't really affect what was happening in the salon, which was great, whereas now it wouldn't work that way.

For me, though, *Big Brother* was always the highlight of my TV year. My favourite ever reality TV moment came on the 2004 series. I remember it so vividly because I had broken my ankle. I used to go to trampolining lessons, because why not? What else would a chubby ginger fifteen-year-old do on a Thursday or Friday after school? That night on Channel 4, 28 May, they were calling it 'Black Friday' because the last ever episode of *Friends* was on and then at 10 p.m., it was the launch of *Big Brother 5*. So, for me, that really was a double whammy night and a half. I'd just come flying off the trampoline and landed with a crack. It hurt like fuck, so I knew my ankle was broken, but I pretended I was OK. I was probably white as a sheet and it must have swollen up though, because my mum wasn't convinced. She kept saying, 'Right, Ross, we're taking you to A&E.' I was just putting on a brave face, saying, 'No, no, no, I'm fine, Mum. Honestly, I am.' She knew I was lying because I was desperate to watch *Friends* and *Big Brother*.

One of the housemates who went in that night was Nadia Almada, the first transsexual contestant to go on *Big Brother*. Unbelievably, she told no one that she was transsexual. It was the first time in her life that she'd gone into a social situation where she could be the woman that she is. She went all the way to the final, and I'll never forget the night that she won, because it wasn't just someone winning a reality TV show, it was someone who was genuinely finally being accepted. Without sounding like I'm getting too deep, it was obviously so much more than a show for her. I just remember watching her walk out of that house, crying with emotion but you could tell it was nothing to do with winning *Big Brother*, something that was built for our entertainment. Actually she was crying because that was her life and she'd felt that she'd been seen and loved for who she was as a human being. No one knew she was trans. That's what's so amazing about a show like *Big Brother*. It was very different on *Celebrity Big Brother*, because when each person walked through the door, you pretty much knew who they were, but when someone walked through the door on the summer show and said, 'Hi, I'm Mike and I'm from Birmingham,' the other housemates had no reason to disbelieve them. When Nadia walked into that house and said her name was Nadia, she didn't have to actually say she was a woman. She just was. It wasn't a question that was in anyone's head. In that sense, it was a massive television moment. And I remember feeling it was a massive moment of acceptance by the British public that voted for her to win.

Then, ten years after *Big Brother* came into our lives, *The Only Way Is Essex*, set around Brentwood, was launched, and a year later inspired its snooty cousin, *Made in Chelsea*. We also imported the *Jersey Shore* format from MTV America and decided to have our own UK version, *Geordie Shore*. And then because of the amalgamation of reality shows that MTV had created, the bosses there thought, let's make a reality show where we can bring all these people together. So *Ex on the Beach* came along. And of course today, you've got your *I'm a Celebrity*, your *Love Island*, your *Circle*, your *Married at First Sight*, your this, your that . . . And it's all great. I'm a big fan of reality TV. However, to me, there has been nothing on telly that is as perfectly imagined as *Big Brother*. I mean, why have a *Big Brother* knock-off when you could have the original back?

The only real reality show left was *Big Brother* because everything else is 'constructed' – the people in those shows are not in a bubble, they see the crew filming them, and also some of them are partly scripted and choreographed. *Big Brother* was never constructed in that way – anything, within reason, could happen in that house and there was nothing *Big Brother* could do to stop it, other than intervening to chuck someone out. More importantly, I suppose, right from when I first watched *Big Brother* over twenty years ago, I liked it because, in the beginning at least, they looked kind of ordinary. They wore the sort of high street clothes I'd see my brother and his girlfriend wearing. You saw them twenty-four hours a day, day in, day out, and yes, you saw them at their best when they all got dolled up for eviction night. But you also saw that they looked like shit when they woke up in the morning and hadn't done their hair or put on their makeup, just like the rest of us. You saw them putting on fake tan, shaving their legs or tweezing their chin hairs. You could even hear them let rip the occasional fart. For real. That's why it was called 'reality TV'.

Obviously, the other fascinating feature of *Big Brother* for me was that once the housemates were in there, they had to compete in tasks to win their food rations, and then the rest of the time, they were left entirely to their own devices. Outside the tasks and the strict rules of the house, nobody was directing their behaviour. Big Brother could throw a task in. He or she could fucking turn the lights off, but it was up to the housemates what they said and did. No producer went in and said, 'Can we shoot that again?' or 'Can you do or say that again for us?', which is what they do on pretty much all of the other reality TV shows. *The Only Way Is Essex*, for example, is very much controlled by the producers and is pure 'constructed reality'; as is *Made in Chelsea*, *Real Housewives* of wherever, and all of those similar shows.

I wouldn't say that I'm a religious *Love Island* viewer, but I've watched it in the past and it is great telly. But it's also completely constructed. When two of the islanders leave the villa to go on a date, you can sense all the production crew in the background literally calling the shots. Sometimes you can almost see the cameramen. They ask the contestants to walk into a shot against a smouldering sunset, and to do it again if the angle's not right – obviously. Who else would be filming the loved-up couple out on a yacht or on a picnic blanket in the middle of some lemon orchard? But that's the set-up for *Love Island* because they're not constantly in the villa. I understand that and it works because it's quite a glamourised show. It's good television because they know how to keep you hooked at the end of an episode. They know all the narrative tricks. A lot of the *Love Island* crew also worked on *Big Brother*, so they know how to make a reality show, but at the end of the day, it's not *Big Brother*. No way would any of that level of direction ever have happened in the *Big Brother* house. *Big Brother* would never have broken that bubble.

I think that was the real secret to that show, and that's why I was so fascinated by it from that very first time I switched it on. But when reality went from being real to constructed, it blurred the lines between reality and fiction. For me, that's where it all went downhill.

Personally, if we brought *Big Brother* back and it was down to me, we would not be getting involved in that constructed reality business in any way whatsoever. I'd much rather have a bunch of housemates sitting staring at a wall for ten hours than start messing about with the format. I'd rather the shock be shit and it be real than producers have to go in and reshoot it. Absofuckinglutely. And anyway, that would never happen because of what *my* Big Brother would throw in at the housemates. I'd be a really fucking evil Big Brother and all. But no, there's no way I'd say, 'Can we all stand up and do that again, please?' No way.

The difference with *Big Brother* is that, yeah, it could have had all these glamorous shots with all the slo-mo and that. But that's not real life. *Big Brother* was gritty, and I mean really gritty, especially when you look back at those early shows I was watching as a teenager.

I particularly remember watching the whole Jade Goody 2007 *Big Brother* racism row when she and her mum Jackiey Budden turned on Shilpa Shetty with the help of *Playboy* model and ex-Miss Great Britain Danielle Lloyd and Jo

O'Meara from S Club 7. I remember that series so well. It wasn't easy to watch. The producers didn't edit what went on in there and they broadcast exactly what was said and done. They didn't immediately choreograph some sort of retraction or apology from the offending housemates. And you know, yes, back then duty of care wasn't what it is now. *Big Brother* accepted a verdict from Ofcom that they hadn't acted quickly enough to protect Shilpa Shetty, or with enough authority by not immediately evicting the offenders. Ultimately, and quite rightly, the public were the judges of that offensive behaviour.

Later that same year, a posh blonde girl called Emily Parr was chucked out after blurting out the N-word when she was mucking about in the garden with Charley Uchea, who is Black. Shocked, Charley just turned and said something like, 'You shouldn't have said that. You're in big trouble.' Charley didn't necessarily think Emily had said it meaning to be offensive to her, she was just young and naïve and stupid, but it didn't matter. It was and is offensive; she said it and she was chucked out for it.

Other times I'd watch it and some guy might be there one minute, and gone the next. The next day it would be announced that he had left the house, and we never really got to know what he'd done to get chucked out. Of course, that then just opened up a whole guessing game, which could actually be very damaging to the contestant in the real world. I understood that obviously there were times when maybe the team had to make a call – for example, when the footage of the incident could embarrass another contestant, and that's why it wasn't shown. I respect that there have to be certain boundaries a TV show will not cross, regardless of whether it's a reality show or not. However, I think in the later years, too much went unexplained and if I was the one calling those shots, I would have let the viewers decide.

God. Writing this, I realise just how much I miss it. I think my fascination with it is that it is that concept of a world within a world. As we know, 'Big Brother' comes from Orwell's spooky dystopian novel *1984*, where he's supposedly the tyrannical leader of Oceania, a totalitarian state where the ruling party exerts total power over the populace. Get me! I told you I was one of the brainy kids at school (actually, I just asked Alexa). No one wants to be controlled. No one wants to be told what to do. No one wants to be told you can or can't do this. But there is something sick in everyone that secretly enjoys watching other people being told what to do. Obviously I don't mean that in a cruel way, don't get me wrong, but there's something fascinating about watching people in that controlled environment. We like seeing people in a bubble, confined in an artificial world, being dictated to by that all-seeing master. We like seeing people do well, but at the same time we like seeing people trip up – or even better, falling flat on their faces. I think that's why reality TV and *Big Brother* in particular became such a phenomenon.

Because you could engage with the programme, via the live feed, at any time of the day or night, it became like you were part of it. And because ultimately we were the ones deciding who stayed and who was evicted, it felt like we had ownership over these people. Like *we* were in control of their fates, not just Big Brother.

It's exactly the same on other reality shows like *I'm a Celebrity . . . Get Me Out of Here!*, for example. And before you ask, NO – that is one reality show I could never do. I'd sooner go on *Celebrity First Dates*, or even *Celebrity Love Island*, if that was a thing, but top of the list of things I will NEVER do is

I'm A Celebrity . . . No makeup, no food? No. I couldn't do that! I'd die. But it's the no makeup that would worry me the most. My luxury item would be a salon-sized bottle of foundation and an automatic spray-tan booth. That'd do me. The thing is though, if I really, *really* had to do it, I would. If I really had to eat a kangaroo's bollock, I'd do it – I could do that if I had to. But a fish eye, again no. Never. Ever.

But that's why reality TV works. It's a bird's-eye view on real people being forced to live in extreme conditions, sometimes having to do things they'd never usually do, with people they'd never usually hang out with. For a dedicated people-watcher like me, that's my idea of a night of telly heaven.

You just wanna look through someone's curtains and have a good snoop into their daily life, don't you? Well, it's definitely what I want to do when I walk down the street at night and people have got their lights on and their curtains closed, but there's a gap – I wanna have a good look through that gap. I just do. It's human nature. Or coming through the suburbs at night on the train, and I can see into people's back windows because they don't think that anyone can see in. I always stare and wonder about all the different lives and dramas going on inside those houses. It's exactly the same if I ever stay at a hotel and you can see onto other balconies or into the flats opposite. I will just sit there. I won't look at the telly. I'll look out the window and I'll watch for hours. When I was in Manchester filming a BBC makeover show called *You Are What You Wear*, all the different people in these flats that were next to my hotel were like my own little soap opera. I gave them all names: 'Oh, look. Dave's back. Maureen's having a cup of tea. Mary's hung the washing up. Hold on a minute, Steve's got a girlfriend.' I was obsessed. Obsessed. That's why I could never live in a block of flats, or in a new apartment building in London, because a) I'd probably get punched in the face, and b) I'd then get arrested for being a peeping Tom.

Well, on *Big Brother*, they were actually letting me see right inside that house. And not only that, I sometimes broke in for a little rob up . . . But we don't need to go into that, babe. That's what it was for me and I found it addictive. I LOVED it.

Lessons I've learned:

- Reality shaped the TV of today and I wouldn't have a job without it
- If you are yourself on these shows, you will always be shown for the person you are – it could be the biggest validation or wake-up call you ever have
- Deep down we are all human, and reality TV shows us mirrors of ourselves. Sometimes we like what we see, sometimes we don't
- We are all NOSEY BASTARDS, and I for one love it! KEEEEEEEPPPP NOSING!

9

THE BIGGEST OF BROTHERS

This is Big Brother.
Would Rylan please come to the diary room . . .

Given my serious addiction to *Big Brother* growing up, becoming a housemate was always number one on my list of things to achieve. When I turned eighteen, I could vote. But most importantly I could also apply to be on *Big Brother*, which was the very first thing I did. I sent in my application video, made it through the auditions, got down to the final selection. I even packed my suitcase and was taken into hiding at a secret location (a hotel called Cragwood Manor in the Lake District). I had all my clothes transferred to the big black glossy *Big Brother* suitcases, the lot! Excitement. But it wasn't meant to be. My identity was leaked and back then, if you got found out, you weren't going in. I was gutted.

Little did I know that a few years later, something even more special would happen. Fast-forward five years, straight out of the trauma of *The X Factor*, and I finally walked into the *Big Brother* house as a celebrity housemate in January 2013. It was genuinely a dream come true. For some people, being locked up in a house and being disconnected from the outside world for five weeks could seem like a prison sentence. But to me, after coming off *The X Factor* and being on the front page of the paper pretty much every day, it was almost like a respite. Although, when you're in it, it's very different to just watching it.

You know, I loved it in there, but sometimes there really was fuck all to do. You were just sitting there, no books or phone, not even some paper to doodle on, and for some people that drove them mad. They couldn't hack it. But with the way my mind works and having been such a superfan all my life, I found all sorts of ways to keep myself amused. I could just sit and look at a door, examine it, and think, 'I wonder how that door locks,' then I'd go and try to work it out.

The locks were obviously controlled by *Big Brother* but electrics can go wrong and sometimes the wrong doors would unlock by mistake. We had a gym the year I was in, and I remember one day I noticed that the eye had turned green above the door. Big Brother only opened the gym door for an hour every day and I knew it wasn't the right time, but I pushed the door open and there was a lovely cameraman standing right there. I started talking to him and he got really frightened and wouldn't speak. Then all I heard was Big Brother's voice, having a right go at me: 'THIS IS BIG BROTHER. Rylan, you must shut the gym door IMMEDIATELY!' So then I got called to the diary room for a telling-off, but I had a go back at Big Brother and said, 'Well, you shouldn't have unlocked the door, should you?' But it happened all the time!

Every time Big Brother spoke into the house, you'd hear a click. That was the sound of the microphone being turned on. It really was just this slightest click, a nothing sound, but I began to dread hearing it, because you'd never know what was coming next. I almost became a little bit frightened of the dictator – because that's what that voice is – and that's exactly how housemates *should* feel, I suppose. As I said, Orwell is where it all comes from and once I was actually in there, I realised that Big Brother's word *was* final. Literally. That's why the show worked. I remember being on *The X Factor* live tour straight after coming out of the house and I heard exactly that same 'click' in a room and I went, 'Shush!'

Automatically, I sat to attention, waiting for this voice to say, 'This is Big Brother.'

As viewers of the show will know, it wasn't just one single Big Brother. There were about ten different ones. I quickly got to know all the voices and I'd try to picture what Scottish Big Brother, say, was like. There was one that we always called 'Mel B' because she had such a thick Leeds accent, and when Mel B called you to the diary room that's when you knew you were in trouble. This voice sounding just like Scary Spice would come over the intercom, 'This is Big Brother. Would Rylan come t' diary room – immediately.' I'd be sitting having my fag, and I'd be like, 'Fuck! It's Mel B. What have I done?' There was another one I nicknamed 'Josh' because I fancied his voice. When I heard it was Josh on the intercom, I'd go all funny and think, 'Ooh, Josh. I might go into the diary room and have a chat.' When you're in there, you just do when you hear a certain voice – or at least I did. I would fantasise and sort of romanticise these different Big Brothers, and make up little back stories for them all. The weird thing is, later, when I got the job on *Bit on the Side*, I actually got to meet some of the people behind those voices. But I haven't got to that bit yet.

For some reason, I could also see through the mirrors. That was another good form of entertainment for me. You shouldn't be able to see through them. No one else could, so I don't know what it was, whether it was my eyes or because of my height or something, but I could absolutely see through the glass. It was just really odd; fucking weird. Guess that's what I am.

There was one mirror by the lounge where we used to sit and I could see the outline of the camera person and his or her hand. See what I did there? I'm not making an assumption about their gender, but to be honest, I always used to imagine that it was a nice, handsome young cameraman. So, every now and again I used to go up to the window and just put my hand on the glass, right up against his. And obviously he shouldn't have, but then when I would move my hand an inch or so to the right or left, or up or down, I'd see his hand move to meet mine. It sounds fucking crazy, but to me it was like a little connection with the real world that helped to keep me normal. The lights are never turned off in *Big Brother* until all the housemates are asleep and I'll never forget being in bed one night and waking up, opening my eyes, looking in the mirror and I could just see him standing there, someone behind the mirror, clear as day. Maybe seeing through those mirrors was my superpower. I wish I could see through fucking time instead, I'll tell ya. Jesus.

So many amazing memories were made in that house. One very important person who became part of my life in there was Claire Richards, aka Claire from Steps. She literally became a big sister to me in that time, and I'm so blessed that carried over into real life. We had so many hilarious moments together. I used to love dressing in her bra and running around the house. She acted like she was peeved, but I know she bloody loved it really. When I walked out the winner, it was a massive honour for me. Not only was it the validation I so badly needed after my experiences on *The X Factor*, but I'd also just won my favourite show on television.

Fast-forward just another few months and it got even better when I was asked to become the presenter of *Big Brother's Bit on the Side*. OK, it wasn't the main show, but there was no way I was going to turn that job down. I was worried, though. After all the hate and abuse thrown at me during *The X Factor* the year before, when pretty much overnight I'd become famous as a 'national joke', I was really concerned about what the public would think. I was also really worried about my capabilities. LISTEN, I knew I could talk about *Big Brother* all day. I'd already been doing it for thirteen years. But could I stand there on live television and actually host this thing?

For me, *Big Brother's Bit on the Side* was the ultimate apprenticeship. I was thrown in at the deep end and had to learn on the job – not to mention get my mouth round talking coherently with a brand-new set of VERY LARGE white teeth. (Don't worry, there's more on my teeth later, they've got a chapter of their own – see p291.) Looking back, it was the best way to learn how to be a presenter and do it with confidence. But my biggest learning from being on *BOTS* is just how important it is to make your workplace a happy place. I was so lucky that the *BOTS* studio became like a second home to me and the team I worked with, and the guests that we had on the show honestly became like a second family. I treated that show like my baby. I would have done anything for it, and I still would.

Before I worked on *BOTS*, I was always really curious to know how it all worked behind the scenes – well, now I know, and I can let you in on some of the secrets. So, imagine your house, but around all the walls there are two-way mirrors. And behind all the mirrored-walls there are corridors, but when you're in that corridor all the mirrors are just like clear windows, so we (the *BB* team) can see in and the camera people can capture every single detail, all the different angles and close-ups. And it's the same around the perimeter wall of the garden as well. Obviously, the housemates can't see us. Well, as I said, they're not supposed to be able to . . .

Inside the actual house itself, essentially there's only the one big 'real' window, a huge glass door, which looks out onto the

AstroTurf garden with the tiny swimming pool. Basically, the whole house is rigged with fixed cameras like orbs. We get the main shots from those, but then if there's a task happening where we know everyone's gonna be together in one part of the house, actual camera people will have the big old cameras ready and they will position themselves at the windows all around to get different close-up action shots. That's how it worked on the main show and that's how it worked for us on my show as well, because I used to love to do behind-the-scenes stuff. I'd go and stand behind a two-way mirror in the bathroom where someone was sitting doing their makeup. I'd go in and be on the other side whispering, 'Oooh look, she's doing a nice job with her contouring.'

Aside from that, every single day I'd go into the *Big Brother* house first thing in the morning, and I'd walk up and down them corridors behind the scenes and look through the windows, seeing how the housemates were getting on and what they were all up to. Then I would normally spend about half an hour talking to the camera crew, checking what was coming up, and how the task room was looking. Everything. I was a nosey bastard, but I'd always like to know what was happening. And not because I needed to but because I wanted to. Even after all that time, the fan in me always got excited. It was just my thing and to be able to do that – well, I just loved it. Sometimes I'd be creeping about all over the shop, having a snoop around, but I had to be very, very quiet. You were supposed to wear a black cloak when you were lurking about in the camera runs to avoid any possible reflection or glare, but no one really did.

After I'd checked out the house, I'd go to the main gallery in the office where there would be about sixty screens with every angle of the house on live. In the gallery, and also in my production office, there were two main streams. You had the 'A' stream and the 'B' stream, and both of them were quad split, meaning each screen is split into four. 'A' is what the production team is mainly following – if there's an ongoing row or something saucy going on, for example. The best way to describe 'A' is as the 'storyline' that the producers have identified and are planning to feature in that night's episode. So, for argument's sake, if Dave and Julie are having a bit of a developing romance, or maybe a bit of cheeky bedroom action is going on, that would be the 'A' story.

On the 'A' quad split, you'd have four different camera angles of Dave and Julie. A close-up of Dave, and a close-up of Julie, and two different wide angles of Dave and Julie from two different cameras and angles. The 'B' story, or the 'B' quad split, would be following something else that was going on in the house. It might be the other side of the 'A' story – so, for example, some of the other housemates in the bedroom discussing what's been going on with Dave or Julie – or it might not correspond with it at all.

Those are the main splits that we'd follow, but throughout the night, twenty-four hours a day, you'd have producers sat there watching *everything* that was going on, all the conversations, all the arguments, and so on, and forming a judgement on which 'storyline' to follow.

Not only that, but in the production office there would be a whole team of 'loggers'. In actual fact, I met one of my loggers when I left the house and I found out that her job was to sit there in front of a computer with a headpiece and to follow me all day, twenty-four hours a day. They'd obviously do it in split shifts – they're not that sadistic. But if I coughed, the logger would have to write in the Rylan Log: '10.32 a.m.: Rylan coughed.' And if I said to Razor Ruddock,

'You all right, babe? How are you?', down it would go in the log: '11.15 p.m.: Rylan to Razor: "You all right, babe? How are you?"' Literally, that is what the loggers had to do. They had to, because we couldn't afford to miss a word. To go back and look for something that was said, or not said, in the tens of thousands of hours of footage, from all the different cameras and angles, was doable – but extremely time-consuming. So that's what the logs were for.

My biggest pet hate with housemates when they used to come on my show, was when they complained about how they felt they had been portrayed on the series. 'They edited me badly' or 'They never showed me when I was dancing on the tables and having a laugh', blah, blah, blah, blah, blah. It was said to me a lot after that very first series that I hosted, so after that I used to go and see all the housemates just before they went in on the launch night, either in their hotel or in the holding rooms at *Big Brother* where we'd normally put them before they actually stepped into the house. Sometimes I'd know some of the celebrity housemates as well because I would have worked with them, but with both ordinary and celebrity housemates I'd always go to say good luck, enjoy it and have a great time. That wasn't part of my job, but I'd do it because I wanted to meet them and get a sense of who they were in person, face to face, and what they were like in real life. Apart from my natural nosiness, I was going to be discussing them every single bloody night – that's what my show was all about. So I always liked to get a real first impression, rather than a *Big Brother* first impression, because people are very different on launch night to what they are a week into the series.

I'd only be in there for like five to ten minutes, but quite a few of them would ask me what was the best piece of advice

I could give them, and I'd always say, 'My one piece of advice is, unless you say it or do it, we can't show it. We can't CGI you punching someone in the face. We can't dub you saying words you haven't said. Unless you say it or do it, we can't show it. So don't say it and don't do it.' Simple as that. But then they'd come out and they'd punched someone in the face, or they'd have said something homophobic or racist, or some other disgusting stuff, and they'd blame the edit. But I just thought, 'Well, it's your own fucking fault. I told you.'

The other thing I'd always say to housemates before they went in was, 'Use the diary room. That's what the show is. That's what it's there for. Use the fucking diary room.' Lots of people wonder who it is the housemates are speaking to when they go into the diary room. Some people tell me that they thought it was a qualified psychologist, but actually it's one of the many *Big Brother* programme producers, because, as I say, it is a really big team behind the show. On any series, there's probably about ten different people that are 'Big Brother'. Obviously, when I got the job on *Bit on the Side*, I really wanted to see what 'Josh' was like. I found out that he was this lovely guy, but sadly I didn't fancy him in the slightest, and then I worked with him for the next seven years. But yeah, anyone can be Big Brother. That's the one thing I would have changed if I was in charge: Big Brother would have been one single voice. I'd have made it so that the voice of Big Brother was vocoded and almost computerised, because that's what stops that mental block, i.e. that Big Brother is actually a real person on the outside.

But back to why we did the logs. On the last *Celebrity Big Brother* series in 2018, for example, when the former *Emmerdale* actress Roxanne Pallett falsely claimed that she had been abused – well, punched actually – by fellow housemate

Coronation Street actor Ryan Thomas, obviously we had all the camera footage from several different angles, but we also had the second-by-second record made by the loggers. And to this day, I still can't understand how anyone can think they can get away with making an allegation about something like that in the most watched house in the fucking country.

It was just awful because we were all sitting there in the production office going, 'What the fuck? This isn't right.' But obviously we let the situation play out in the house, and that was the right decision, because actually it went to show how much of a real-world situation that was, because sadly that kind of thing, people making false allegations, does happen in the real world.

I think that's what was different about that show. We had to make some really tough decisions about whether to break the bubble and intervene, or whether to allow a pretty horrible situation to play out in real time and let the viewing public make up their own minds about the rights and wrongs of what was unfolding in front of their eyes. And yes, maybe sometimes some people thought *Big Brother* should have acted faster to safeguard the wellbeing of contestants, but on the whole I think it was judged fucking well. When you go into something like *Big Brother*, you sign your life over to us for the four weeks or however long you end up in there. There's no hiding in that house. The truth will always come out.

If we have to chuck someone out of the house, I believe we should always show why we're chucking them out, every time, without fail. As bad as it is, as good as it is, as whatever as it is. I don't like secrets on *Big Brother* because that's when the fans lose trust. But over the years there were a lot of things that happened in the house that weren't shown, and will never see the light of day, for reasons out of our control. But if the show was to come back, I don't think that could happen any more. Transparency is key, and always should be.

Of course, things have changed so much even since the last series of *Big Brother*, and thankfully now telly makers have to take their role in safeguarding contestants incredibly fucking seriously. We all know about the fallout of reality TV shows and especially the suicides of two of the former *Love Island*ers. I know myself from my time as a housemate how hard it can be, even when you're still actually in the bubble. That's why I always drummed it into the housemates before they went in that they should use the diary room, as often as they needed to. That's what it was there for. On *Big Brother*, if someone was really upset or struggling, they could speak to Gareth, who was our main psychologist. He was always on hand, twenty-four hours a day. He would talk to the house-mates via the diary room, and sometimes we would let him actually go into the diary room and sit with the housemate, though obviously for patient–doctor confidentiality reasons we would never show that.

There were also times when other doctors had to go into the diary room, because someone had hurt themselves or was complaining that they had something wrong with them, a tummy ache or whatever. Of course we did – we had to look after people. But the doctor would usually go into the diary room as opposed to the person coming out. The only time we would ever bring a person out was on a doctor's order. Say, if someone had broken their leg in there, then they'd have to be taken to hospital to get an X-ray and have treatment. And in that case they went to hospital in a blacked-out car with a blanket over their head. They were put in a private room at the hospital, they didn't speak to no one other than the doctor, and then they went back into the house if they were fit and well enough.

Some of the housemates were paid a lot of money to take part in *Celebrity Big Brother*, but I'd normally find it was the people that were probably paid the least, who went in there with zero inhibitions, who'd give us the best content. The stars who were paid more money didn't need the show so much. They could take it or leave it, so they would tend to sit back and not get that involved in the game – because it *is* a game show after all, a televised competition. They didn't need to win it, or even go on there in the first place, so they didn't have to step up and give it their all. For example, Evander Holyfield, aka 'The Real Deal', the American former heavy-weight boxer, was paid a shitload of money to go in. Don't get me wrong, he is a really sweet guy, but he didn't really do anything once he entered the house. The other housemates were so bored by him he was voted out after a week, and that was that. It was just one of those things.

The beauty of *Celebrity Big Brother*, however, is that you could sit there and see all these big names on paper and think, 'Wow! That's going to be some series.' But then there would be some people that you might not be as familiar with, or some you'd never even heard of, and they'd be the ones who'd end up winning it, because they were just themselves. It would happen every single year – it always does. Those are the people that do best in *Big Brother* – and in any other reality contest, for that matter. As I've said before, if you're that good an actor, you should be in Hollywood, not Borehamwood.

Over the years, I've made so many fond memories and, more importantly, so many friends on *Big Brother*. What could be more amazing than working on your favourite television show with a bunch of brilliant people who would end up becoming your best mates? One person in particular is Nads. He was my runner and we instantly clicked. There was something about his personality and his love for the show that I was instantly drawn to. (As I've mentioned, he's now also one of my managers, but more on that later.)

There are so many crazy stories from my time working at *Big Brother*. Some of the stories about housemates I could never repeat, much as I'd love to – and I'm not just talking about things they got up to in the house; crazier still were some of the things they got up to when they came out – but from a legal point of view I'd better not. Still, I can reveal some really hilarious moments that won't give my publisher's libel lawyer a heart attack.

For example, one night we booked a car to take an ex-housemate home after appearing on my show. Simple enough, you might think, but the driver had to pull over on the side of the M25 and ask the ex-housemate and their partner to leave the vehicle after engaging in a sex act in the back of the car. Getting that phone call to the office was quite exciting and funny. Not only did we have to apologise to our regular car company, but we then had the issue of one of our guests being stranded on the hard shoulder of the M25 in the middle of the night. As I said, not mentioning any names, but it was a celebrity housemate . . .

Another of my funniest memories of working in the *Big Brother* office was the afternoon Daisy, our production manager, took a phone call from the hotel where we put up our guests overnight before the show. I was sitting opposite, being a nosey parker as usual, and could see that she had a really confused look on her face. It looked like she was lost for words, so I told her to put the call on hold and explain what was going on. She said it was the hotel manager calling to inform us that our forthcoming *BOTS* guest – an ex-housemate – had left a pile of human faeces on the floor of his room. Yep, you read that right – a great big dump on the floor. I told Daisy to tell the hotel manager we would call them back after we'd spoken to the guest in question. Daisy put the phone on speaker and we called the ex-housemate and told them what the hotel had just told us. The first excuse was brilliant. It went something like this: 'Oh no, that's not poo! I got a kebab last night and I must have dropped it on the floor.' OK, fair enough, we thought, maybe the hotel mistook a cold kebab for human faeces. We called the hotel back, explained what the ex-housemate had told us, but the manager of the hotel cut us off abruptly mid-clarification and, completely deadpan, said, 'Guys, this is NOT a kebab. Someone has taken a shit on the floor of the hotel room.' Just reading these words as I'm typing is actually making me laugh out loud. So then we called the ex-housemate back and explained that the hotel were adamant that someone had defecated on the bedroom floor. That's when the story changed. The ex-housemate then said that late the night before, they'd been walking down the hotel corridor and noticed a dog sniffing about. What must have happened, they claimed, is that they left their door open when they went to bed, and the dog must have walked into the room in the middle of the night, looked around and done a whoopsie on the carpet. I was dead. I couldn't contain my laughter. But that was the point at which we knew the game was up and we just needed to pay the cleaning bill. Don't get me wrong, as much as we love this ex-housemate, there always seems to be some type of drama surrounding them. But to go to the lengths of trying to persuade us that a dog was walking along the hotel corridor, had broken into their room in the middle of the night while they were sleeping, taken a crap on the floor, and then left again, really was one of my favourite excuses of all time. That was just a typical day in the *Big Brother's Bit on the Side* office.

Then there was the unforgettable day of the 'David's dead' saga. I was in the office early on 10 January 2016, when we found out that David Bowie had passed away. It was Day 7 of *Celebrity Big Brother* and his ex-wife Angie was one of our housemates, so she needed to be told. In real time, on our office plasma screens, we saw that she had been called to the diary room. When she walked back out into the house, she decided to tell one of her closest friends in there – Tiffany Pollard, star of US reality dating show *Flavor of Love* – about the news. 'You can't say a word,' Angie said, 'but David's dead.' Tiffany immediately went to pieces, collapsing on the floor and wailing like a banshee. We couldn't believe what we were seeing. We genuinely thought Tiffany must have been SUCH a big Bowie fan. I mean, even his ex-wife wasn't reacting like that! In real time, Tiffany's sobbing went on for about half an hour. We were all glued to the screens, actually worried that she was having a full-on nervous breakdown. Then Tiffany decided to go and tell the rest of the housemates that David had died. Watching as things unfolded, we thought it was extremely disrespectful to do that, but the girl was in such a state. It was only when those now iconic words came out of her mouth that we all finally realised what the hell was going on. 'David's dead,' she gasped. Naturally, the other housemates all went into shock. Because there was another David in the house, Mr David Gest, who for the previous few days hadn't been too well with a cold. That's when we realised that Tiffany thought DAVID GEST HAD DIED IN THE HOUSE. All our jaws dropped to the floor. I remember screaming 'NO, NO. NO FUCKING WAY! THIS ISN'T HAPPENING!' The *Celebrity Big Brother* house descended into chaos, housemates clattering into the bedroom only to find the apparently dead body of David Gest lying under the covers in his bed. It was like a scene from *Silent Witness*. Darren Day pulled the covers back to reveal an ice-white, slightly waxen and dishevelled-looking David Gest. Admittedly, he didn't look great, but he was very much still alive. I think it was genuinely the best piece of unscripted television that has ever graced our screens.

Me and the team got up to our own hilarious antics too. One of my favourites was a regular ritual called 'Audience Dog'. Each Friday during an eviction night, we would go round to the side of the studio on my buggy. The members of the live show audience would be queueing up on the opposite side of the fence, but they couldn't see that we were there. We would creep along, put our hands underneath the fence, grab the queueing people's legs and start barking, hence the name – Audience Dog. If it was a warm night, we would also take a water gun with us. We would drive along the line of queueing people and start spraying them – but not in a nasty way. It was fun and we knew that the audience enjoyed it. It literally became tradition. Every Friday, come rain or shine, Audience Dog was on! I know it sounds crazy but genuinely it was hilarious and it really made my eviction nights.

Don't get me wrong though, our team also worked really, *really* hard. There were about thirty-eight of us and we always made sure that the show was top notch. And when the shit hit the fan, we knew how to deal with it. And believe me, there were a lot of times where things went wrong – and I mean SERIOUSLY wrong.

One show I'll never forget became notorious as 'Fight Night'. It was after eviction night on Day 27 of *Celebrity Big Brother* 16 in 2015; model Janice Dickinson and US 'Queen of Porn' star Jenna Jameson had left the house, so *Big Brother* was covering that live from 9 to 10 p.m., and then my *Bit on the Side* show was going out at 11 p.m. When housemates come out, we want to make sure they are still fresh and on form, so instead of waiting an hour, we carry straight on with filming and pre-record the show 'as live' at 10 p.m.

That night, alongside Janice and Jenna, on the panel were Farrah Abraham, the US reality star of *16 and Pregnant* and *Teen Mom*, former *Big Brother* contestant Aisleyne Horgan-Wallace, and actress Vicki Michelle, best known for her role as the saucy waitress Yvette Carte-Blanche in *'Allo 'Allo!* For legal reasons, I can't share all the details of what happened, but let me just say that Aisleyne and Farrah didn't exactly hit it off. About forty minutes into our recording, so at about 10.40 p.m., in a discussion about 'anger issues' – oh, the irony! – Aisleyne called Farrah a 'nasty bitch', adding, 'You've got your cheque, you've had your cheque, now get on the plane and fuck off!' To which Farrah replied, 'Hag, be quiet!'

Readers of the tabloids will know that after that someone threw a glass of bubbly at someone else. And *I* know a big fight broke out, because I was caught right in the middle of it. We stopped the recording of the show and, before I knew what was happening, Aaron, my security guard, wrapped his arms around my waist and chucked me out through the fire exit door. Two seconds later I decided to go back into the studio because I couldn't let what was happening unfold in front of my beloved audience. I walked back in to find Janice Dickinson crowd-surfing across the audience. I couldn't believe what I was seeing. Chairs were flung all over the floor, broken glass was everywhere, and the audience seemed to be loving it. Within seconds the police turned up, and that's as far as I can go with this part of the story – that footage will be somewhere, but it's not public.

That was a real turning point for me because that's when I realised that as much as this show was all about having a laugh and taking the piss, sometimes it could get intense, and that night things got *really* intense. Back in real time, at 11 p.m., what we'd already recorded started playing on Channel 5. It was suddenly 11.15 and we were right up against it. We still had the police in the studio when we realised, 'Fuck, we're gonna catch up live soon.' And that's basically what happened: we caught up live and still had fifteen minutes left of the show to fill. So viewers at home saw a glass being thrown across the studio, then suddenly the test card came up, and then eight seconds later it cut back to me, standing there in the studio that looked like it had been hit by a tornado. I just looked into the camera and said, 'Something's happened. We were on a bit of a pre-record delay tonight and unfortunately we have caught up live. I'm afraid we can't explain what's gone on . . .'

It was totally surreal. For the last fifteen minutes, I just winged it, made it up as I went along, asking the audience questions and getting their opinions on what had been going on in the house. This is how good my *BOTS* audience really were. They were fucking massive *Big Brother* fans, who loved the show as much as I do, the same faces most evenings. And of course I smashed it. Because I'm a pro, and because at heart I'm a fan before a presenter. And for that final part of that show, I was especially proud to be one. It was the fans that kept the show going that evening.

I'm also proud of the little bits of me that I brought to my *Bit on the Side* empire. We had lots of traditions. Whenever a housemate was evicted, I thought it would be funny to get them to go and sit in a well, basically so at the end of my show I could say, 'That's it. It's time for your final farewell.' We just thought it would be funny. And it was.

We also had the Dildo Olympics. Yep, you read that right, the Dildo Olympics. In 2016, one of our legendary *Celebrity Big Brother* housemates, the self-proclaimed HBIC (Head Bitch in Charge) aka 'New York' aka Tiffany Pollard, came on the show after reaching the final (she came fourth, behind actor and singer Darren Day; runner-up actress Stephanie Davis; and the winner, *Geordie Shore* star Scotty T). Don't ask me why, but for some reason we made her film a segment with a massive pink rubber dildo. I think she was doing the sex segment, so one of the runners went out and brought back this real 9-inch dildo. I think it was a real one anyway. You can't really get a fake one, can you? I mean, I don't know how big they normally are – I don't use them – but our Wendy from the audience team looked pleased to see it, so . . . I'm assuming it was real.

Anyway, I got a bit distracted there. But back to that pink rubber penis. It became very much part of the office furniture and one of its many bonuses was that it had a massive suction pad at one end. Me and the team would take it in turns to chuck the dildo up in the air and see if we could get it to stick to the ceiling. We all did quite well in the Dildo Olympics heats, to be fair. Special mention again to Wendy – she fuckin' aced it. (Oh, and while I'm at it, Wendy, a sincere (non-) apology for constantly throwing a potato sack over your head, wrapping you in a blanket, tying you to an office chair, making you eat spoonfuls of cinnamon and then bundling you into a car boot. We love you. And you really are the best. Sounds worse than it was – she loved it, lol.)

One day during a round of Dildo Olympics, six or seven people walked into the office, all in suits, looking very serious. No one had decided to inform me that the Endemol lawyers were coming to take a tour of the studio. There I am, standing on a table, 9-inch dildo in hand, and my bosses' legal team have just walked in. I had two choices: 1) place the dildo on the table and jump down to the floor and apologise, or 2) invite them to play. Within a minute the serious besuited and booted lawyers were vying to get up on the leaderboard. The image of these high-profile legal eagles frantically tossing that 9-inch dildo at the ceiling was the epitome of the *Big Brother* office. That's how we worked.

We used to really rinse the main show. If we got our time slot pushed back or something, for whatever reason, we used to get our water guns, run up to the main show set, soak people and run away. And I used to make placards, saying, 'Justice for *BOTS*!' We'd march up and down the hill outside the main show's office, shouting, 'Justice for *BOTS*! Justice for *BOTS*!' The execs in there would be furious, telling us to shut up because the housemates would hear us, but I'd just shout even louder. It was hilarious.

If things were a bit slack in the office during the day before filming, we used to play sardines. I'd get the whole office outside and then one person would go and hide. Then we'd all split up around the office and the *BOTS* studio, and try to find them. Then how sardines works is that when you find the first hider, you hide with them. There was one place that someone found one day that was underneath the audience seating. I just walked past and saw a bit of their trouser-leg poking out. I don't know how they even managed to get in there in the first place, but I had to go around the back of the set and then under this hole and wriggle in. The next thing I knew, there were twenty of us, all crammed in there underneath the tiered seating, trying not to make a sound. I was having to hold my nose (it got a bit sweaty Betty under there TBH), but also trying not to laugh. We loved it.

We had so many games in the *Bit on the Side* office. We'd play rounders outside. We used to go and sneak up onto the roof of the George Lucas studio, look into the *Big Brother* garden and shout at the housemates. We had two crows as well, Sheryl and Russell, that we used to talk to. The *Strictly Come Dancing* lot used to come in right at the end of the *Big Brother* series, so before I worked on that show, I used to drive my buggy up to their set and drive across the dance floor. I'd be like, 'Here they come, the *Strictly* lot, ready for their show.' I'd sing the *Strictly* theme tune – 'Doo-di-doo-di-doo-doo-doooooo-doo-doo-doo-doo-doo . . . Boo!' – and then drive off.

When they were filming the first series of *The Crown* there, we used to abuse all that lot as well, because we thought that they thought they were something special too: Claire Foy, Matt Smith, Ben Miles, Jared Harris, John Lithgow, Eileen Atkins – all of them. Lovely people I'm sure, but they filmed next door to us in Elstree and they just used to come in and swan about like they owned the place. They built all these big sets all over the shop – everywhere you looked another whopping great palace would have popped up. They took away our bit where we used to play rounders in the summer and put Buckingham Palace there. 'You cunts!' was my general attitude. So I hated them, and then I started watching it and fucking loved it. But we used to see them walking about all the time, so you'd be sitting there, then someone would pipe up, 'Oh, there's the Queen!' 'Oh look. Yeah, there's Phil again.' I used to break into Buckingham Palace and Downing Street all the time. On my last day of *Big Brother*, I snuck over and wrote 'Rylan woz here' on the tunnel that led into Buckingham Palace. Have that, you fuckers, coming in here and taking over our studio space! I got very territorial.

Yeah, we were terrible, but the studio management at Elstree loved us, because we would literally brighten their day. I used to go up on the roof of the studios and throw water balloons at people and hide. And then one day I got the fucking director of the entire Elstree studios straight in the head by accident and he still doesn't know it was me.

As the host, I didn't care whether you were my runner or my executive producer – *everyone* was treated the same. Everyone's ideas were valid, and everyone had a big input on the show. Work can sometimes be heavy, and like on any show I've ever worked on, but especially *Big Brother's Bit on the Side*, I always wanted people to enjoy it. We worked when we needed to work, we played when we were allowed to play, but ultimately we enjoyed every single second of it.

I had an amazing time at *Big Brother*. Even after six or seven years, I never lost the buzz of excitement at being part of it. Every day I went into work, I'd drop my bag off in my dressing room, then without fail the first thing I would do was head over to the *Big Brother* house. Even after all that time, the feeling of walking around the house immediately transported me back to the first time I walked through those doors as a housemate back in 2013. There was something so special about that house; it wasn't a TV studio. It felt like home, and even though we changed how the house looked for each series, I always had a special connection to that building. Maybe it's because for a long time the only place I've ever felt safe was when I was securely locked in the *Big Brother* house.

In fact, my love for that house is so deep that I modelled my own house on the set – the garden was landscaped by people who worked on the show and I even built a diary room in my hallway for me to sit in. I love it. It's full of shit at the moment, but you press the eye button on the wall and everything to get in, just like in the real house. That's how much I fucking love that show. Anyway, I just go in there to think. And talk. I can even set it up so other people in the house can listen in if I want them to.

My saddest memory is the time we found out that *Big Brother* was coming to an end. Of course, every year we always knew that there was a possibility of it not returning, but it was an institution, the mother of all reality shows, so none of us ever really expected it to be axed, and we definitely didn't see it coming back then. I'll never forget that moment. It was the day before we launched the final series, and both Emma Willis and I had a phone call from the head of Channel 5 to tell us that the show wasn't being renewed. I was devastated. *Big Brother* had been part of my life for so many years and now it was being taken away from me. That's the thing about *Big Brother* – to me it wasn't a television show, it was a way of life. It was *my* life for six months of every single year and, with pretty much the same team of people returning for each series, it was way more than a job.

The next day I went into the office to prepare for our launch night. There was this real sombre atmosphere among the team as none of us could believe that this was it – the last and final series. I walked in and saw Emma. She looked at me and I looked at her, then we both just stood in silence and hugged. I think neither of us actually believed that it was really over for good. Deep down I thought it might turn out to be like when the show moved over from Channel 4 to Channel 5. I was just convinced that it would end up somewhere.

Looking back, I can be honest and say that the show did lose some of its shine over the years, but it was the fan base that kept it going. Five nights a week, my loyal *Bit on the Side* live audience would be there, sat behind me, screaming, cheering, laughing and crying. There were so many familiar faces in that audience over the years and many became my friends as well. Barbara, for instance, who was always sat right in the front row, ready to make a song and a dance, and that's why we loved her. These people didn't get paid to do this. They were there because of their love for the show, and they would be there without fail every week. It would never have worked without the audience, and to each and every one of you, I thank you for being part of such a special experience.

I've said it before and I'll say it again, I might have been the presenter, but on the inside, I felt exactly like one of the audience members – the undying fan – and believe me, it's a real celebration that we got through that last series. But then finale day came and, fuck me, it was bittersweet. The last day on any show always feels weird, but this one was different because we knew it was potentially the last one *ever*. There was tears from everyone and to this day I don't honestly know how I got through that last show. It just passed in such a blur because I couldn't really fathom that this was the final time I'd be in that studio, hosting the programme that I loved. But we did it.

Live on air that night I promised that *Big Brother* would get back to you, and I'm still confident it will. And I pray that when it does, I will be a part of it. That evening we had our wrap party and boy, did we party. I had already asked Nads to come and work on my management team as he had become such a close friend and I knew I could trust him. At about 4 a.m., me and Nads walked up to the house and let ourselves in. I needed one last time in the *Big Brother* house. All the lights were off. A few things had already been robbed – shock – but it was beautiful. I'd never seen *Big Brother* like that. I sat in the garden for the very last time and had a cigarette. It felt almost like saying goodbye to a mate who was moving abroad, that I knew I was never going to see again, or at least not for a long, long time. Before I left, I walked into the diary room, sat in the chair, looked at the camera, and I thanked *Big Brother* for everything it had given to me. So at least that clears up who the last housemate in the diary room was. Then I walked through the lounge and exited via the fire escape. That was the last time I ever saw my beloved *Big Brother*, the show that changed my life, my career, my relationship, my confidence, my heart. I miss it every day.

I don't know where I'd be today if I hadn't gone into *Big Brother* as a housemate. I certainly wouldn't have married my ex-husband and I doubt I'd be doing the jobs I'm doing now. That show was genuinely like my child, my baby. It was live every weekday night, so that was my routine, my life, my everything. I can tell you now that when it finished, it definitely fucked me up a bit. It was when I was in the process of building the house I'm sitting in now, so it's not like I even had my own home to go back to because I was living in a bedroom at my ex's in-laws. Just nothing felt right.

I've made no secret that it's the job I'd love to have again because I still miss it so much. I still see lots of the team, but the thing with that *Big Brother* lot is that I could go years without seeing them, then I'd see them tomorrow and it would be like it was yesterday because we were so close. They were like my second family, and they always will be. As much as I love working on everything I've done since, my loyalty will always be with *Big Brother*.

There have always been rumours of it coming back, and finally it's been confirmed. At the time of writing, however, I don't know if I'll be part of it. I will always love *Big Brother*, no matter what, and what happens, happens. They know I'd be there – in a heartbeat. But if I'm not asked to be the presenter on any new series, then I wish all the best to whoever does get the job. And I hope that they love the show just as much as I did.

Lessons I've learned:

- *Big Brother* was everything that me as a little gay ginger boy wanted it to be
- If it ever comes back, I hope whoever is there does it justice
- Nothing can better prepare you for being a TV host than working on *Big Brother*; it's the best training ground. Anything after *Big Brother* is a breeze
- They say don't mix your work life and personal life. I did – and although things don't always work out the way you plan, I have no regrets

LESSONS WE'VE LEARNED . . .

Nads Dehdashti

Friend/Manager – Team Rylan

I first met Rylan – or Ross as I call him when I am trying to have a serious conversation – back in the summer of 2014. After freelancing as a production runner for two years, I had finally landed my dream job of working on Big Brother.

Arriving at the Bit on the Side *studios, all raring to go, I was surprised to find out that one of my main responsibilities would be looking after what I thought was a pop star wannabe who was trying his turn at presenting. What I was greeted with was a charming, sweet, and very talented man, who wanted a Chicken Selects meal deal from McDonald's for his rehearsals. I didn't think that would be the right time to tell him I had voted for Speidi to win his series of* Celebrity Big Brother.

What bonded us immediately was our obsessive love of Big Brother, *constantly trying to outdo each other on our knowledge of previous housemates and tasks. Luckily, we were in the only place in the world where this was not considered (that) weird. On top of that, while we were living totally contrasting lives, Rylan was only four years older than me and with me being only twenty-one, we were both going through the growing pains of living through our twenties. Even though he might have had those sparkly veneers, a somewhat questionable tan, and a celebrity profile, I quickly came to realise that we weren't that different. We were both trying to navigate the ups and downs of life. And as fate had it, we would do this together for the next eight years.*

On paper, it seemed like Rylan had his whole life together. His dream job, married at twenty-five with a stepson and about to embark on building his own house, while I was still only just managing to pay my rent and bills and manage a somewhat non-existent dating life. He had fast-forwarded that 'adulting' phase. But life is not as simple as a straight-line trajectory, as we would both quickly learn.

After three years at Big Brother, and being promoted to assistant producer, I felt like I was on cloud nine – until the rug was pulled from under me. On a random Wednesday morning in January 2017, I was sat in the shoebox of a dingy workshop that they called our office, when I got an unexpected phone call from a family friend. Instantly I knew why. She yelled down the phone at me, 'Your dad's dead' – think the 2016 CBB 'David's dead' moment from Tiffany Pollard, but without the hilarious comedy of error. Because there was no mistake here. I looked around, slapping a smile across my face, conscious that I didn't want anyone to see me upset.

That whole hour (and month) is a bit of a blur but all I can remember is the crushing claustrophobia of being stuck in a shoebox in the middle of Elstree, an hour from home. Luckily for me, our team at BOTS was already like a second family who were there to soften the fall. I remember I wanted to leave before Rylan got in. I packed my stuff to go and meet my friend, then rushed out of the office only to run straight into him arriving in his infamous taxi. Instantly he knew something was up and minutes later, I was rushed to his dressing room. He lit us a cigarette, got me a Red Bull and with some Persian music playing from his phone, he danced around the room. This rather strange but hilarious gesture was the distraction I needed. Later that night, I got home and got a text from my boss telling me to turn on the TV. They had changed the credits to include my father's name. This will stay with me forever.

After it was announced that Big Brother was being cancelled (I won't go into what an injustice this was to a television staple), I knew I was at a fork in the road. I had to decide where I was going with my career. Just like magic, in the weeks leading up to *the finale, Rylan introduced me to Holly Bott, his manager and now the managing director of YMU management company. When I met Holly, initially I was intimidated. This was a strong and powerful woman with a fierceness that rivalled the best. No wonder Rylan had the career he had! But it only took an hour to realise that this power lady was all mushy inside. Rylan had spent years talking to me about coming onto his management team but when you're in production, that's like moving to the dark side. It was tempting, but it was meeting Holly that sealed the deal. After a few interviews with various members of the team, I was lucky enough to be offered the position in Rylan's management team, and the rest is history. Four years later, I'm still standing.*

In 2021, it was my turn to be there for Rylan during one of life's more challenging times. After eight years, for various reasons that are probably in this book, Rylan and his husband decided to split. This sent Rylan into a spiral, and a spiral like I had never seen for any person. To me, it seemed like an accumulation of years and years of work, fame and his personal life, all merging inside this intense pressure cooker. Just as he had done for me all those years before, I knew that all I could do for him in that moment was help him navigate his feelings as much as I could.

I think that is the lesson we learned together: first and foremost, growing up can be tough and at any moment, on a cold morning on your way to work, or while you're sat in the bath on a Sunday night, life can throw a curveball at you. The truth is simple, though: going through it on your own makes all those moments that bit harder. We have a much better chance of riding these waves if we're surfing them together.

With love from Nads x

10

A FEW OF MY
FAVOURITE THINGS

Pants, Peroni and PlayStation? . . . YES LAD

Palais Rylan

One of my best moves ever was building my new house in Essex and then moving my mum to her new house just around the corner. When I first saw it, it was a cottage-style bungalow with a loft. It was all a bit dated, but it was a good size and had a lovely drive, with just under two acres of secluded garden with beautiful big mature trees at the front and back. I immediately knew this was the one.

As I explained in my bestseller (just had to drop that in again) *The Life of Rylan*, growing up, I always wanted to be an architect. So when I found this house, I just instinctively knew what I could do to transform it. I had to keep some elements of the original building because of planning regulations, so I just worked with it. I completely gutted the old building, saving only some of the original structure, and knocked down pretty much all the old interior walls to open the rooms up and bring in more space. I also knocked through in the hallway to make a double-height ceiling, which means I've got loads of light. A masterstroke, if I may say so. It looks amazing.

I did all that design work myself, all the architectural layout, the interior decor, the kitchen design, fixtures and fittings throughout, everything. Every tiniest detail from the bathroom taps to the electric sockets, I hand-picked it. I built my dream house, my luxurious five-bedroom Essex palais. And it's gorgeous and I absolutely love it.

TEN

I'm set back along the gravel drive, so I don't ever hear any traffic, and because I've got the big garden and all the trees all around the house, it feels private, which is exactly what I want. It's like a sanctuary where I can just disappear to. I feel comfortable here. I could walk round stark bollock naked all day outside, if I wanted, and no one would bother me.

Because I built it from scratch, I thought of everything. I built my own little train station and a bus stop at the front on the drive. I got a flagpole put up so I can fly a flag when I'm in residence, and I put up the Union Jack in honour of Her Majesty's Platinum Jubilee – but also, and I'm not gonna lie, when we all get pissed I'm out there bringing it down and wrapping it round me to do my Geri Halliwell impersonation. I've thought of everything. Literally.

Let me give you a peek through the keyhole *chez moi*. I live in quite a smart home, and by smart I also mean 'smart', as in all the mod cons. A lot of the doors in Palais Rylan are automatic and the whole house is voice-activated. Literally, if I can't talk to it, I don't want it. That's my life. That's how my house works. It's all smart – well, apart from my gardener, that is. Half the time he's here, I look out the window and think, 'What the fuck is he doing out there?' Like yesterday, he mainly seemed to spend two hours standing staring at a tree. And I'm sat there trying to work out what the problem is. But anyway, otherwise the house is all run by Alexa.

I have to be careful even typing her name because I'm scared it'll start her off. But basically, I just sit here and say, 'Alexa, turn on the lights, Alexa, turn on downstairs, Alexa, turn the heating off. Alexa, lock this door. Alexa, unlock that door.' In the kitchen, the oven and all the appliances are all actually smart too, but they're the one thing I just switch on and off normally. Everything else – lights, music, telly, heating – Alexa's in charge of all that. I love it. I like living in the future. What's the point in living in the past? My mum can't stand it. She don't get it. She's like, 'In the time you spend telling Alexa what to do, why don't you just get up off your arse and effing do it yourself.' But I don't know. I'm lazy, what can I say?

The only problem is that if ever the Wi-Fi goes down, sometimes I can't remember how to turn the lights on like a normal person. When that happens, I'm stood here pressing random buttons and screaming for Alexa to help.

The worst time, though, was the other night, when there was a power cut leading to a fucking disaster of a front gate malfunction. It was June 2022 and I was on my way home after I'd spent the day on the Jubilee Bus, then I'd gone on for a few drinks and a bite to eat with my old mate AJ Odudu. It was my brother's birthday, so I'd said to him to have the day off and I'd booked a car to get me home. I finally got back in the middle of the night and there was a bit of roadworks going on up my road. So I told the driver, 'Don't worry, I'll jump out here, mine's over there.' So, he's gone and it's pissing it down, and when I went to put in the code to open my front gates, there was no power, nothing was illuminated. What the fuck? I couldn't get into my own fucking house and I had to climb up and over the wall. That's the problem when you build a smart home. If something fails, you're fucked.

But as I say, I've thought of everything in my luxurious 'smart' abode, from an open-plan kitchen to a beauty room, nail bar and gym – and of course, my *Big Brother* 'diary room', complete with flashing-eye button to let me in and the original chair from the series when I won, which is priceless. Visitors are usually a bit shocked when they see my diary room. I think everyone thinks I'm joking when I tell them about it. But then, when they see it, they always want to have a quick selfie in the chair – it's a Palais Rylan tradition. I love a perch in my diary room. Every day I can just push that button and feel instantly at home. And above every door in my house I've got the same famous *Big Brother* 'eye' that flashes red or green when it locks and unlocks.

I've got a cinema room, but that's not where we watch telly for *Gogglebox*, we do that in the kitchen for some reason.

Moving to the outside, a few years after we moved in, I had the garden landscaped by the same people who do the *Big Brother* house. Now it looks beautiful, but back then I spent £14,000 on hedges grown to my exact measurements, but I didn't water them and they died. I thought nature would water them naturally. But because they were part of the wall design, planted in a trough filled with soil and not rooted in the ground, they didn't suck up any water. We won't dwell on that expensive oversight, though, will we? Moving on swiftly in my tour of the grounds, at the end of the garden, I built a swimming pool, but I don't swim as often as I should. It's like one of those things, innit – when you've got it, you don't use it. But no, I do love a good swim and whenever the family and friends are over we always end up in there. Especially the kids.

I love having everyone over for a bit of a do. I love an occasion with all the family. As I said, last Christmas was a total wash-out, for obvious reasons, but usually what I like to do is really go to town with the lights and the decorations, the whole lot, inside and out. First impressions are important, don't you think? So, round my front-door porch area I like to decorate the black pillars with twinkly white fairy lights. Then I get some nice evergreen foliage fronds, some pine branches and what have you, swathe everything in a bit of that, and then dangle a load of big, coloured, metallic baubles all around. I like to settle on a colour scheme too, you know, which I then bring into the rest of the house, so one year, I went for a bit of a pink, brown and silver palette for me baubles. But I think that's nice, to make a bit of a statement with my front entrance. It cheers people up when they come through the gates.

It's the same for my birthdays. Late 2021, for my thirty-third birthday bash, I decorated the hallway and my staircase with these beautiful slightly shimmery black, gold and white balloons – all perfectly complementing the sandstone floor and all the black accessories round there, like my big entrance-hall mirror, the console tables and my piano, which is black, obviously. Well, not obviously, because I suppose it could be white, or pink, or anything, but anyway, I've got a black mini Steinway grand under the stairs. Hark at me with my Steinway! Just call me Elton.

And because I designed and built every single detail of my living space from scratch, I'm always thinking of little tweaks and improvements. I'm constantly looking for the next thing. 'Right, what can I get for in here?' It's like my brain never stops when it comes down to my house, ever.

I'm on my own now, as you know, so a while back I got three moon jellyfish to have in the entrance hall. I got a little tank and had to work out how to get their new living conditions just right for them, so I had to adjust the water and all that. I also went all David Attenborough and spent hours in the library researching my new housemates. Actually, that's a lie – I spent five minutes on Wikipedia. Here's what I learned:

Aurelia aurita (*also called the* **common jellyfish**, **moon jelly** *or* **saucer jelly**) *is a species of the genus* Aurelia. *It is capable of only limited motion, and drifts with the current, even* *when swimming. The jellyfish is almost entirely translucent, usually about 25–40 cm (10–16 in) in diameter, and can be identified by its four horseshoe-shaped gonads, easily seen through the top of the bell. The moon jelly feeds by collecting medusae, plankton, and mollusks, crustaceans, tunicate larvae, rotifers, young polychaetes, protozoans, diatoms, eggs, fish eggs, and other small organisms with its tentacles, and bringing them into its body for digestion. When a moon jelly has had its dinner, you can see all these food items in the jelly's stomach, which is the flower-shaped organ in the bell.*

Moon jellyfish typically live about twelve to fifteen months, provided they are kept in an appropriate aquarium. [Hmm, I fucking did all that, top-range living conditions and all, but read on, because mine didn't!] *Jellyfish of different species regularly prey on each other, but jellyfish of the same species do not. This is because their venom only affects other species.* [Ditto: keep reading . . .]

Biology lesson complete, I was ready to welcome my new family members, who I named Beyoncé, Kelly and Michelle. They looked beautiful in there, swimming about in their tank, so I lit it all up with a bright pink light and posted a video of them to a sound clip of Destiny's Child's 'Bootylicious': 'I don't think you're ready for this jelly . . .'

Well, I certainly was not ready for their jelly, because the whole thing was a catastrophe. First, the tank kept getting manky. THEN . . . It upsets me to inform you that Kelly ate Michelle, Beyoncé then ate Kelly, and finally Beyoncé disappeared. I have no idea where she is to this day. I lay awake at night with worry, thinking a freak-size jellyfish will awaken me from my sleep to inform me that I didn't clean the tank correctly, and then proceed to smother me to death with its tentacles. (FYI: I realise that during my earlier intensive research, I must have missed this bit: *jellyfish are made up of 90 per cent water, so they often dissolve quickly after dying.*) Anyway, RIP to the girls.

I love living in this house. It was not only the best financial decision ever, but the best life and wellbeing decision I could have made. It's mine, and it's my home, and as they say, an Englishman's home is his castle. This literally is my very own little palais. And when I started going through the divorce, that was the thing that constantly ran through my head: 'Am I going to have to sell the house?' But no, I thought, I've worked too hard for this. I'm a council estate boy from Stepney Green. Things like this don't happen often to someone like me, and I'm not letting anyone take it away from me. The only person I'm gonna let take it off of me is me. No one else. Even God will have to fight me for it.

Now, after giving it some thought, my next home improvement plan is that I want to build a club. Like an actual nightclub at my house: VIP booths, dance floor, everything – a proper nightclub at the end of the garden. So, I'll have my train station at the front of the house, the swimming pool at the back, and then I'll have my nightclub on the side. A proper little Leicester Square. I want my own little Disneyland. And why not? What can I say – I don't go out a lot.

Cleaning products

I love a bit of a clean. I have a cleaner now, but I never used to. I actually love cleaning – in fact, I'm a bit of a hygiene fanatic and can be a bit obsessive. Once I get the Marigolds on and get going with the Flash, there's no stopping me. I'll be cleaning the kitchen and suddenly think, 'Ooh, I wonder if there's something I can buy to remove that stain on the tap?'

Sometimes you just need all the gear, and there's nothing I love more than a browse in the cleaning products aisle of the supermarket. Then I'll spend £300 on cleaning products just to have a jolly. I love a bit of bleach. I love a dishwasher tablet. I love a bit of limescale remover. I love a bit of oven cleaner. I love a new sponge, a posh feather duster, a good squeegee for the shower and windows. I love looking at cleaning products and will order every possible specialist cleaner and gizmo for every possible scenario – windows, stainless steel, wood floors, stone floors, toilets, showers, baths, washing-machine disinfectant . . . you name it, I've bought it. And you know when you can see a 2-litre bottle of Comfort for three quid? Honeysuckle and sandalwood? Oh yes, get in! I love it.

Shopping for home bargains

I really miss a little walk around a B&M, The Range, Home Bargains, TK Maxx, and all those types of places that you normally find in retail parks where you can get things like discounted biscotti, but also all the kitchen shit – a pink salt and pepper mill set, balsamic vinegar for a fiver, a candlestick that I'm never gonna use, but still. I fritter money away on stupid things like LED light bulbs in different colours. Oh my God, that's a bit of me.

Homeware and hardware shops, and pharmacies when you're abroad

Following on from that, I absolutely love a nosey about all those types of shops when I'm working away, or on holiday on the continent. For me, there is nothing so exciting as spending an hour or two in all those foreign homeware and hardware shops

– even a foreign supermarket will get my heart racing. And don't get me started on cleaning products abroad. Oh my God. I love it. I will buy something from the cleaning aisle in a foreign super-market, just for the sake of buying it. And try keeping me out of any French, Italian or Spanish pharmacy I spot on a street. Oh my God. It's the best thing. There was one in Turin that I went to with Scott Mills and his fiancé, over the road from our hotel. It was A-MAZ-ING. I wanted to spend all day in there looking at all the shampoos and the serums and the creams. I was in heaven.

It's the same old shit but it's exciting because you're not at home. I always think a foreign pharmacy feels so much posher than our boring chemists over here. And I'll do really sad things like buy a toothpaste and toothbrush because I like having them in my bathroom when I get home. It looks nice and it makes me feel all cosmopolitan. I love all that shit. That's where I'm a sucker.

Even when I go and get a bag of crisps in Spain and it says Lay's rather than Walkers, I'm all, 'Oh, get me with my exotic foreign tastes!' Or, I get an ice lolly and instead of it being Wall's, it's called Frigo; Sure deodorant is called Rexona. It's basically all the same products, but with different names that all the Europeans can pronounce – that's why Jif is now called Cif over here, because no one in Spain could say it with the 'J'. Though someone told me they thought it was because it meant 'spunk' in Croatian, or something. It might do. If it does, let me know? It might come in handy.

Stationery

I love a bit of stationery and a really nice paper product. Love it. I'm the sort that will buy a really posh pad of thick laid writing paper, and a box of matching envelopes, the ones lined with tissue paper inside. And a really nice pen. But I don't post anything; I don't write letters – and thinking about it, I hardly ever actually use a pen – but I like to know I've got them in a drawer. Growing up as a kid, there was nothing better than when we were coming up to September and me and Mum went to WHSmith to get a new pencil case and fill it with a whole new set of kit – pens and pencils, a new sharpener and rubber. That was the best feeling. I used to absolutely love a scented rubber. One year, I remember over at Blockbuster they were selling a *101 Dalmatians* push-button pen: you pushed the button, and a sharpener popped out. I was very proud every time I got that out of my pencil case, I can tell you.

Fragrance

Fragrance is what I'm all about. My very first scent that I ever had was a near-empty bottle of Fahrenheit Dior which my brother let me have when I was about nine. I absolutely loved it and I think that's why I've been obsessed with fragrance ever since. He also gave me his old bottle of Kouros by YSL, but that smelt like piss, so I didn't use that.

My mum always smells nice. She has always smelt exactly the same as well. Ever since I was really small, she's worn Aromatics Elixir by Clinique, which I absolutely loved as a child and still do. She also likes Estée Lauder Azurée. That's been discontinued now though, so whenever she wants a bottle of that I have to really go searching for it. I remember one Christmas when I was at school, I gave her that little gift coffret with miniatures of Loulou, Anaïs Anaïs, and Paris, YSL, that every mum I knew had. The Loulou bottle was claret and blue, and then Paris was clear with the black and red top. I think I got it in Argos or somewhere like that. But the thing I really remember from my childhood is how she always smelt after she got out of the bath. She would always use Bronnley English Fern body cologne in the green bottle, and now that smell always reminds me of growing up and of Mum. Over the years, I've bought her every fucking fragrance under the sun, but she always goes back to those three – Aromatics Elixir, Azurée and Bronnley English Fern.

When I was really little, when she got me out of the bath, she would always smother me in a Spanish baby cologne called Nenuco, which smells very citrusy. We always used to buy it in Spain and I still adore that scent. It smells so clean.

Then there was my nan's scent. She wore Angel by Thierry Mugler and I've still got her last bottle of it in my drawer from when she died. That was her fragrance and it will always remind me of her. In fact, that's just reminded me of another fragrance memory – of me wearing A*Men, the men's version of Angel. How weird is that? I'd totally forgotten about that but I'm going to buy a bottle right now.

My go-to fragrance hall is in Fortnum & Mason in St James, London. Their fragrance floor is amazing because they have everything. Selfridges is the same. Liberty is nice as well, but I find it a bit busy, very touristy, whereas Fortnum's fragrance floor is a very relaxed experience because not a lot of people know it's even there. I buy a lot of my fragrances online, though, because I'm the sort who will think of a scent out of nowhere, and I have to immediately get it. I know what I like and I know what I will not like.

Ten years ago, my go-to scent was still Fahrenheit Dior, then over the years I went through stages from dark fragrance to a really light, summery fragrance. In terms of my preferred fragrance now, I'd say that I'm a very sort of oud-y, woody kind of guy. I don't like changing my scent throughout the year. I like sticking with one scent, but now I'm very much in a cycle of three or four very similar fragrances, but with slightly different notes, as they say. I'd like to say that my signature scent is 'Loughton Brothel' and I'm happy I smell like that. That's what I'm known for. Anyone that knows me will tell you, 'Rylan smells good'. People at work always say that they know when I'm in the building because they can smell me in the lift – though it means that I'm terrible at playing hide-and-seek because I always get sniffed out.

Fragrance is a massive thing for me. I will be sitting somewhere one day and I will smell something – it could be when I'm outside, it could be food, or when someone walks past me in the street, and it will trigger a fragrance memory and I'll have to go and buy it. Whenever I meet someone, the first thing I think is what do they smell like? Some people smell like clean washing, which isn't a bad thing. Others smell of the scent they always wear, and as I've said, fragrance invokes memories. So, obviously, with my ex-husband, there were fragrances that I would buy him that now remind me of him. Now I can't have them in my house.

Fragrance to me is almost like listening to music. It reminds me of people in my life and takes me right back somewhere, to so many different places and times in my life. The first fragrance I bought for myself was a long glass bottle of DKNY Men. It was when my brother took me on holiday and it cost twenty-odd quid at the airport. Now the smell just reminds me of being young and of Greece, more specifically Rhodes. We were staying in some shitty hotel and there was this song by Bran Van 3000 that was playing all the time round the pool. And there was a three-legged cat, and a collection box in the reception area for the manky creature – that's what DKNY Men conjures for me. Tom Ford Tobacco Vanille and Passion by Louis Cardin, remind me of me. And so does Fahrenheit and obviously of my brother giving me that very first bottle when I was a kid.

Things like Lacoste's Touch of Pink and Britney Spears' Fantasy remind me of every girl at school and take me back to my teens. I've still got a bottle of Touch of Pink because I always loved the smell, and, no word of a lie, Britney fucking Spears' Fantasy is still one of the best perfumes ever made. I still sometimes wear it in bed because it's such a sweet smell. Jean Paul Gaultier's Le Male also reminds me of being at school, and Spicebomb by Victor & Rolf reminds me of a bloke when I was younger. Fierce by Abercrombie & Fitch reminds me of one of my exes and I know he still wears it. Every time I smell it, it reminds me of him.

Another of my favourite scents from my schooldays was a special Spice Girls edition of Impulse, and I've still got a bottle of it from twenty-odd years ago. I was never really into Lynx back then, but I remember when they brought out the chocolate-scented one because all the boys wore that at school. I was not a fan, but the one I do love now is Lynx Africa. If I don't get a gift set of that at Christmas, I'm disappointed. Everyone takes the piss, but I think it's a really nice smell. They actually do a perfume of it, too. If it had Versace on the front of the bottle, it would be a bestseller. I'm telling you now, it's a really, really good perfume. It's woody, it's oriental. Oud-y, and bergamot. It's nice.

Michael Kors takes me back to when I was in 4bidden in Ibiza. One of the boys had been sleeping with a girl, and she had left her bottle of Michael Kors perfume in our apartment. Then she flew home and we didn't know her address, so I started wearing it. Now, every time I smell it, I think: 'Oh, boyband!'

The one I can't stand from that era is Joop. An ex over there used to wear that and don't get me wrong, he didn't do anything bad. But the smell reminds me of when I was once so hungover in the morning and had to walk back from his apartment to mine in the 40-degree heat of Ibiza – I could smell him on me, and that's why I can't stand that smell. I only have to think about Joop and that smell memory takes me right back there, otherwise there's no way I'd remember that day.

You could literally name any popular fragrance, and I'd probably have a story. It's funny, isn't it? For other people, it could be the taste of a food, but with me it's smells. It's like my super sense. Like some people are super-tasters, well, I'm a super-smeller.

As I said, I used to work on the Benefits cosmetics counter, so I used to get to know all the fragrances when they came in. I remember I once stole a bottle of Clinique Happy from the stockroom. Didn't give a fuck. And now I can't wear that because it reminds me of me robbing it. We had one called Maybe Baby on our Benefit counter and we all used to spray ourselves in clouds of it. I think it got discontinued – and when I say people were in uproar . . . It was the most brothel-y, prostitute-y smelling perfume. I loved it. Then they started bringing in new fragrances called different 'houses'. Maybe Baby was number 42 and it was the best, and that also reminds me of every girl at school.

I sniff people. I will sniff them and I say, 'You're wearing X, Y or Z.' They're always surprised, like, 'How the fuck did you know that?' But it's because I just know it. I've always had quite a good nose with fragrance. I can smell a fragrance and know what's in it.

That's why I've got my fragrance company, Luxenoa. It's such a massive passion of mine, so I wanted to turn it into a business, which I've done and I adore it. Luxenoa has been going for three years now, and from start to finish it is all me. Anything I do, I'm the one who designs it, helps to make it and signs it off. If anything has my name on it, be assured that it's 100 per cent me that's done it without anyone else getting involved. I actually go into a lab and mix the fragrances. It's quite a skill and I love it. I've got a great team of people that work with me on the concept side of the business and we're rebranding everything and relaunching this year. We sold out completely last year, so now we're ready to start again. Coming back with a bang.

What with my super-smelling abilities, obviously I also adore a scented candle and a diffuser. I like my house to smell nice the minute you walk in the door; I've got one of the diffusers from my new Luxenoa range on the side table in the hallway. Even the utility room needs to smell gorgeous, because another smell I hate is that awful badly washed clothes smell. You know when you leave something in the washing machine for too long and you get that horrible damp stench? It's a nightmare. I've done it before when I've left sheets in there and I thought I was going to have to throw that load out. Thank God for booster pearls, is all I can say. I popped them in and it was gone.

Smelly bathrooms are another no-no. I like a scented candle when I'm in the bath. But I'm a sucker for that whole home fragrance section in a supermarket – give me half an hour and next thing I know is I've bought half the Air Wick range. Years ago, when they brought out their sandalwood fragrance, I bought a hundred just because they were limited edition – I'm sad.

Alexa

I love Alexa, I really do. I mean, I'd be lost without her. I couldn't have written this book without her, for a start. Who else did I turn to to remind me of when Tiffany Pollard thought David Gest was lying dead in the *CBB* house, or what is actually in a crab stick (see p275)?

And I did really take over the voice of Alexa for April Fools' Day. I work with Amazon so I became 'Alexa' for the day. And even now, if you ask her certain things about me, it will be me that replies.

So if I say, 'Alexa, how old is Rylan?'

She says, 'Let's ask him.' Then my voice says, 'Well, last time I checked, I'm thirty-three years old. I know I look a lot older. But, what can I say? It's been a long ten years.'

They got me in and got me to record certain replies and bits that they can piece together.

They've been great to work with and, who knows . . . maybe Ry-lexa will make a re-appearance.

Call of Duty: Warzone

During the first lockdown, it did get a little bit boring. While I was laying in bed, I could hear my stepson playing a game on his PlayStation. 'What the fuck is he playing?' I thought, because all I could hear from his room was, 'You bastard! You fucking this or that. I'm going to blast your head off!' It turned out it was *Call of Duty*, and within *Call of Duty* there's this separate game called *Warzone*, which is basically a live interactive game that you play with other people using a headset. You're put on a random team with two other players, then you and your teammates go around shooting people and earning money, and you all shout at each other. It's literally that ridiculous. However, I decided to play this a couple of times with my stepson, and lo and behold, I was hooked. Me being me, as you know I like to be a bit extra, so I bought the brand-new PlayStation, got *Call of Duty* and started playing *Warzone*. I absolutely loved it, the fact that in this game I could be in this fantastical world where I could run around and do what I wanted, really. I'd sit up at night playing it, along with my team. I had no idea who these people were. For all I know, I was sitting there playing with a bunch of eleven-year-olds while they were all screaming at me, 'Bastard! Flank him! Flank him! He's got no armour, you fucking dick!' because I'd failed to shoot someone to death. But there we go.

It's crazy. But when you're playing it, you want to win. And it's really addictive. I became a bit obsessed with it to the point where I decided to tweet about it. The second I did, well, I think my follow count just went through the roof. I went from 'Uncle Rylan' to 'OMG, Rylan is a G! I can't believe you play *Warzone*! What's your killstreak? What's your loadout? What's your this? Your that?' I had no fucking idea what half of them were talking about, but I absolutely loved it. The Activision team who created *Call of Duty* then got in touch with me and asked me to launch their brand-new *Warzone* map. They wanted me to be the travel agent and introduce people to the new map. That was really, really exciting for me.

The Activision team have been absolutely amazing to work with. They always slyly update my game with maybe a few extra credits and a new gun here and there. I don't get to play it half as much as I'd like to, but when I do, don't expect me to answer the phone because it's not gonna fucking happen. You read it here first. I'm trendy and I'm cool. Leave me alone.

11

THE FAMILY

To break into the circle, you're gonna have to be pretty fucking special . . .

For me family is very, very important. Obviously, I've got my blood family, but then I've also got a close circle of friends that are *like* my family to me. I trust these people with everything, and they are everything to me. And when I talk about family, this is who I mean. But I have to be totally honest here: it's only as I've got older, and in the last twelve months especially, that I've realised just HOW MUCH I need my family. And after last year, when everything fell apart, if it weren't for them, I wouldn't be here today, 100 per cent.

Ages ago, I was asked to do one of those newspaper questionnaires, for the *Guardian*'s Weekend magazine. One of the questions was: 'What is your greatest fear?' I remember that I answered: 'Being alone.' Well, last year I came face to face with my greatest fear, because the truth is, when my marriage ended, I didn't just lose a husband, I lost a whole new family too. I basically lost the whole life that I was living. Outside work, my relationship with my ex and the relationships we shared as a couple had become my whole life. I'd allowed him to just consume that whole side of our relationship, so it was *his* family and *his* friends at the core. Everyone I socialised with, any family events, any Sunday afternoons, it was all centred around his side. My friends were his family friends. Why was that the case? I don't know. It just was.

I lost all my friends pretty much in the course of my marriage. And don't get me wrong, I can't pin all of that on my relationship. I mean, I'd already either drifted apart from my teenage friends, or we'd fallen out. People like Sam from River Island, for example, who I talked about in my first book, and who I fell out with back then because I went out with his ex. Then there was my best friends Katy and James, but I also fell out with James over stupid things. I look back and I just think that could have all been handled so differently, but back then I really couldn't deal with it.

But you know, you grow up, things change. Now I talk to Sam every now and then. (I saw him not long ago, actually, and he's good, we're good. He's forgiven me.) And I speak to Katy every now and again as well, although not loads. But I haven't seen James at all. There's been the odd message over the years – nothing horrible, actually quite nice ones. And I could easily have gone back and met up with him, but I was frightened to, I think. I still am. Even though in some ways I'm a bit more like the old me again, sometimes people do just grow apart. And there are people that I really can't imagine being friends with now, that's the God's honest truth. Not necessarily because that's what happens when you become so-called successful or famous: I don't think it's because *I've* changed. But my life has changed. And with that, I've grown up. And I don't know, some people are lucky to have best school friends for the rest of their lives, but I don't think it's *that* uncommon for some of our early friendships to fade with time. As I said, sometimes friends just grow apart. The way I was in my marriage was the nail in the coffin, though.

It's only when I split from my husband that it hit me: 'Oh FUCK. I'm on my *own* own.' It suddenly dawned on me that, literally overnight, I had no friends to speak of, really, since I no longer could count on the friends we'd had as a couple. I've had a lot of time to think back on it since then, and I know now that over the eight years I was with my ex,

I didn't really make time for MY people, MY friendships. I didn't even make time for my own blood family at points. That's what's so sad about it. I realise now that for a while, I forgot the Clark side of my life.

But then, in times like that, you learn the simple truth: your true family is always there for you. And that's when I fully understood that when the shit hits the fan, that's who I've got. My mum, obviously, but she's got a whole chapter to herself. She's that important to me. My brother Jamie, my sister-in-law Jayne, and their kids, Olivia and Harvey. Harvey was twenty-two this year, and Olivia has just had her eighteenth birthday. When they both hit seventeen, I wanted to buy them a car – from Cinch obvs. That's me, always on brand. Honestly, though, I love Cinch, they're such a good company. So, Olivia has just got her new car. I bought her a Mercedes that she's driving around in. Get her!

I know it's not going to be long until Olivia starts going out on the town with me. And that's the end. She's been going out for a while now. The other night she rang me at two in the morning saying, 'I'm in Soho. Where are you?' And I just replied, 'No, we're not ready for this yet. There's plenty of time.' But she's brilliant. They're both just really good – no, GREAT – kids. I love the relationship they've got with my mum. They both adore her. At the minute Harvey is working on the Elizabeth Line, doing building stuff on the new stations, so he stays with my mum quite a lot in the week because it's easier for him to go to work. Olivia is just about to leave school, so she keeps asking for a job. I'll end up employing the whole fucking family at this rate.

Beyond that, I've got the wider Clark clan: my two aunts, my mum's older sister Susan and her little sister Pat, and their other halves and kids. I was always the baby of the family; all my cousins are around my brother's age, and he's fourteen years older than me, so when I was younger, they'd all go out and I was always the kid left at home with the oldies. It's different now, obviously, since the age gap doesn't matter any more and we're all a lot closer.

Then there are close family friends who are basically another part of my family. My mum's best mate Pat, who's like an aunt to me, and her daughter, Kimberly. Me and Kimberly were born two weeks apart and everyone knows us as Barbie and Ken. She's blonde with the tits; I'm dark with the beard. We've been inseparable since birth – except when we had a massive fallout at my ex's fortieth and didn't speak for two years. We only started talking again when it went public that my marriage had broken up, but now we're closer than we've ever been before. And I'm so glad that Kimberly and Pat are back in my life.

Them and the Clark clan are the family I've got around me now. And actually, they never left me; I just lost sight of how important they are – always have been, and always will be. And it was then that I also understood that I can and do have an extended family as well: Claire from Steps; Bernice, a close friend and my makeup artist; my close friends and managers, Nads and Holly; Ruth Langsford and Eamonn Holmes. They were that bubble for me last year.

My relationships with all of them were very strong anyway, even before what I went through, and what they saw me through. I already considered Ruth and Eamonn as two of my closest friends in this industry – well, almost step-parents really. I can't remember the first time I met them, but after *Celebrity Big Brother* when I started doing bits and bobs on *This Morning*, we immediately hit it off. Over the years, we became very close through working alongside each other on the show. I don't know, our friendship just happened. It feels like we were supposed to meet.

Last year, when I was really ill and had moved in with my mum, she secretly arranged for them to come and see me at my house. She didn't tell me, because I obviously didn't want to see *anyone*. She told me that she was taking me back to my house and that we were going to spend the day there. And I didn't want to. I just didn't want to be there. I told her I couldn't, but she said, 'You're going.' She drove me round there, and then Eamonn and Ruth suddenly turned up. I remember how their faces looked when they saw me, seeing how badly ill I was, and then Eamonn became very upset. I'd never seen Eamonn get upset like that before, and that was like a wake-up call. I remember thinking, 'Fuck. Do I look that ill? Am I that bad?' It was just awful. They stayed with me all that day.

Ruth and Eamonn are the two nicest people in this industry you could ever wish to meet. They've got time for everyone. They don't care about status or who's who in the pecking order. They get on with it. They're just the funniest, sweetest, kindest people. I mean, I thought I talked to people, but fuck me, walking down the street with Eamonn is something else altogether. He will spend the whole day talking to EVERYONE. It takes about half a day to get anywhere. Someone says hello to him, and Eamonn will stop and have a full-on, in-depth conversation: 'Oh, hello. Where are you from? Oh, what have you done to your leg? That's terrible. Oh, my brother was in that hospital . . .' And then I'm standing there while he's happily chatting away for two hours. Eventually, I have to tell him, 'Dad! Come on. We need to go now.' And it's mad because before I got to know him, I didn't think Eamonn was someone I would get on with. I thought that he was a bit of a different person to who he actually is. But he's one of the best. And very much like me, he can't stand the bullshit; he tells it like it is. He'll say, 'I don't like that person. He's a cunt.' He doesn't care. And I say, good on him. Fucking say it how it is, Eamonn. That's what I like about him.

The special thing about Ruth is that she always knows the right thing to say. She's so level-headed. She's always been there for me when I've needed her. On the flip side, I've been there for her when she's needed me too, most notably when her sister sadly passed away. That's what friends do. You make sure you're there for each other. And in a time of crisis, Ruth Langsford is the person you need around you. She'll give you a cigarette, she'll sit you down, and she will tell you what's right and what's wrong. I'll never forget that day they came around when I wasn't expecting them. We sat in my garden and I remember shaking the whole time. She tried to calm me and she did. I'll never forget that. I'll never forget the pair of them taking time out of their lives to come and do that for me.

I met Claire Richards, AKA my Steps sister, on *Celebrity Big Brother* in 2013 and our friendship went from there. She really is just like my big sister, and I'm her annoying little brother. That is literally what it's like. We can go a week or two without talking to each other and then we're talking all the time. Claire always moans at me that I don't ring her back, then when I do ring her back, she has a go at me. And then she doesn't ring me back. It's the classic brother–sister relationship. It was like that right from the beginning and our relationship has stayed exactly the same over the last ten years. Nothing has changed with me and Claire. I love her to bits and she was *so* there for me last year. So it was quite a big, emotional thing for me when I was asked to present the

Icon Award to Steps at the Attitude Awards in October 2021 in London. It was my first big public event since the split, so for support I took little Lucy Spraggan, my old *X Factor* mate, along with me as my date. She held my hand the whole night, because I was dreading having to speak to anyone, let alone address the whole fucking room. When I got up on the stage in front of everyone, I knew I wanted to say something personal to thank Claire for being there for me, but it all got a bit too much. 'One of the members of this band is like a sister to me and for the past four months, for probably the toughest time in my life, she's supported me,' I said. 'And without her, I don't think I'd be here presenting this award.' Then I started to cry, but not big wail-y cries, I just welled up and got a bit choked. I'm glad I said it, though. She means the world to me, and I know I could trust her with anything.

Trust is the main thing to me. With my friendships and my family it is all about trust. I'm a shit judge of character when it comes down to celebs, because they are generally all nice to me, because I'm also a 'celeb'. So I'll hear stories about people that I've thought I always got on with, and it turns out that in fact they are total arseholes to people. But that's the thing: if the public knew the fucking truth about everyone in this industry, there would be a lot of people not working. Because it is very backstabbing. It's very disloyal. So, when you can find a handful of loyal ones, fucking hold on to them, because there's not a lot of people you're going to find in this industry like that. Unfortunately. I know I could trust Ruth, Eamonn and Claire with my life. I know I could tell the three of them absolutely anything. I could tell them that I'd killed someone, and they would still stand by me. Without a shadow of doubt.

Nads is one of my best friends. Genuinely. When I first met him, I just knew. He was my runner on *BOTS* and I just remember thinking, 'There's something about you. We're going to be all right.' And all these years on he's now my fucking manager, bossing me about. The amount of rows I have had with him. But I wouldn't want it any other way. It's just like my relationship with my mum – we can shout at each other and we can both be pig-headed pricks, but it works. I trust him to always be honest with me and I can take it. People always use our friendship against us, in the sense of 'Well, it's different now that you have a management relationship. And it might be difficult because he's your friend.' But we're not stupid. We know what business is and we know what friendship is. So sometimes we'll be on the phone, and I'll say, 'No, Nads. I'm not doing that.' Then he'll say, 'Listen, as your friend . . .' I hate it when he plays the friend card, the bastard. But yeah, he's a really, really good person to have by my side. He's really good at looking after me and managing me. And at getting me to do things I don't want to do. Honestly, we're so close, some people have tried to suggest that we're an item. But no. Let me just clear that up, once and for fucking all. For a start he's straight, and secondly, he's about twelve. So no, I am not sleeping with Nads. Lol.

Holly's amazing too. We've become so close over the years. She gets me. She gets it. She is the voice I need in my moments of madness. Holly is a Rottweiler, the sort of person you do not want to get on the wrong side of; not because she's a nasty person, far from it. She is the complete opposite. She's a lovely person, but she's fucking brilliant at her job. And sometimes I forget how good she is at her job because I just look at her as a friend. But ultimately, she is unbelievable at what she does, which is why she's in the position she's in. She has been there for me and fought my corner tooth and nail, and if I've got a lot of tooth, she's got a lot of nail. I don't think I'd be where I am now in my career if it wasn't for her input over the years she's been working with me. I've always been the sort of person that, when I've got a team around me, if you're on Team Rylan, I need you to be my friend. Yes, there are times when I need you to be my manager and tell me I'm wrong. But I like to work on a friendly basis. I don't want to answer the phone, and say 'yes' and 'no' and then not talk to you again. For me, having a relationship with the people that I work with is just as important as the jobs I'm doing. Holly is the epitome of that person. I can go a week or two without speaking to her, but I know that she's always in the background, watching with one eye. And every time I see that phone ring, I shit myself, thinking, 'What the fuck is she calling me about? What have I done now?' Normally, when it's an early-morning call from Holly, you know you're in the paper for something that ain't good. That's how I know she's always got my back. I couldn't imagine her not being part of my life.

And Bernice, my makeup artist, she's also family. She's only been working with me for a couple of years, but she's been my friend forever. Bernice and I met in 2010 on the Essex scene. She was already a makeup artist back then and it was her ex-boyfriend that put in my long blond hair extensions for the shoot before my *X Factor* audition and all that. So yeah, Bernice is responsible for the hair. And we've been friends ever since. It would have been so much easier if I'd just had her doing my makeup from day one, but I just didn't think and it never came about like that. Then when me and Mummy started doing *Gogglebox*, one morning the makeup artist they had booked for my mum had to cancel, and randomly I rang Bernice. She came in, did Mummy's makeup and that was it. Because after seven years I had parted ways with my old makeup artist that I'd met on *The X Factor*, so just like that I asked Bernice to come and be my personal makeup artist and she said, 'Yes!' Now she does my makeup for anything I do on telly.

The thing with Bernice is that I've known her for so many years, but it's only in the past few years that we've got close again. And I'm so happy because I look at her family now as part of my family. I absolutely adore her husband, Ant, and their boys, Malachy and Jude. We have these little moments where we just laugh at things that aren't even that funny, but because it's us two we find them fucking hilarious. That's the sort of person you need around you. She was totally there for me during my break-up, ridiculously so. In fact, more so than I ever thought she could or would be. Now, especially after last year, I literally cannot imagine her not being in my life because she is so good for me. She's normal. And she's just brilliant. It's surreal – it's as if she's *never* not been with me. Nads loves her, everyone loves her, and that's why now it's a case of 'protect Bernice at all costs'. She comes everywhere with me. She's so much more than a makeup artist – she's a stylist, she's a therapist, she does everything. Bernice gets it all. And if there's anyone that you want to get the gossip from, it's someone's makeup artist. They know fucking everything. But I should warn you now, you're gonna get fuck all from her because she's a loyal one.

Something that will keep coming up in this book is the word trust. I've learned that that word has got many, many meanings. But for me, when it comes down to friends that are family, trust is really all that matters. To be a good friend, in my eyes, I don't need to talk to you every day, I don't need to see you every week. I just need to know and you need to know that if either of us needs each other, we're going to be there. We pick up where we've left off, and it seems like no time has passed. To be a real friend is just to know that someone's always there for you – they don't necessarily have to *literally* be there. The friends I've spoken about in this chapter – Bernice, Ruth, Eamonn, Claire, Holly, Nads – I met them because of my job, but they're not people I associate with my job any more. And that's when you know you've got a real friend.

Last year taught me that I only need one handful of people close to me and I've got them. So I know now I'm gonna be all right. They're all just nice people. And there's not a lot of nice people about. But as I say, trust is also a massive thing for me. And it's gonna take someone really fucking special, really every fucking box ticked, to get into that circle now, because I can't just let anyone in it. I can't go through that again. I won't make it out next time. I know I won't.

The other thing about my close circle is that most of them have got kids, and I really want my own kids. I've always wanted kids. Obviously, my ex had a son, Cameron, and I was stepdad to him. He was thirteen or fourteen when I met my ex, so basically, I helped bring him up. I did the 'difficult years'. And then in that marriage I just sort of got to that point where I thought I was never gonna have kids of my own. I had Cameron.

Now all of a sudden – and this, I guess, is yet another silver lining – actually I can, or could, still have kids. I'd have them now, but now isn't the right time. I know I'd love it and that I'd be a natural parent, though, because I did a pretty good job with my stepson. There was ten years between me and Cameron and ten years between me and my ex, and I was very much the man in the middle. I was quite often the one keeping the peace, so in that and all other respects it was just the same relationship as being a pretty normal dad. I moaned at him to clean up, he cleaned up. He used to cut the grass, I paid him. It was just your very bog-standard father–son relationship.

So, I know what my parenting style would be. If I had a girl, I'd lock her up until she was forty. If I had a boy, I'd lock him up too. I used to tell Cameron that I'd cut his dick off if he made me a grandfather before I was thirty. Seriously though, I know I'd be a really good dad. My mum and my nan were my role models growing up. They were strict but not ridiculously so, though my mum shouted at me all the time. Still does. Literally. My family always takes the piss – when they want to get my attention, they always shout, 'ROSS!' because that is what my mum was like with me growing up, always bellowing my name. I always joke that that's why I changed it to Rylan.

I know how lucky I am. I am extremely lucky to have my family and my chosen family around me, especially after the breakdown of my marriage. I'll never take them for granted. Growing up, my mum took me on holiday a few times to Spain, and I went with my nan Rose to Lanzarote to see family who lived out there. Jamie would take me away as well to places like Butlin's and Haven, which I loved. Though I don't remember all of us ever going on holiday together at the same time. Now, I would love to take my whole family – my mum, my brother, Jayne and the kids – away for a couple of weeks, maybe to a villa in Spain. I'd love to do that. It would be my small way of saying 'Thank you'. For everything, always.

Because BELIEVE ME . . . I won't ever forget the Clark side again.

Lessons I've learned:

- I've only got one lesson for this chapter: you can't choose the family you're born into, and for that I'm glad, because I couldn't have designed mine better myself, and the ones I've chosen to be part of it, I wouldn't change for the world

LESSONS WE'VE LEARNED . . .

Jayne Clark

Friend/Sister-in-law/Sister

Let's start with a positive. On the plus side of having a celebrity in the family, we have had the privilege of going to sought-after events and being able to experience these in executive/luxury surroundings. We have also had the privilege of meeting some very nice celebrities and important people in the business who make all this happen. Some of them have become friends. It's so important to stay grounded and true to yourself in these situations and not become absorbed in this life, because for the relatives, this is not our real life, it is just a few moments of fortunate experiences.

On the downside, we have witnessed how complete strangers can be so cruel, via social media, press and peers. Our children have told us of how older school peers have mocked them about who their uncle is. Fortunately, our children are very grounded and mature and have either stood up for themselves or ignored them. They are also very quick-witted, and luckily often have a good comeback for anyone who dares to challenge them. This is definitely a Clark trait!

The worst are the social media trolls, who aren't brave enough to display their faces or go under their real names. These trolls hide behind a fake persona and attack. They don't stop at the celebrity, they go for anyone who dares to stand up to them. The only thing to learn from this is not to give them any time, response, or attention, unless there is a safety concern. Once you engage with these people, they thrive on it. That's what they want, then it's a slippery slope into a dispute, and it's game over! Ross has taught us all to just ignore it. As much as you want to react, don't – it's not worth it. And he is having the last laugh.

I think that the biggest thing we've all learned as a whole family is that no matter how strong you think someone is and how well they appear to be coping with things in general, in life one change in circumstances can bring your whole world crashing down. Unfortunately, we all saw this last year following the breakdown of Ross's marriage.

If anyone would have told us what we were about to experience with Ross's breakdown months before, we would NEVER have believed them! Ross has always been a strong-willed, strong-minded person who has always been in control.

We knew from when he was little that he was going to be on TV somewhere, somehow, even if it was for five minutes because he was a born entertainer. He always wanted to put on a show or be the centre of attention. Don't get me wrong, he wasn't always entertaining! He could be quite annoying and exhausting at times. But he followed his dreams and made it happen. I'd like to think that we have played an important role in his life, with advice and guidance. When he came out of The X Factor *and was preparing for the live tour, I can remember Jamie (Ross's brother) saying to him, 'This is what you've always wanted, and you can make this work for you if you want it. Just don't be an idiot and fuck it up.'*

Ross went from being the joke of The X Factor *to being an amazing presenter. He hadn't been famous for long before he met his ex, and he'd never really learned who he was in this new lifestyle on his own or with his family. No sooner had this new career come along and he was straight into a whirlwind relationship. Ross went from being a party boy (pre-fame) and socialising, to hardly ever going out. It was difficult to get him to go out and maintain some kind of normality with his own family and real friends. He wouldn't go to family meals out or celebrations, unless they were in certain settings; he didn't really want to deal with any of the attention and harassment that came with the fame. He changed and became almost reclusive, sticking to his work, home or the homes of close family members,* where he felt secure. There were times when it felt like he prioritised others before his own family, but knowing what we know now, as a family we have a better understanding of his actions during these times. Ross always maintained an appearance that everything was OK, and after a while never really confided much in his family or friends.

He continued to work very hard, taking a lot of the opportunities that came along for him, as he was always mindful of how fickle this business can be. The showbiz, happy-go-lucky person you saw on the TV was not always the reality of what we were getting. He was exhausted a lot of the time, from working long hours and travelling. This eventually all became too much and he opened up to us, and once he did this he literally stopped functioning. He became someone we didn't recognise; he crumbled like a child and became so withdrawn, we couldn't believe what we were witnessing. The strong, clever, intelligent, vibrant, funny Ross we all knew disappeared. This had a massive impact on us all.

None of us had ever really experienced someone close to us completely breaking down. Not only does this affect the person who is going through it, but it has a catastrophic impact on their loved ones. For the first time, I personally experienced real fear for another person's safety and wellbeing. Ross didn't know how to deal with anything; he wasn't even able to carry out basic functions. He was frightened of everything and refused to see or communicate with anyone other than his mum, Jamie and me. He was even frightened to seek medical attention. After a long period of this hell, and that is the only honest way to describe it, little bits of Ross started to come back. It wasn't overnight, it was over months, and it wasn't unaided.

We were very lucky to have the trust and support of a few others in the same profession as Ross, who expressed their genuine concern and reached out to us, his family, which we were – and still are – very grateful for. We as a family couldn't relate to his fear of how the media were going to portray him, as we've never been in his shoes *and simply could never know what that feels like. But unbeknown to Ross, we were able to make arrangements for his close friends in the industry to visit him, as he was refusing to see anyone. It was very difficult for him initially to face anyone, including family, as he really didn't know how he was being perceived, but I'm so glad that we persevered with this. These friends were able to reassure him that he was going to be OK, and that there was real, genuine concern for him in the industry. And most importantly, yes, he could go back to doing the job he loves so passionately, and hold his head high again. Although his family were telling him this, we couldn't really relate, and he knew that.*

His biggest hurdle, and the start of his healing, came at my and Jamie's wedding, seeing a large amount of family and friends for the first time. We were so mindful of the damage and the setback that this pressure could cause that we talked it over with Ross and reassured him that if it was all too much, he didn't have to do anything he didn't feel up to. He came through, put on a very brave face, and made a heartfelt speech at our reception. That was when we knew he was going to be OK, and that he could come back from this.

It hasn't been easy on any of us at all, but what me, Ross, Linda, Jamie, Olivia and Harvey have learned is that with the right support, and a strong network of family and friends, you can get through anything together – you just have to KEEP TALKING.

Love, Jayne, your sister-in-law and friend, always

Behind the scenes
at *Big Brother*.

Just casually hanging out
with the BB zebra.

Me and Nads in the Diary Room at
4am on the last night of *Big Brother*.

Shared so many memories
with this one – Emma Willis
will always be my first
telly wife.

On the set of *The Wave* in Portugal.

My second Eurovision – Tel Aviv 2019.

With the wrong'uns at Radio 2.

Bringing back *Supermarket Sweep* was a childhood dream . . .

. . . plus I also robbed
so much.

Me, Jamie and Jayne.

Just me and Madonna.
Casual.

With the big boss, Holly Bott.

For God's sake, she
don't leave me alone.

Joining the team of *Strictly Come Dancing*.

With my second telly wife, Zoe Ball.

Goggleboxing with Mummy Linda.

The Great Celebrity British Bake Off, 2019.

Can't believe Pudsey still hasn't sorted out his eye.

KaRYoke.

With my Steps sister, Claire.

Ready. Steady. Orgy.

My beautiful brother and sister-in-law on their wedding day, with my niece and nephew, Harvey and Olivia.

With my third telly wife, Janette.

Me and B.

Me, Nads and B having a quiet one.

Bonjour, Kimberley.

Ten years on, still by my side.

Turin 2022. With my Eurovision husband, Scott.

Of course, it pissed down on the first night.

12

SINGLE

If this thumb swipes one more time
it's gonna fall off

Christ. Just typing those words, I can't fucking believe it. Who'd have thought I'd be sitting here in my underpants, aged thirty-three years, starting a new chapter all about being single now, a place I thought I'd *NEVER* be again? Here I am in my kitchen, all alone. Apart from the occasional visit from Susie the squirrel on a quick stop at her nut table outside by the window – she never stays to chat for long, ungrateful little mare. Well, that's not quite true. There's the pigeons too. I know them all now, but I have a more special relationship with the one I call Percy, the one with the dodgy foot. He's got a bit of a limp. There's a one-legged pheasant as well. Genuinely. And there were two ducks yesterday making a scene out the front, standing under the flag. Anyway, all alone apart from the local wildlife, let's put it that way. And work people, but only remotely. They can't leave me alone for five fucking seconds, honestly.

I look homeless-slash-Danniella Westbrook. I got myself this new little shortie tracksuit from Burberry, white with a red graphic pattern, to cheer myself up. I've not worn it before now, so I thought I'd put it on and now I'm too hot. I've got no tan on, no makeup on. I'm due for my hair and due for everything, and this is why I'm single. In fact, at one point that's what I thought we should call this book: *This Is Why I'm Single*.

So, where do I begin to even tell you about it? All that new me, new beginnings, new life, new loves, blah blah blah. What can I tell you? Well, I've done what most people coming out of a marriage do: I've been on a few dates, and yes, I've fucked around. You know, I'm on dating apps and I do meet people out and about. But it's all still pretty new to me, and I am rubbish at things like that. I know it sounds ridiculous because I'm the biggest flirt in the world – I mean, I can flirt with anything, even with Susie. Or even with my fake yucca plant in the toilet, if I'm at a really low point. I mean, I even try it on with half the male callers on my Radio 2 Saturday afternoon show. I practically propositioned the lovely Lewis after he got through five rounds of our weekly Couch Potatoes quiz. With some not-so-subtle questioning, I cleverly found out he didn't have a partner, and well it could have been the start of something special. But I genuinely don't go in for much casual sex and I am totally shit at dating. And now I have to learn how to do it all over again. I'm literally starting from scratch. I am not confident when it comes down to that side of things, so I am just trying to take baby steps.

Not long after the break-up happened, I joined Tinder. I put in my bio, 'Tall, normal bloke – 6'4" – am I actually on this thing?' But then within two days I got chucked off because they thought I was a catfish. I looked at my profile and it said: 'Your Tinder account has been banned for activity that violates our Terms of Use.'

So then I joined it again and immediately got chucked off for a second time, so I actually had to get someone on my management team on the case. Someone emailed Tinder for me and told them, 'That's actually him.' How embarrassing is that? And even now, even though I've got the blue tick or whatever the fuck it's called, every single time I match with someone, they still message me saying, 'How can I prove this is really you?' And I'm just so bored of it. I just feel like writing back and saying, 'You know what? I'm fake. Don't worry about it. I'll have a wank instead.'

Later that October, after the whole Tinder catfish debacle, when I was presenting the Icon Award to Steps at the Attitude Awards, when I stepped up onto the stage I was looking down at my phone, looking like I was preoccupied with what I was reading. Then, as a joke, I said something like, 'Sorry, guys, I was a little bit distracted; I was trying to download Grindr – it's been ten years!!'

The truth is, yes, Grindr exists, but I'm not on it. To me, that's just sad. That is just sex. Anyone can go and get sexy sex anytime they want. If I wanted, I could go and find sex anywhere. I'm not frightened of sex in the slightest, but do I just want sex? No, of course not. It would be nice to have more. I wanna find someone that I want to be with. I mean, put it this way, I doubt anyone's going to find a husband on Grindr. But good luck to you if you can.

Even Tinder is difficult. I just don't know if that's how I'm going to meet the right person, but seemingly the days are gone when you can just go to a bar and talk to someone. I've been in bars and seen people and thought, 'Oh, they're nice-looking.' But they won't come up and talk to me, and then two days later I get a message on Instagram saying, 'It was nice seeing you the other night.' Well, in that case, why didn't you come over and we could have had a chat? Just stop being a pussy and come up to me, for fuck's sake. And grow a pair of bollocks. People will talk to me on social media, but won't in real life. I'm sure you must be thinking, 'Well, why don't *you* grow a pair of bollocks, Rylan, and go and talk to them yourself?' The answer is that I've always been crap at all that. I might be a terrible flirt with callers when I'm on the radio, but I'm totally hopeless at it in real life. The God's honest truth is that I've never been able to make the first move with anyone – I'm not self-confident enough about how I look, about whether someone will find me attractive, will like me and want to talk to me.

So I wish I could tell you some of my funny dating stories, but I haven't really had any – not yet, anyway. Obviously I've had my fair number of cheeky DMs since being single. Actually, I wish I had more, so please slide into my DMs, any time. And maybe that could be the tentative first steps of a beautiful romance. Maybe. But it always just ends up with willy pictures, doesn't it? Honestly, within two texts it's, 'Hmm, what's the way to win Rylan's heart? I know! I'll go straight to the dick pic.' And they've got the cock out. That's gays for you. Don't get me wrong, nothing wrong with the odd willy picture, but I wouldn't mind a Peroni with them instead. And then, obviously, you get the ones that are married or in relationships . . . You know, those guys – the ones who'll say, 'I don't normally do this, but . . .' Oh, all right mate, I see. Fuck me, I've done all that before – but years ago, you know, been the bit on the side, the secret boyfriend, all that bollocks. But not now, not any more. No way. I'm not gonna be anyone's secret. It's all fun and games but I'm done with all that.

The thing is, I genuinely never ever, ever ever thought I'd have to do all this dating game again, and to add to that, I never ever thought I'd have to do this again being Rylan, as in being 'famous' and single. Because not only do I have to start meeting new people all over again, which is an effort as it is, add to that *I am Rylan*. It's all a little bit weird. Firstly, there's the whole press and social media side of things, so I can't just date in private. No, as far as the media is concerned, for some reason it's as if my relationship status is suddenly a matter of pressing public concern. I could just go for dinner with a mate, and next thing I know someone has taken a photo of us and they're Rylan's new 'mystery man'. Seriously, I did go on a couple of dates with someone not long ago and it frightened me because that person was a little bit known. Two days later, I had my PR boss on the phone telling me that someone had taken a photo of us together in a restaurant and the papers were gonna run it. Obviously, they didn't. The PR supremo managed to shut it all down, but it just made me think twice about dating anyone, famous or not. However, a few weeks later they got another photo and decided to print it. Since then there's been stories saying our families had met, we've known each other for ten years, and I've also heard of one newspaper trying to come out saying we'd moved in together. All that from a date. It's laughable. I doubt if I can even have a fag outside a pub with someone, never mind a snog, without it ending up in the press. Because ever since the day it was announced that I'd split up with my ex, the press and the paps have been following me left, right and centre. All of a sudden, I'm prime suspect number one because they wanna know who I'm with, and they're hiding in fucking bushes. It's ridiculous. I've never had that my entire life but now they know I'm single, out there, back on the market, they're monitoring my every move. Don't get me wrong, I understand why the press might want to see if I'm with anyone, who I'm with, what I'm getting up to, but I don't really understand what the point of knowing is – just another shit story to fill pages?

Secondly, unlike the first time round before I got married, things are now complicated by the fact that I have that extra layer to think about. Is that person wanting to see me because they want to see me? Because they actually like me? Do they genuinely fancy me? Or do they just fancy the job of 'Rylan's new partner'? I mean, if I couldn't trust the man that I lived with for eight years to be with me for the right reasons, how can I trust some random or other that I've just met in a bar? So now it's twice as hard to find that someone as it was ten years ago. I'd love it if I weren't recognised on a first date, to be honest. I'd love to just walk into a bar and meet someone who genuinely had no clue who I was in my day job. Someone who'd maybe been living off grid on a remote desert island for the last ten years and so had never watched the telly, listened to the radio, or seen a single newspaper with my mug in it. Imagine that! They'd just meet me, see if they liked me and fancied me, if they thought I was funny and sweet and genuine, and if we'd get on. I'd fucking love that. I just wanna find someone who just wants me and loves me for me, Ross Clark. Someone who wants to be part of my *whole life*, for good and for bad, and not just for the surface celebrity aspect of who I am with my job – but who supports me in that too. And I want to be part of *their* life; I want someone who shares things with me, and I want to share all of me with them. I want to find someone that who, if I'm at a work event and I have a drink afterwards, isn't ringing me every five minutes asking, 'Where the fuck are you?' I want them to either be there with me, or telling me to go and enjoy my night. I want someone who wants to take me out for dinner. Or I take them out for dinner and if someone comes over and asks for a photo, doesn't start tutting and rolling their eyes, but actually says, 'You're cool. Don't be silly. It's not a problem.' Who understands it, gets it, and accepts that's now part of me being Rylan. Sorry, I'm getting on my high horse now, but that's it. That's what I want.

So, as they say on *Love Island*, what's my type on paper? All my friends would sit there and say that my type is a typical Mediterranean-looking bloke, the type you might bump into at midnight ordering a kebab. That's always how they take the piss out of me, because, looks-wise, I like dark features, a bit hairy, that's definitely my type. But I think since I've been single I've realised I don't actually have a 'type'. I'm not looking for a 'type'. Though, obviously, you don't stand in a bar and look across the room and go, 'Fuck me, he's got a well nice personality.' You sit there and go, 'Fuck me, he's handsome.' Of course you've got to be attracted to someone. That's the initial pull. That's what gets me walking over to them to find out more. But the truth is, I've been with the good-looking people that are arseholes; I've met people that have been really great-looking, but they're either dull and I'm bored, or they're just dickheads. None of that matters. Looks fade. So for me, it's more about what they're like. I've met people that I wouldn't necessarily think I'd fancy, and I'm so attracted to them because I like what and who and how they are to spend time with. In that respect, I think I've grown up. I've gone through that stage of just falling for what's on the surface. I mean, a lot of people say it, don't they? Once you've been married and it doesn't work out and you get divorced, the second time around is always better because you've learned so much. And I've learned that what I thought I wanted, I still want, but I actually want other things more. So rather than having the super good-looking, sexy husband, with . . . yeah, I'm not gonna go there, but I actually want other things more.

So, what do I want? What am I looking for? What do any potential lovers need to do to sweep me off my feet? Well, I just want someone who wants to lay down at night with me on the same sofa and watch a bit of telly. Not someone who's sitting there a mile away on the opposite sofa. I want to be able to go on holiday with that person, just the two of us, and not be worried that it's going to be boring or that we ain't gonna have anything to talk about. I wanna laugh with someone. I don't care if he works in Sainsbury's or he's a Hollywood A-lister, but my dream man is someone fucking decent, who is proud of me, who is happy when I walk through the door, who treats me with respect, who loves me, makes me laugh and I do exactly the same for them – that's my dream man. I don't care who it is, as long as they're honest and kind.

I still want to find 'the one' – but most of all, I need to trust someone again and I don't know how long that's gonna take me, unfortunately. I can't rule it out just because of what's happened to me in the past though, but trusting someone again plays a big part in this stage of my new single life. Also, I have realised that now I'm in no big rush. Time will tell when I'm ready to meet that special someone. (I was going to write that when the time is right 'it'll come', but then I changed my mind. Oops.)

People have asked me if I would be up for going on something like *Celebrity First Dates*. Well, the answer is that I wouldn't right now, though I wouldn't rule it out entirely. Never say never, as they say. And actually, I had what I thought was a brilliant idea for me, Judge Rob Rinder and Alan Carr – because, as you might know, we've all just got divorced and we're all gay. (Well, I say we're all divorced, but I'm still in the middle of the nightmare, Alan's just finished his and Rob's came through a little while ago. It turns out we all ended up with the same divorce lawyer, and we didn't even realise.) But anyway, back to my genius idea. As I said earlier, I sometimes feel that the only way I'm actually gonna find that relationship and love again is if I meet someone who doesn't know what I do or who I am. So basically the pitch is, think *Gordon, Gino & Fred's Road Trip*, but the gay version and with romance. All three of us would go away somewhere abroad, ideally really hot and sultry – sun, sea and sand, all of that – where no one had heard of us, and the series would just be us meeting and dating people and seeing what happens. You never know, I might find my late-night kebab seller! Like Shirley fucking Valentine. I just think it'd be fucking hilarious. And I would have no shame in doing it. First stop for me would be Italy, so maybe it would have to be a pizza seller rather than kebabs. And even if I didn't meet the one, I'd still have a bloody brilliant two-week holiday with that pair. Eat some nice food, drink a load of wine. I think we could get away with it. I'd just love it.

In the real world, though, as opposed to telly land, it's probably a case of just doing it, going for it, giving it a go. I just have to keep an open mind and an open heart and keep meeting people, put myself out there. And have fun while I'm at it. So now, coming out the other side of the break-up, I've turned into a yes man. Whereas before I would say 'no' to things a lot, as in 'no' to going out for dinner, or 'no' to going clubbing, now I think, 'Fuck it. I'm thirty-three, not ninety-three. Go and enjoy yourself!' I wanna have a life. I'm going to keep on flirting and having a laugh. As I said, I can't help myself – you know me. And you know, I'm sure the 'one who shall not be named' is doing the same. I don't know, but I want to say that I honestly don't give a fuck.

With time, the trust will come. And I'll just know when that trust and that right person for me is there, right in front of my nose. This time, I'll listen to that gut feeling. From now on, the minute I get the slightest whiff of something being off – if I feel I need to check someone's phone or if I think that someone's lying to me – that's it. I'm out. Because if I feel the need to do that in any relationship, what's the point? I want to be able to not even have to worry that I'm the only one for him, and he definitely will be the only one for me. Of course, people will make mistakes and as you now know, I've made mistakes myself. But whatever happens next in my romantic life, the most important thing for me is just to be honest. You have to own your mistakes and not fuck with people's heads. Just be normal. Be honest and be real. That's all I can be, and it's all I'm looking for in a partner.

But nobody has managed to tick all of my boxes just yet. Don't get me wrong, I've been lucky in that – I was about to say, 'I've come across', but again that's definitely the wrong choice of words – I've met some nice guys, but I think maybe I met them too soon. Now, I have had more time to reflect on certain aspects of my first marriage. Looking back over everything that happened in the last year, I feel I've learned so much when it comes down to relationships. What's right and what's wrong. As I said, it takes time to recover from something like the kind of break-up I had. I was with the wrong person for eight whole years and yet I thought I'd found the one. So after what I've been through it's going to take someone who's going to really make me go 'Wow!'.

I'd love to find someone. Of course I would. But when I do and it's the right time and they're the right person, I think I'll know. I hope I'll know. But I don't want any regrets. That's why I'm quite calm with it all at the minute. And who knows what's gonna happen in the future. Also, next time, I'd get a prenup. Silly prick.

Lessons I've learned:

- Make sure you know what way you're swiping when you're pissed – it's awkward the following morning
- Don't be scared to trust, but don't give it all upfront (emotionally, not sexually . . . You get yours, babe)
- If you see one red flag – run

13

CELEBRITY

Would you rather be rich and famous or . . .
just rich?

In another life, I probably would have been an architect. Growing up, I loved looking at buildings, all those places in London like Richard Rogers' Lloyd's building, No.1 Poultry, Stratford station, Stansted Airport. I loved all those modern designs. I was obsessed. I used to sit there drawing and designing buildings. But somewhere, somehow, along the way, all that early childhood ambition went out the window. By the time I was at secondary school, my main focus was on becoming a celebrity.

Back in the late nineties, when I was still at primary school, celebrity was still an untouchable thing. TV was the main media in our house. My mum used to get newspapers every day – the red tops, natch, usually the *Sun*; it was never the *Guardian* in our house! On a Sunday it was always the *News of the World*. I can remember so clearly the morning when Diana died. I'd woken up really early that Sunday, 31 August 1997 and I got up and went to the living room to play a game on Teletext called *Bamboozle!* It was an early quiz game, with multiple choice questions where you just pressed the red, yellow, blue or green button on your remote to answer. I don't know why I loved it so much, but it was something to do. Anyway, when I put on Teletext, I read, 'Princess Diana dead in car crash', then I carried on with my game – I know! I was only nine for fuck's sake! Every time I finished a quiz, I had to reload the Teletext page and all I kept seeing was that breaking news headline. Eventually, I thought I'd better go and tell my mum about Princess Diana. I woke her up and told her what it said on Teletext and I remember she said, 'Oh my God, no,' and she jumped out of bed and ran downstairs. I remember Mum crying. Then my nan got up and then she was crying too. I just couldn't understand it.

Mum went to the shop to get the papers. All of them ran the story of the crash, that Dodi Fayed was dead and that Diana was gravely injured, but the *News of the World* must have printed a late second edition, because the headline was 'DIANA DEAD'. I just remember looking at the photographs of this crash, thinking that people had actually died in that car. Back then the press and the paparazzi who followed Diana didn't care. It was that sense of ownership of her; her privacy and any sense of respect for the family was secondary to selling newspapers. I just always remember that, and it's still the case, I think – to a certain extent, people in the public eye are owned.

With the new millennium and the phenomenon that was *Big Brother*, that whole sense of celebrity as some unreachable magic thing all changed. I remember being at secondary school and suddenly all these normal people who went into the house became really fucking big celebrities, more or less overnight. Now we were in the era of the tabloid obsession with the housemates' every single move, indiscretion and argument. And that, of course, led to the explosion of the celebrity mag market featuring all the latest gossip and candid paparazzi shots.

On a Tuesday, me and my school friends would go and buy them all – *Heat, Hello!, OK!, Closer, Now, New, Look*. All of them. They'd all be the same fucking thing, but I used to read every single magazine front to back, back to front. In those days, there wasn't that whole sidebar of shame clickbait thing going on in the same way. You had to get the actual newspaper or magazine to read all the juicy stories and latest gossip, and *Heat* was always my favourite because it followed the same pattern every week. You had the 'Circle of Shame' and all that shit. Magazines can't do that kind of thing now, but back then, I loved it. There was always a *Big Brother* story in *Heat* as well, with pictures of ex-housemates papped out and about. I loved it all. Couldn't get enough of it.

At school, my mind developed from education, education, education to fuck education. I remember that my English Literature teacher – who was also my form tutor – chucked me out of her class one day during GCSE year and said I'd literally amount to fuck all. But out of the two of us, I'm the one who wrote a book that went to number one on the best-seller lists. I then went and did my written English Literature coursework on *Big Brother* and *The Salon*, genuinely. And then because I forgot what day it was, I missed the English Literature exam anyway.

I knew what I wanted to do. I wanted to be famous. I didn't know why, or how, or even what I wanted to be famous *for*. But I didn't care. I just knew. It was about being, not doing. I wasn't alone in this obsession, either – a few of my friends were interested in being famous too. My gay best friend James wanted to be a dancer; I was gonna be the pop star. But it was almost like everyone at school knew that I was actually going to do it. In our yearbooks, I was always the one my classmates chose as 'most likely to be famous' and 'most likely to sing', 'most likely to "make it"'. Shit like that. Even my teachers used to say it. The only subject I put any effort into at school was drama, and my mum paid for me to go to outside drama lessons as well. Every Sunday I was part of the Pineapple Performing Arts School in Covent

Garden, so I always used to bump into celebrity-type people there and I thought, 'I'm in the right place but I'm not there yet.' And for me it was always music that I wanted to do. I looked at people like the Spice Girls and thought: 'That's the life I want.'

I always wanted to be in the magazines. I always wanted to be pictured out and about, getting drunk in a club, rolling out of there, and laughing about it the following morning. I thought that fame was something special, something that was unreachable, but also strangely reachable in my little head. Looking back now, I don't understand why I wanted it so much.

As I said earlier, my first proper brush with fame was back in 2011 when I went on *Signed by Katie Price*. The whole premise of the show was to decide who would be the next modelling superstar, but it was an ambitious format, something like *The Apprentice* meets *Big Brother* meets *The X Factor*. Me and the other wannabe stars were sent to Bootcamp in Frome, and then along with the other eleven finalists, I moved into the contestants' house, a grand six-bedroom mansion in Roehampton, complete with a pole in the front room (for dancing up) and a jacuzzi in the back garden. Like *The Apprentice*, we were set many challenges along the way: design a clothing brand, create a viral YouTube video, and for the final, design and pitch our own personal fragrance brand – I was quite pleased with mine, which I named 'Rylan: ID', tag line: 'Be who you wannabe'. But I didn't win. I was the runner-up and the prize money, modelling contract and black Range Rover went to my rival, a stunning eighteen-year-old who looked like Cindy Crawford's younger sister. I remember the night before I went away to do the show and I thought, 'Well, finally! This is IT.' It wasn't.

When it was eventually aired later that year, on Sky Living, the show wasn't that well received and didn't get many viewers. After the series finished, I remember being invited to go on *Daybreak*, now known as *Good Morning Britain*, and thinking it was the best thing in the world. It was so exciting. Because for some reason, that was attractive to me – I wanted people to know who I was. I wanted people to know where I was, what I was about, what I liked, what I disliked.

Then I went on *The X Factor* in 2012 and I got it. Finally, literally overnight, I got given that thing I'd been craving ever since I was a small council house boy in Stepney Green. I remember seeing my face on the front page of the newspapers, the endless news articles written about me, looking online and googling my name and seeing people talking about me, and my photograph everywhere. I remember doing my first shoot for *Heat*. It was me, James Arthur and Jahméne Douglas. And it was a proper interview story. I couldn't believe it – I was on the front cover of *Heat*! What the fuck? It was just thrilling to get something like that. I was trending on Twitter and I couldn't stop myself reading every tweet. It was the first thing I'd do when I woke up. It was crazy.

For those first few weeks on *The X Factor* it was absolutely everything that I'd thought it was cracked up to be: the invites, the premieres, parties and photo shoots. All of that and more. But then I started to realise that behind the overnight fame, I had made it through to the live shows for a reason, and not necessarily my singing voice. No, the producers had a job for me to do on that show. And at that point my job wasn't to be a singer: it was to perform every single Saturday night in front of the nation and make a bit of a scene about it. To be the gay diva. My job on *The X Factor* was to be the one that everyone spoke about, whether they loved me or hated me.

That was my real job on the show. I was lucky in that I got wise to that quite early on and I thought: 'Fine, we'll roll with it because I'm only going to get one chance to do this.' And while the hysterical crying at Judges' Houses in front of Nicole Scherzinger was absolutely all true – it wasn't an act, I mean if I was that good an actor I'd have been in fucking Hollywood, not on *The X Factor* – I played a character when I was on the live shows. I knew I only needed a week on the live shows to earn a bit of money and set myself up for a while. I also knew I had to be the gay stereotype that was on the front of the papers every day. And I did my job well, I played the game – too well, perhaps. That's where others had failed in the past – they believed the hype. They genuinely believed that they were going to be the next Beyoncé. I knew I wasn't going to be the next Beyoncé. But at the same time, I always knew that I could be the next *something*.

It wasn't easy. As much as I was just being myself on that TV show, playing up to the character that so quickly was expected of me was really difficult. I needed to play to the cameras, to be the joker, to go along with the arguments and the criticism, especially from Gary Barlow, and to a certain extent play the public at their own game. In real life, I got on quite well with Gary and I'd never walk around wearing those wacky outfits Wardrobe dreamed up for me – a light-up boiler suit, hello? (Well maybe sometimes, if I've had a drink) – but that was part of the game I had to play to gain fame. And I understood that to keep going, to keep putting myself through the show week in week out, I also had to learn how to navigate the rules of the game. It was a bit like snakes and ladders: sometimes you roll the dice and you get to go up the ladder, but there's always a snake at the top of that ladder somewhere, waiting to send you crashing back down.

Don't get me wrong, mostly I had the time of my life on *The X Factor*. I made some amazing friends, and met some amazing people who work in the industry – I mean, I met Nicole Scherzinger, who's a close friend now. She's always helped me and pointed me in the right direction whenever I've needed her, and I'll do the same for her. And it's an honour that I can sit here and say, 'I could give Nicole advice if she asked for it', because I know what she means now.

But after the first live show, the media and public had turned on me and the name 'Rylan' was now trending for all the wrong reasons. The abuse was vile and violently felt. I was suddenly the world's number one most hated person. As the weeks went by, and as week after week people voted to keep me in the competition, sending home some genuinely brilliant, talented singers, the headlines of Sunday papers called me a 'National Joke', and the programme became dubbed '*The Fix Factor*'. And it was all my fault because, as I said, I was in on the joke. I played the game. The coverage was awful enough, but the death threats from my Twitter trolls, with people genuinely wishing that I was dead, and the fact that my family were dragged into it, was what nearly brought me to my knees. I look back now and I ask myself, why did I carry on? Why did I still want fame?

When I did the *Grounded* podcast a few years ago with Louis Theroux, he asked me if not having had a father figure in my life had affected me. Whether I thought that might explain my wanting to be famous, growing up? If it maybe stemmed from a need, from lacking attention? But no, I don't think it was that. I got a lot of attention as a kid and I had a great upbringing and a great family. And as for the lack of a father figure, well, I said that was definitely a big no because my big brother Jamie always acted sort of like a dad to me. I never wanted for anything because he bought me things and took me on holiday.

So I don't know what it was that kept driving me on. But the problem is that the second you walk out of something like *The X Factor*, you are on your own. I was very lucky because I'd already been invited to go into *Celebrity Big Brother*. If that offer hadn't come along, I genuinely don't know where I'd be today. I just can't imagine it.

I jumped at the chance. I had barely unpacked one suitcase before I was packing another, practically the week after. I knew that if I went on *Celebrity Big Brother* it was my chance to let the public see the real me, not the pantomime version they'd seen on *The X Factor*. And I still think that was one of the best decisions I ever made, because I was completely, 100 per cent myself on that show. Obviously I wanted my fellow housemates to like me, and vain bastard that I am, I definitely cared about how I looked on the show, but I didn't care about coming across bored, or grumpy, or getting into arguments. I was the 'real' me, and that's why people in the real world started to like me. Well, not everyone was going to like me, but it didn't bother me, still doesn't. Anyway, enough people changed their minds about me to vote me the winner of *Celebrity Big Brother* 2013. That's when I really knew I'd won the biggest fucking lottery pay-out ever. And I was still in that bubble of thinking fame was the be-all and end-all.

Again, I was lucky. After all the interviews and appearances on *This Morning*, I joined *The X Factor* live tour and so the attention and the photo shoots, and the fans wanting selfies and autographs continued. I'll never forget seeing myself in one of the weekly celeb gossip magazines for the first time. I can't remember if it was in *OK!* or *Closer*, but someone had taken a photo of me in a car park with one of my dancers on the tour. He had his dog with him and I was just stroking this dog. It was the 'Pic of the Week', so the person who'd sent it in had won the weekly £200 prize. I remember thinking, 'Oh my God! I made it. AND I'M PIC OF THE WEEK. Amazing!'

But when I finished the last gig and I went back home, sitting there in my childhood bedroom, I realised that the second you leave a show like that, you're nothing. It was the first time I'd been in a room on my own for eight months, without anyone watching me. I remember waking up at 4 a.m. and thinking: 'It's over.'

If the phone hadn't rung with the *Big Brother's Bit on the Side* presenter job a few weeks later, I don't know what I'd have done. But it did, and I went for it, and then some. I lived the celebrity cliché. I had my teeth done (MUCH more on that controversial subject later, I promise). I bought a Range Rover – the Essex dream – and had it customised so that the silver lettering on all the badges that normally say 'Range Rover' said 'Range Rylan'. I couldn't tell you how much it cost, but I was so adamant about getting it done that I just said, 'Take whatever you need.'

Then I started my first proper full-time job in television, and this time I was the one doing the interviews, not the one being interviewed. And that's what saved me, from myself and from this lifelong delusion of what fame actually meant. Because when I started hosting *Big Brother's Bit on the Side*, I realised I had misjudged what fame would bring and that it hadn't actually turned out to be what I had thought or hoped it would be at all. You know when you read in the papers about this or that celebrity that's gone to the drink and drugs, how they've got all the money in the world and they're not happy with their lives? I used to sit there and think: 'That's a bit much, isn't it? You've got all the money in the world, and you're moaning?' Now I totally get it.

I hate people knowing who I am. Which is the one thing I actually wanted as a child. I've got a lot of fans that follow me around – I call them Rylan's Sirens. And I feel like I genuinely know these people because I see so much of them. They'll come to my work and stand outside for a photo. The other day after my Radio 2 show, when I went for a meeting at the BT Tower, one of them was outside – I didn't even know I was going there, so how they knew I have no idea. They follow me around. They'll be outside Wogan House when I go in and when I come out. Then they'll follow me or they go home. Don't get me wrong, it's actually really sweet. I stop and say hello and take a selfie with them, both on my way in and on my way out. But it's crazy.

There's one young girl who knows my schedule better than I do. Genuinely. I will sometimes get messages from her on Twitter saying: 'Can't wait to see you tomorrow on *The Lateish Show with Mo Gilligan*,' or something. I'll be straight on the phone to Nads complaining that he hasn't told me that I was doing that show, and he'll say, 'Oh, yeah. Sorry, I was gonna ring you about that!' Honestly, half the fucking time she knows what I'm doing before I do. I don't know why the firm don't get her to work for them because she seems a lot more efficient than any of that lot! (NB Nads: JOKE!)

Even interviewing Madonna, one of the most famous singers on the planet, on *The One Show* for her new album, *Madame X*, in 2019, I got mobbed more than the Queen of Pop. Not because I'm more 'famous' or recognisable, but because I'm in people's houses every day. So people think they know who I am. And to a certain extent, they do. And when people think they know you because you're on the telly, they think they've got a say in your life. They don't realise it's a show – I might be playing myself, but I'm doing a job.

It was funny that day when I interviewed Madonna because I remember that earlier in the day I'd been doing a job for McDonald's, because I do a bit of brand work with them. I spent the afternoon working in one of their restaurants in Ashford to see what it's like to be a McDonald's employee. I wore the uniform and everything, then I got changed and went and interviewed Madonna. I literally had both ends of the spectrum, from working in McDonald's to interviewing a pop superstar, in the space of two hours. When I got to her hotel, she was a bit late and all her PRs and various assistants were telling me, 'She's really not in a great mood.' I'm like, 'Great. Why the fuck are you telling me that? Like, I'm about to interview her?' She sat down and I just said, 'Nice to meet you,' and the first thing she said was, 'What star sign are you?'

'I'm a Scorpio,' I said.

'I don't like Scorpios,' came Madonna's response. So I said, 'Well, you're gonna fucking love me!' And then I interviewed her and at the end, she said, 'You're the nicest Scorpio I've ever met.' So if Madonna said it, it must be true.

Anyway, what I mean is, one day I'm interviewing Madonna, Sir Paul McCartney or the Kardashians, the next I'm going to see the Spice Girls, because Geri got me a ticket. Basically, ten-year-old me is having a wank. This is me meeting my idols. The people I was obsessed with as a kid. But as I said, outside that hotel, more people were waiting to scream at me than at fucking Madonna. That's not me having a humblebrag. It's just crazy.

In 2003, the Pet Shop Boys released a song called 'Flamboyant' and I remember when I heard it recently, me being a complete ego-maniac, I thought, 'It feels like they've written that about me.' There's a line in it that goes, 'Just crossing the street, well, it's almost heroic'. That hit a nerve because sometimes I will literally feel anxious just about getting out of my car, for fear of people going, 'Rylan, Rylan.' (With Jamie now my driver, at least if I can't face getting out, I can just sit in the back and cry.) And fuck me, I'm not under any illusion that I'm an A-lister; I don't think I'm even on the alphabet scale. It's not that, it's just that people recognise me and sometimes you just don't wanna be recognised. Sometimes you want to just disappear and go into the shop. Just going to get a pint of milk at the shop across the road is a drama sometimes. I know it sounds so fucking silly, but sometimes it is. I feel like I have to put on makeup to go in there because it only takes one person to take one photo and then the next thing you know it's in the papers with the headline: 'RYLAN LOOKING SAD AS HE SHOPS FOR SEMI-SKIMMED IN TESCO' or 'CONCERNS ABOUT RYLAN'S HEALTH AS HE POPS INTO CO-OP LOOKING REALLY ROUGH'. That's literally it and then I'm sitting here shouting, 'No, I ain't. I've just got no spray tan on and I just woke up, you cunt!' It's all these things you wouldn't normally think of, then suddenly it's all you think about a lot of the time. When really all I should be thinking is, 'Fuck. I've run out of milk. I need to go out to the shop and get some.'

From the moment I left *The X Factor*, for some reason lots of people have always wanted to follow me, to know what I'm doing, and to talk to me. I get it. You are owned, you are public property, you're a product, at the end of the day. So you just have to accept that as part of the job and go with the flow. But when I'm out, in private, and not working; when I'm not Rylan, just me, I'm constantly being stopped by people wanting to say hello or take a selfie with me. And I'm constantly having to apologise about it to whoever I'm with. In fact, I spend more time saying sorry than anything else. 'I'm so sorry' / 'It's fine, it's fine' / 'I'm really sorry.' At the same time, everyone's lovely – touch wood – they're all really nice people, but sometimes you just wanna go out and forget. And just enjoy yourself. And going out locally doesn't make it easier. No, it doesn't matter if it's local or international, it doesn't matter where I am. There's always someone. I might be all right if I was in the local pub every single night for two months, then people might get used to my ugly mug and ignore me. But then I'd go in two months and a day later, and lo and behold, someone new would be in there and they'd be like, 'Rylan, oh my God, it's Rylan!'

It's just normal to me now and I try not to worry about it, but I can spot it before it even happens. I know who's going to come up to me before they've even seen me. It's so blatant. And it's the same thing every single time. They say, 'Rylan, I would *never* normally do this, but . . .' It's always a variation on that same line: 'I would never normally interrupt you during your dinner' or 'I would never normally do this, but Rylan, I've got to come and say hello because my husband or my wife or my mum or my kids or blah blah blah, please can I have a photo?' And of course, I say, 'Yeah, no worries.' It always happens like that and it's really strange. In the past, if it had been the other way round, I'd probably have done the same – but I don't, partly because I now get how that feels.

In fact, weirdly I was in that very position not long ago. I took my mum and her friend and my cousin to Paris in early 2022 and we were sat there on the Eurostar – I'd treated us all, so we were travelling in first class. This guy was at the table across the aisle from us and he had a cap on and stuff like that. You know when you look at someone and you're like, 'I know that man.' Well, there's three things I always think: a) Are they famous? b) Have I fucked them? or c) Have I fucked them off? That's what runs through my head. On this occasion, it turned out it was the first one. He was famous. It was Tahar Rahim, who among other things, had played the serial killer Charles Sobhraj in the BBC TV drama *The Serpent*. Me being the beady-eyed bastard I am, I was looking over and I could see he was reading a script on his phone, so I thought, 'It's definitely him, I know it.' He's French, so it made sense because we was on the Eurostar to Paris.

I gave my mum a nudge and nodded over to him, and she's all, 'What?'

Let me tell you, my mum is the LEAST nonchalant person in the world, so I slyly said to her, all hushed tones, 'It's him from *The Serpent*.'

'What???'

And again I'm, 'That's him from *The Serpent*.'

And then she goes, 'Oh my gawd it is!!!'

I was shushing her: 'Mum, shut up. Shut up!'

Then Pat, her mate, starts going, 'Say hello! Say hello!' And, to be honest, I was really tempted to say exactly that, 'Listen, I'm so sorry to bother you . . .' – maybe at the end when we were all getting off or something like that. But even though I thought he was fucking great in *The Serpent* and I'd not met him before, I didn't. I mean, it's different if you are at an event or out and about somewhere in a bar or something, fair enough. But sat on the fucking Eurostar – no way, because there's nowhere to go. It's not like he could just get off. So I didn't talk to him. And I think that comes from being that person on the receiving end. You can tell when someone doesn't want to be spoken to. He was wearing a cap, he had his head in his phone, not making eye contact, keeping himself to himself. Yet I do that – I've got a cap on, a pair of sunglasses, four jackets – and people still fucking come up to me! I mean, can you not tell I'm trying to go under the radar?

I just think people feel that somehow I'm different, and they can come up and chat. I think it's because I was in people's houses on the telly early in the morning every day and then I was in people's houses late at night before they went to bed. And being that person there in the morning and there at night, it's almost like I became like one of the family, and they think, 'Oh, he's normal, he's all right.' That's why they feel comfortable enough to approach me. I get that, and that's actually a massive compliment to me. But people genuinely feel like they know me – in real life, not just from the telly. And I think a lot of the time people forget that they don't actually know me; they've never met me, and I've never met them.

I still don't really understand it. I can't seem to remember what it was like to be on the other side of it. It's also partly because the world has changed, and everyone is a photographer now. Everywhere you go, you're watched by people who record your every single move, and it's frightening. I got rid of the Range Rylan when people started driving alongside me with their phones out trying to get a piccy. It made me panic at the wheel. But when I go to something like a family wedding – lovely people, great conversation – when it gets late, that's when it starts. People who've been there all day start asking for photos. It's that constant reminder that: 'Oh shit, you're Rylan.' I've lost a lot of friends over it. I've got one handful of people who I can cry down the phone to and know it's between us. But then I think, 'I did this to myself.' I went on *The X Factor* and sold my soul . . . to the *beast*. And that beast is called 'fame'.

There is this constant pressure to try and impress and be the perfect specimen, whether that's how I look, speak, or behave. In my early years in this industry, it's something that I took extremely seriously. Sometimes I took it too far. I would rarely go out and would try to make sure that I had a squeaky-clean image. And even though I honestly have been pretty squeaky-clean for ten years – I don't really get into arguments, I keep myself to myself – it doesn't stop newspapers like the *Sunday Mirror* from concocting front-page stories about me being some kind of junkie, asking for 'gear' on a perfectly innocent drunken night out. Sometimes I genuinely don't know how some of those journalists sleep at night.

As the years go on it's something I try to care less about, but I quite like the fact that I make mistakes and I like the fact that I fuck up. And I own my mistakes; even when I'm presenting live and I misread the autocue or my teeth get in the way and out comes some fucking garbled nonsense from my mouth, I own it. I just make a joke of it and carry on. Sometimes, and on reflection I think that's what the public like, I'm normal and I screw up. No one wants to watch Mr or Mrs Perfect. Making mistakes is probably why I'm still doing this job ten years on, because you learn from them. Sometimes you learn the hard way. Sometimes, then, that pushes you further. But the press intrusion seems to be getting worse, following me around, the paparazzi hiding in cars taking photos of me when I'm drinking with people in a bar or standing outside having a cigarette. Genuinely no one seems to care that I'm just out enjoying myself – and you know what? I fucking deserve to enjoy myself for a change.

Hand on heart, I don't class myself any differently to anyone else around me, whether it's a friend, a family member, someone who works in the shop over the road . . . whoever.

I class myself as someone exactly the same because I *am* exactly the same. I've just got a different type of job to most people, a job that a lot of people know about because they see me on the telly in their living room or hear me on the radio. But I'm no different to anyone else. I know I've said that a lot of times, but I really do have to repeat it, because I genuinely believe that certain people I meet think that *I* think I'm different to them – more special, or whatever. But that's BOLLOCKS. And it's through no fault of my own.

I find that when I meet people, especially for the first time, they do treat me slightly differently, and it usually goes one of two ways. Either they will be all over me, SO interested in me, and want to be my new best friend. Or they go in the complete opposite direction and try to be as uninterested and distant as physically possible, because they think that's what I want. It's so obvious. But I'd like it to be somewhere in the middle, what I call the normal ground. And it's always hard meeting new people, because a lot of the time people genuinely believe that they already know me, which to a certain extent they do because I've shared a lot of my life through my work. I find that makes me feel like I'm always starting on the back foot, though, because I know nothing about them. But while people might think they know everything about me, in fact they don't. As much as I am who I am on television and radio, that's not ALL of me. There's a lot more to me than my work and that big mug you see all the time on your screens – also, I'm a MILLION times more gorgeous in the flesh! When people meet me in real life, the first thing I notice is their surprise at how tall – and hunky – I really am; secondly, that my voice is a lot deeper than they expect; and thirdly, why not, I'll say it again, allegedly I look a lot better in real life. Now, that's not me bigging myself up. If anything, it makes me worry that I look like a short, high-pitched gargoyle on the telly, but I'll take it as a compliment.

More and more over the last ten years, as my career's progressed and the job opportunities have continued to come my way, I know for sure that I really don't actually want all the hysteria any more. In the beginning, the fame was the exciting part but in fact now I want and cherish the work much more than the fame. Because now the job is the exciting part. And if I had the choice, I would happily let the fame go and keep the job rather than the other way round. I know you might think, well, that's a bit rich coming from someone who went all-out in pursuit of it, and yes, in the early days, it was all I ever wanted. I wanted people to know who I was. And the first six months of my career were a public vote. I never forget that. But now, much as I'm grateful for it, what fame meant to me as a twenty-three-year-old isn't necessarily what it means now, which is the one thing I wish I didn't have.

Is this a classic case of the grass isn't always greener? You finally get given something you've always wanted and then realise it's not all it's cracked up to be? Don't get me wrong – being known has many, many perks. Being invited to places you never thought you'd be able to go, or being able to some-times walk straight in somewhere and not have to queue is nice. Yet sometimes it's important to stand in the queue. Sometimes you wanna feel like everyone else. Sometimes you want to just fuck off over the garden centre to buy a plant. Or go down the high street shopping. I'm now a mister online person – for everything.

I'd love a little walkabout, though. The last time I was in a branch of The Range, this woman kept asking for selfies. So she had her selfie. And then as I was down every aisle, I could see her taking photos of me. I mean, she'd had her photo,

I just wanted her to fuck off. Because then I'm also worried about what I pick up, because next thing it's on social media and people are asking, 'Ooh, I wonder why's he getting that Vanish Gold?' The amount of times I've gone into a shop and asked for twenty Marlboro and the person behind the counter says to me, 'Oh, *you* shouldn't be smoking.' Why?

I mean that's bad enough, but imagine if I walked into a shop and said, 'Can I have a pack of condoms, please? Make it twenty of your best ribbed ticklers. Oh, I'm gonna have that dildo as well. Thank you.' Could you imagine? But that's how I have to think. You can just imagine the rumours. So no, I can't remember the last time I nipped into Zara or a TK Maxx, or did anything really normal like that. And I mainly get people over to mine for dinner rather than go down to a bar or a restaurant. Fame doesn't mean the same thing to me now that it did back then, and that's not from an ungrateful stance.

I've thought about it a lot, but it's weird because I've never really talked about it to other presenters like, say, Eamonn Holmes and Ruth Langsford, or so-called 'famous' friends who are in the same shoes. Because everyone's different. I mean, I could walk down the street with a presenter I work with and she could be wearing a big puffa jacket, a woolly hat and no makeup, and no one would know it was her. Not because she looks so different from how she appears on telly, but just because she blends in with the crowd. And that's not a bad thing, because that's what she's trying to do. But if I try and blend in with the crowd, I look like a terrorist because I look like I'm smuggling some type of bomb. I'm 7 foot tall, my teeth are massive, the beard . . . I can't hide.

What's more, apart from being strip-searched for explosives, airports are the fucking worst places in the world because there is just NO getting away from being recognised. You are literally stuck. If I get on a plane and I hear the words 'stag do', I know that's it, I'm fucked. And hen parties – oh my God, they're just as bad. I was at an airport one time and I saw a hen do heading towards me through the concourse. They actually didn't see me because I was sat in a Starbucks and they all walked through, but there were about forty of them, all with Rylan cardboard cut-out face masks on them. And on the back of their shirts was printed 'Mrs Rylan To Be'. I didn't know what the fuck was going on. I thought I was on *Ant and Dec's Saturday Night Takeaway*, but I guess the actual husband-to-be just had a beard and his mates probably rinsed him and called him Rylan. I was gonna go up and surprise the bride-to-be and her hens, but I'm glad I didn't. It was just one of those surreal moments where I thought, 'Do I?' But by the time I thought, 'Oh fuck it, I should . . . I'm gonna do it!' – because that probably would have made her hen-do weekend – they'd gone on through to their boarding gate. I felt bad, but maybe it was just as well, because to be fair I doubt I would have got out alive.

Those Rylan masks are another thing. People sell any old shit, don't they? You've only got to type in 'Rylan' on Amazon and literally, you can buy life-size cardboard cut-outs of me. Just earlier today I went to do a job and there was a gag involving two cardboard cut-outs of me that they'd got off Amazon. One of them was in an outfit I wore two weeks ago. And I knew exactly when it was because I had my brand-new watch on. What the actual fuck? So they're doing a fucking quick turnaround them cardboard people, I tell you. People are crazy.

I also feel like the world and the concept of being famous has changed so much in the last ten years. Back then when I did *The X Factor*, being 'famous' was still quite rare. And before

I continue, don't get me wrong: I am fully aware that I'm no Hollywood superstar. Far from it. But remember that ten years ago, digital television was just starting up; barely anyone had even heard of *Netflix*, and unless they had a BSkyB satellite dish, most people only had a choice of five TV channels, and one of them, Channel 5, was still a baby. Reality TV was also still really just getting started: *The Only Way Is Essex* and *Bake Off* were two years old; *Made in Chelsea* and *Geordie Shore* were just one; *The Voice* had just been born. *Love Island* wasn't even a twinkle in the ITV2 commissioner's eye.

Social media is one thing that is particularly difficult to deal with. I understand how the fame game works and even more so when it comes to social media – it's a work tool, but at the same time it's a tool for anyone to say ANYTHING they want to with zero repercussions. There are a lot of people online who find it fun just to sit there on their phone or laptop and hurl abuse at people. I'm a thirty-three-year-old man. I'm big enough, strong enough and ugly enough to take criticism. I'm also aware that some of it might not be genuine criticism and it could just be insults to get a reaction. But sometimes you can catch me at the wrong time, and I'll see something that for some reason really affects me. I don't really know why I let comments on social media hurt me so much. Probably because I'm human, like everybody else.

I feel like I've really grown up in the last ten years. I'm lucky and I'm so grateful to have what I have, but there's just something about the word 'fame' that makes me uncomfortable now. As I said, if I could do my job and be forgotten about the second I'm off air, I'd definitely take it. Would I miss it? Well, I'd like to miss it, if that makes sense.

I read once that with 'fame' or any level of celebrity, however great it is, you're not going to come out unscathed

– unless you're a sociopath-slash-psychopath, that is. It can't NOT affect you, in varying degrees. You either go off the rails with sex or booze or drugs, or you completely crack up. And if you don't, then, well, you're probably not right in the head. I feel like last year when I had my breakdown, obviously it was triggered by my marriage failing and what was going on in my personal life, but I think it was also nine years' worth of a breakdown coming. 100 per cent. I think it was everything that had been building up, and then I crashed because for the first time in nine years, I stopped – actually stopped dead in my tracks. And when that happened, I had no intention of even coming back to it all. None whatsoever. Crazy. Well, I changed my mind and now I'm back. And I won't change my job for the world.

Lessons I've learned:

- Be careful what you wish for, because sometimes you get it and it's not what you think
- Fame is something that I wanted, but not necessarily the thing I want still. Don't get me wrong, it's always lovely meeting people and of course sometimes it's flattering to be given the full VIP treatment, and I understand that everything comes part and parcel with my job, but if I could press the button to switch all that off, I'd do it in a flash
- Also . . . don't be ungrateful. Lol.

LESSONS WE'VE LEARNED . . .

Ruth Langsford

Friend/Colleague/TV mum

[D] admiration (noun): respect and warm approval

I admired Rylan the first time I saw him on The X Factor and I continue to admire him to this day. He has become a true friend to me and Eamonn and that doesn't happen very often in showbiz!

I didn't know Rylan when he was on The X Factor in 2012 but I liked him immediately – he was cheeky, funny and didn't take himself too seriously and I now know that's exactly what he's like. His personality shone through on that talent show but it was his kindness and loyalty on Celebrity Big Brother which made me love him. When he stood up against that awful American couple 'Speidi' for effectively denying Claire from Steps her letter from home, I knew he had not just personality but heart, and in the time I've known him he has shown me that heart many times.

I finally met Rylan in person when he came to work on This Morning, reading out viewers' messages in the live interaction hub. He was an absolute natural . . . not just at presenting but in how he was with the team, the crew and the guests. I believe you can tell a lot about a person by how they treat others around them. In this industry I have met many who are sweetness and light to the presenters of the show and come across to the viewers as lovely people, but then I hear they've been absolutely vile to the people backstage. I've witnessed people not thank the runner who brings them a drink or totally ignore a makeup artist who's helping them to look good. Believe me, this happens a lot. Not with Rylan. The following story proved to me that he was a good, decent human being:

A very good friend of mine asked if it would be possible to bring her mum in to watch This Morning *one day – she'd been a big fan of the show for many years, so it was my pleasure to be able to arrange that for them. We always try when possible to get people a photo of the celebrity guests who are on a show; it's a lovely memento of their day, which they treasure. The celebrity guest that day, however, was rushing off to another appointment, so I didn't want to hold them up to have a photograph with my friends. Disappointing for them, but I thought, 'I'll grab Rylan when the show's finished and at least make sure they get to meet him.'*

So the show ended and my friends got an opportunity to sit on the famous This Morning *sofa and get lots of photographs before they switched the studio lights off. While they were doing that I saw Rylan walking across the studio floor to leave. I called out to him and asked if he'd please have a photograph taken with my guests.*

He said, 'Oh, are they your friends? I've already done it, babe!'

It turned out that before the show Rylan had walked into the guest green room to make himself a cup of tea, and my friends were in there too. Not knowing they were my guests he asked them if they'd like a cup of tea while he was making one. They said, 'Yes please', and after chatting to him for a while they asked if they could possibly have a photo with him – he said yes without question and then dashed off to the studio for the start of the show. My friends told me how delightful he was and that he made a great cup of tea!

That is Rylan right there – down to earth, grounded despite the fame that's come his way, and so kind-hearted.

I have been on the receiving end of his kind heart many times since I met him. When Eamonn took time off from This Morning *to have his double hip replacement operation, Rylan stood in to present the show with me. But more than him being a great co-host and enormous fun to work with, it was his concern for Eamonn that really touched me – always asking after him, texting to see if* he was OK, asking me if I needed anything. He genuinely cared. This is when he started to call us his 'TV mum and dad' and we nicknamed him our 'TV son' – we still call each other by those names to this day.

I said before that I believe you can tell a lot about a person from the way they treat others around them. Well, I also believe that when you have difficult times in your life, you find out who your real friends are.

The most difficult time in my own life was when my darling sister took her own life. Eamonn was away in Belfast, which meant I was in the house with just our son Jack when I got that shocking call. It was midnight when Eamonn rang Rylan and asked if he would call and talk to me while he called my three best friends to ask them to come over. I don't remember a lot about that conversation but I know Rylan kept me on the phone until my girlfriends arrived. I can never thank him enough for doing that – it was the act of a true friend.

Eamonn and I had the chance to reciprocate Rylan's care and kindness when he had a difficult time himself following the breakdown of his marriage. I hope he felt the love and concern coming back to him.

I suppose the lesson I have learned from Rylan is that sometimes friendship can come into your life from the most unlikely people. When I was admiring him from afar on The X Factor, a complete stranger to me, who knew that ten years later we would be the closest of friends? Thank you, Rylan.

Love you, Son, your TV mum, Ruth x

14

A FEW OF MY UNFAVOURITE THINGS

I've had a lot in my mouth before,
but that ain't going in, babe

Crab sticks

Obviously we've established by this point that I don't like to eat fish, in any way, shape or form, but crab sticks are a law unto themselves. Even the thought of them makes me gag. Linda loves them. I still have traumatic memories of her sitting peeling a crab stick in front of me as a child. That was a real East End thing when I was growing up. Every Sunday there was a fucking Tubby Isaacs fish stall on every street and those guys who used to walk around with a tray full of crab sticks round their neck like a fake belly. And you always had crab sticks on the buffet at family parties. Why? I just find them absolutely bizarre. It's not even crab. I don't know what the fuck it is, but I can tell you that there's zero crab in them. I'm pretty sure it's just things they find on the beach, bones and boiled up bits of cod with a bit of gelatine. I'll ask Alexa: 'Alexa, what's in a crab stick?'

She says it's 'pollock with fillers such as wheat and egg white'. Pollocks to that. Bullshit. I don't trust her. I mean, 'pollock' – who named a fish that? Anyway, that's a NO from me. I've already said it, but I'll say it again: CRAB STICKS ARE THE DEVIL'S FOOD.

Set-up pap shots

I'm sorry if I'm repeating myself, because I put this in *Room 101*, but it needs saying again. You know when you see so-called 'candid pictures' in the paper of girls working out in the park, and they've got a full face of makeup on and a high pony-tail? Come on, love, we know that's not how you work out. You're fooling no one because we all know that's not how it happened. I don't mind people trying to further their career. I mean, good for them. However, a set-up pap shot of someone taking the bins out with their tits out just don't cut it for me.

People not saying thank you at zebra crossings

I put this one in *Room 101* and all. I know the pedestrian's got the right of way, I know my Highway Code and that's the law. But how hard is it for them to raise their hand or give you a nod to say thank you to the considerate motorist, and acknowledge the fact that you slowed down or stopped instead of deciding to knock them over? But most people don't. And I just think that's really rude. Every time someone does it, it winds me up so much that I wind down my window, shout at them, then drive off. Because manners cost nothing. Lol.

Crumbs

I've got the biggest phobia of crumbs. I don't know where it's come from, I don't know why it is, but if I get up in the morning and I'm just wearing my underwear and I eat a piece of toast, I have to spread my legs wide open like I'm doing a gymnastics routine, for fear of a crumb falling on my naked thigh. It makes me feel physically sick. When it comes to my crumb phobia, my mum is the worst. She eats a bag of crisps, and she puts her whole hand in the bag. What the fuck is wrong with you? Use your two fingers – your index finger and your thumb. They're the only things that can go into the crisp bag. I remember sitting on a train once on the way home from school and there was this elderly woman eating a bag of salt and vinegar crisps and she put her whole hand in the bag. I had to move carriages because the thought of the crumbs stuck to her greasy hand was just disgusting – yuck! It makes me feel sick. So I don't know why it is, and I know I sound like an absolute weirdo for saying this, but CRUMBS ARE JUST NOT RIGHT. They're vile. And as for anyone that eats and drops crumbs in bed, well, they can get the fuck out of mine.

PDAs

I don't mind all public displays of affection; I actually generally think it's quite cute. But at the same time, now I'm single, it makes me think, 'Fuck off, you're happy. Good for you. Gold star.' But maybe I'm saying that because I'm bitter and single. I mean, don't get me wrong – if you're giving your partner a discreet kiss on the street, that's absolutely fine. I'm not that bitter. But I don't need to see you sucking him off at the train station.

Poor personal hygiene

Listen, if I can smell your dirty hair, that's not good. Wash it. Have a bath, have a shower, and while you're at it, wash your *whole* self properly, and put a bit of fucking aftershave on. And if you ain't got time to wash your hair, do me a favour and at least spray something on it. Honestly, there's no excuse. It's really not hard.

Slow walkers

I don't walk along the street that often any more, but if I do go shopping or something like that, the slow walkers in the middle of everything really wind me up. If you're gonna walk slow, go along the wall. Get out the fast lane and stop blocking the pavement. If I'm going somewhere, I like to get there fast. And I hate it when I'm going around a department store or a supermarket and people just stand in the middle of the aisle doing nothing. Have you not been brought up with any respect for anyone else around you? Fucking move, and move your fucking trolley and all! I just don't get it. People do my nut in sometimes. That wouldn't happen in my supermarket, put it that way.

People watching me eat

I can't stand it if I go to a restaurant and I look over and notice someone looking at me and my food. Do you mind? Can I eat in peace? I get funny when people watch me eat – and actually, it's not just when I'm eating out; I hate people looking at me even when I'm eating in my own house.

People who insist on telling the shop assistant, 'Hold on! I think I've got the right change'

Please. If you're in front of me in a check-out queue, do me a favour, just give the fucking assistant a pound coin or a fiver and take the change. Again, my mum is one of those people. I mean, I've worked in a shop, a lot of people have worked in shops, and when you go to pay for something, don't start rummaging around and counting out the pennies. Do you think the shop assistants want that? They don't give a fuck if you've got the exact change or not. They really don't care. There is a till full of change, for fuck's sake. Pay with a pound coin, that's absolutely fine. We will give you 13p back. Please do not pay 87 pence in 2ps and 5ps and 1p pieces, because it pisses us off. And it pisses off the people who're stood behind you waiting to pay. Please, don't do it. That really annoys me. But thank you, Jean. We appreciate the thought.

That advert

There are some TV ads that I don't really get, but the one that REALLY pisses me off is the one from the government advertising workplace pensions. There's this professional sous chef woman in a white chef's top and blue cap, working in a really busy, steamy restaurant kitchen somewhere, making some kind of sauce. Then she has this little mini-me version of herself, in the same chef's whites and blue cap, but about the size of a pepper grinder. She gives her mini-me self a taste of her sauce, then throws a tiny little silverskin onion at her and then slices it in half with her giant knife. And oh my God, that little version of herself looks like such a cocky git! I don't know why, but the very first time I saw it, I just took offence at this smug-faced cocky little chef bastard. Now every time it comes on I'm like, 'Fuck off!' I would have got the pan and fucking flattened that mini-me. I hate that ad, to the point where I want to smash the telly up. Little fucking cocky chef. I would have stood on it. I don't know what it was but it really grated on me. There's a few ads that do that to me, but that's the absolute fucking worst.

15

ALL AT SEA

Get me off this fucking boat

Before the unfortunate fish counter incident in my early childhood, I used to eat fish. And I *wish* I still could because, actually, I know I'd love it. But I just cannot eat fish or any of its
marine mates. I'm not right, am I?

I remember when I was on honeymoon in the Maldives,
one evening we went to an underwater fish restaurant in the
middle of the Indian Ocean. I thought, 'God, if I liked fish,
I'd be in heaven right now.' You had to get a boat out to it.
You stepped off onto a wooden pontoon, and there were no
railings or anything, so you could just fall off. But basically
there were tables with little lamps on this wooden deck and
then you went down the stairs and there was a glass dining
room with floodlights lighting up underwater. Obviously,
because we were in the middle of the ocean, you could see
sharks and all the tropical fish swimming right in front of your
face. That was pretty cool – beautiful, in fact. Plus I felt safe
because I had a pane of glass between me and the seafood.
I can't remember what I ate that night – probably a plate of
chips and some salad.

I remember when I went swimming on the first day of the
honeymoon, a shark swam past my foot. Not Jaws or anything,
just a baby one, but it still freaked me out. The people at the
hotel said, 'They're fine. It's no problem. They're scared of
you. It's when they're grown up that you've got to worry.'

Two days later, we had a day out on a private boat to see
dolphins. Worst fucking day of my life. When we got out into

the ocean, suddenly the sea changed colour from a crystal-clear turquoise to a deep blue-black, just like that. I thought, 'OK, we're out deep now.' And it was only this tiny little private speedboat, no bigger than a dining table. It just didn't feel safe, what with my fish phobia and all. It was choppy and I was clinging on to the side for my fucking life, then suddenly all these dolphins appeared round the boat, so close I could almost talk to them. That was lovely, I don't mind a dolphin – it's not really a fish – and all of a sudden they started diving under the boat and then re-emerging a few metres away. I was sitting thinking, 'Oh, that's cool.' But then the boatman pipes up, 'You know why they do this?'

'No,' I said.

'Very, very big shark,' he said.

I looked over the edge of the boat and all I saw was this fucking big fin. When I say it was Jaws, it could have eaten the boat in one swallow. And I just said, 'Turn this fucking thing around and take me back – NOW!' But we'd gone so far out we couldn't see the islands no more. You couldn't see anything. We were miles out, literally in the middle of the ocean. There was nothing around except us and this shark about the size of a small bungalow. I was in pieces. I thought, 'If this boat fucks up, we're dead. We're not getting back. No one would know where we are.'

It scared the shit out of me. And this was all before break-fast. Oh my God, I got back to shore and let me tell you, I've never been more happy to put my foot on a bit of sand.

But in late 2017, in spite of my mixed feelings about all things aquatic, when I first saw the idea for this new game show called *The Wave* for the W Channel, I thought 'this seems like a fun idea'. The premise of the show was quite simple: teams of two would join us on a beach near Lisbon, they'd be split up and we would throw one of the contestants (victims?) into the Atlantic Ocean off the Portuguese coast, make the pair of them answer some multiple choice questions to win money, and then the one swimming would swim all the way back through the mile-high surf to land. Basically, to win, the swimmer just had to try not to die. Easy, right?

Well, I mean I wouldn't have to go anywhere near the fucking ocean – I'd be sitting pretty on a nice sandy beach in me sunglasses, sipping a pina colada and talking to the partner or friend of the person risking their life out at sea. Count me in.

The series was broadcast between January and March 2018, but we filmed it over a week in the previous September, at a beach called Foz do Lizandro, about forty-five minutes outside Lisbon on the Atlantic coast, well known as a surfers' paradise. The day before we started filming, I was sitting there on the sand where they'd built this whole film set-up, a little flimsy, blue beach cabin thing that they'd made for me out of plywood, electric wires and cables everywhere. I was looking out at the sea, watching the waves crash in, and it was very choppy, so I said to the crew, 'That wave looks very big, guys.' I mean, it was REALLY big. But they just said, 'No, it'll break. Don't worry, Rylan, we're fine – it'll break.' But it didn't. It was a mini tsunami that wiped out the whole set. And if it weren't for the quick-thinking electrician pressing the kill switch, anyone that was on damp sand would have been killed. We'd all have been electrocuted to death.

Undeterred by these hazardous conditions, the production crew pressed on with the competition and the contestants prepared themselves for their fate. So, imagine that I'd be on the beach with your partner. Your partner would be answering questions posed by me. You, meanwhile, would have swum out – in a wetsuit, thank God – to a floating pontoon, which looked a bit like one of the emergency life rafts from a cross-channel ferry, in the middle of the Atlantic Ocean. On the pontoon there were two hatches, A and B. If you and your partner got the question right, you opened hatch A, and in there was the cash prize, say £1,000. You put that money in your waterproof belt bag, and then you swum to the next pontoon, then the next, further and further out into the ocean. But if you got a question wrong, you opened hatch B, and instead of cash, you collected a kilogram weight.

At that point, the swimmer out on the pontoon had to make a decision: whether to stop and swim back, or carry on to the next float and the next – the first one was 200 metres from the shore, the last one 325 metres away – because whatever you decided, you had to battle the not insignificant ocean currents to swim back to shore in an allotted time in order to keep any money that you'd won.

One day, we had one couple where the swimmer swam out to all seven pontoons, took all seven questions and got all seven wrong. So they ended up in the middle of the Atlantic and had to swim all the way back to shore with a 7-kilogram lead weight round their waist. And they didn't have life jackets. Nothing. But at any point contestants could forfeit some of their hard-won dosh to buy various bits of kit to help tackle the ordeal, from a pair of goggles (£300), to small flippers (£500), big flippers (£750), and even a bodyboard (£1,000).

A few days in, we were in this bay, and it was beautiful, clear blue skies, sun, sea and pure white sand. One of the male contestants – called Josh, I think – had completed all the questions and was out at the last pontoon, but just as he jumped in to start swimming back, it was as if God thought he'd have a bit of a laugh, because this dense fog descended over the entire bay. We couldn't see the contestant anywhere; the waves were crashing every which way and he had completely vanished. I mean, I couldn't even see my hand in front of me, never mind what was happening to him out there in the sea.

Josh's girlfriend, Natalie, was standing beside me on the shore, the drone had lost the contestant and the lifeboat that was supposed to track him could not find him anywhere. I had it all going on in my earpiece: 'He's disappeared. We can't find the contestant. We can't find the contestant.' I just had to carry on, telling the girlfriend and the audience, 'Five minutes left on the clock; four minutes left on the clock . . .' cheerfully adding, 'I don't want to alarm you, but I think the mist is getting even thicker. He'll be feeling very tired now . . . Oh, I think we've even lost him on camera . . .'

I was standing there with Natalie, thinking, 'Fuck. What do I say?' I just kept saying to her, 'We're giving him a bit more time to get to the shore because of the fog,' hiding behind my sunglasses, keeping up the confident smile, but I'm sure the worry was painted on the rest of my face. Natalie, too, looked terrified – the pair of us stood there frantically scanning the non-existent horizon since by then the visibility was near zero. All the while, none of us had any clue where Josh had disappeared to. Literally.

He turned up in the end, thank fuck – a mile down the beach, gasping for air and suffering from mild hypothermia, looking like he was going to throw up. And I'm sure he was fucking traumatised; in fact, he's probably still suffering some form of PTSD, or at the very least a new crippling phobia of the sea. The waves and the mighty Atlantic current had dragged him in completely the wrong direction. When he was finally washed up on the beach, they had to send a car to go and get him. Genuinely, that's what it was like. I was terrified, thinking, 'No, this ain't the one. This is not the one. I am NEVER doing this show again.' It was C.R.A.Z.Y. I still don't know how we got the insurance for it to this day. And needless to say, we just did the one series.

It was just the most surreal show, to be standing on a beach, chucking people into the middle of the Atlantic Ocean with heavy weights tied round their waists. And these people were someone's husband, wife, girlfriend, boyfriend, their best mate, their loved one, basically someone you don't want to be dead. And then they'd end up a mile down the beach in an ambulance. I remember this other mum and daughter team. The mum was a real fitness woman, I think her name was Debbie. Debbie was *very* hench, very healthy and at the end of it she was basically bundled into an ambulance, wrapped in the Bacofoil cape. That's when I think we all realised this was no joke: 'Fuck, what are we doing here?'

Of course, I'm sure all the health and safety forms were filled out and the risk assessments were watertight. I was assured that while it was a struggle and quite hazardous, the contestants weren't actually in any real danger while swimming in the open waters of the Atlantic Ocean. The production team made sure to cast some really strong swimmers and, obviously, we had so many lifeguards and people around them at all times, including Olympic swimming silver medallist, Keri-anne Payne, who was on set to ensure the safety of the contestants – but at the end of the day, they were on their own in the ocean.

On the shore, we always had standby contestants in case something went wrong, someone pulled a muscle, or got sick, or a contestant pulled out. They were there for the whole week of filming and it was getting to the point where they were all sitting there shitting themselves: 'I hope I'm not getting called up next, cos I'm not going in.' Absolutely ridiculous, but it was a lot of fun.

OK, there were no sharks in Portugal, at least I fucking hope there weren't, and I am a strong swimmer and I love swimming, but no way would I have got in that sea. No way! Because our very own Olympian Keri-anne told me she didn't want to do the course – and well, that said it all.

Lessons I've learned:

- Don't trust the fucking sea

16
TEETH

*The tooth, the whole tooth and
nothing but the tooth*

At the end of 2021, newly single – new start, new me and all that – I made another dramatic change. New teeth. I was obviously going through a midlife crisis – trying to dye my hair blond, buying three pet jellyfish, and now having the old tombstone veneers knocked out. I had to have two operations under a general, a third under a local, and then the £25k veneers were hammered, then chiselled off.

As I'm sure you all know, I famously had my first set of veneers put in after winning *Celebrity Big Brother* in 2013 – I can tell you now, since I already blabbed on Louis Theroux's podcast anyway, that I got a hundred grand to go on that show. I'm not gonna lie, I felt as though I'd won the lottery, though it was quite shocking for me to realise how much money there is in television.

Anyway, as I have said many times, that was both the best and the worst decision I ever made, because I didn't *hate* my own teeth. Honestly there was nothing wrong with them, but they were never 'perfect'. I've always wanted that 'Hollywood smile' and had always loved the look of veneers. I don't know why but it was almost a status thing. It was something I wanted done, and suddenly after *Big Brother* I was in a position to afford it. And so, when I got out, that's one of the first things I did.

After five weeks of hell in Harley Street, I had what I'd always dreamed of: a gobful of BIG WHITE PERFECT TEETH. And when I say BIG, I actually mean GIGANTIC. Initially, it was really difficult because they were so in your face. I started hosting *Big Brother's Bit on the Side* and everybody was saying, 'What the fuck has he done?' Everyone and his uncle had an opinion, most of them uncomplimentary, especially on Twitter. People wrote things like, 'Funny how Shergar vanished and next thing Rylan turns up with his teeth . . .' And 'Fun Fact: The glare from the teeth of Rylan Clark-Neal means he is banned from Exmoor National Park during the hours of darkness'. Or that my teeth and my mouth had different postcodes. Yeah, OK, they *were* white and huge, but you know what, at the end of the day, half of the people that were piping up about my teeth hadn't even got a tooth in their heads!

Actually, my teeth were trending so much on Twitter, that they decided to set up their own account: @Rylan_Clarks_Teeth. Honestly, those teeth really do deserve a full fucking chapter of their own. They literally were more famous than me. They still are.

I mean, yes, they were massive but at the same time I would be wearing my old foundation colour, which I knew matched my face, but it didn't go with my new teeth. So, I had these enormous bright white teeth with this orange face, and the whole thing just did not work. I used to have my lips really filled at that point as well, so they were massive too. My beard was a lot thinner and sculpted along the jawline, another combination that didn't work visually, but I didn't have the time to know that because I was working so hard, having been thrown in at the deep end on *Bit on the Side*. I mean, I was learning how to deal with someone talking in my ear at the same time as I was talking with a brand-new set of teeth that looked like they were coming round the corner before I was. And you know, I was pretty shit at my job in the beginning. I was a fucking awful TV presenter, but the only upside was that for the first three months, because everyone was talking about the teeth, I got away with it. It gave me time to learn my craft without anyone calling for me to be sacked. I literally learned on the job and by the time they'd stopped talking about the teeth, I was actually a really good TV presenter. So, you know, swings and roundabouts . . .

Looking back now at some of the old photos, they did, in all honesty, look pretty ridiculous. Under the studio lights, I looked like I had swallowed a flashlight. They were a bit out there, but you know what, I liked them. At the end of the day, the blinding gnashers became one of my trademarks and made me a talking point. At that time, you know, it was kinda 'all publicity is good publicity', and they were one of the first things that always came up every time I did an interview. Then people started saying to me, 'I can't believe you had your teeth done, they look so much better!' But they were the same teeth. It was just that I'd changed other things: my beard was fuller, and my foundation was toned down, my lips were slightly smaller.

But over the years, I've taken plenty of stick about them, which I mostly took on the chin. And then last year after my break-up, I thought, 'Fuck this. I'm going to do some stuff for myself.' And even though I was always happy with my teeth, if I'm honest I'm never fully happy with any aspect of my appearance, so I thought I'd get them redone. Why not? I'm in a position to, so in November 2021, after eight years, I took the decision to say goodbye to my teeth. As I posted on Twitter at the time: 'It hurt, so much, but sometimes you just have to let go.' And I did. Mentally, I'd had this massive new start in my life, so I thought let's change my body physically to how I want it to be. That's why I started the fitness regime with my trainer, Scott, and also why I got my teeth redone.

TEN

The first time that I had my veneers fitted, it took over five weeks and the whole experience was horrendous. So, this time I got knocked out and I don't remember any of it. It took three days in total. Day one was removal of the old veneers, which apparently took six hours because they were stuck on solid, like cement. That's why they had to take a mallet and chisel to them to get them off. Obviously, because I was under anaesthetic that was much easier for the dentist, because then he could just chip away. It makes me feel sick just thinking about it, so thank God I was out for the count. I don't even remember coming home. Apparently I was all over the place, so my brother rang Bernice and said, 'Look, Ross is very out of it. I think he needs someone to keep an eye on him.'

Bernice came over, got me upstairs and into my bed, and she ended up staying with me that night. I woke up at about two o'clock in the morning, fully clothed in my bed, and I had no idea what the fuck was going on – what time or what day it was, where I was, or how I'd got there. I was all hot and confused, so I stood up and stripped down to my pants. Then I took my pants off, turned round to get back into bed and all I saw was Bernice's little face smiling up at me in the dark. 'Hello darling! You feeling all right?' I nearly had a heart attack. I was so embarrassed; I said, 'Oh my God, I'm so sorry you had to see that!'

I didn't even know she was in my house, never mind actually snuggled up in my bed with me. Of course, Bernice was just pissing herself lying there. It was the actual fact that the dirty mare hadn't said anything, just thought to herself, 'This will be really funny', let me literally take all my clothes off, then waited for me to spot her there when I was already stark bollock naked. So that was all fun and festive.

The second time I went back, it was temps off, new veneers on, again under a general but this time without incident back at home. I had the veneers on for a week to check that I was really happy with the placement and the shade. After two days, one of them fell off, because they weren't placed on for real, and I nearly swallowed it. Then on the third and final day in the dentist's chair, it was just full bonding, a little bit of bite adjustment and that was it.

Before he put me under, I asked the dentist if I could keep the original veneers after he'd chiselled them all off. So the next time I went, he handed a clear ziplock bag to me with what was left of my old teeth. In the meantime, I treated my mum to new teeth for her birthday. She got a set of veneers, like me. It was the same dentist, so, like I said, I keep winding her up, telling her that they've put my old ones in her mouth. She actually believes it. But in fact I have the broken shards hidden at the back of a kitchen drawer at the minute. I'm actually gonna get a little glass display case and have them placed in there, with a brass label, saying:

2013–2021
RIP
The teeth that were more famous than me

Gawd, if those old teeth could talk, they could tell a tale or two.

This time I went for smaller ones. Slightly less white and a lot squarer. These ones are a lot flatter, not as bulbous as the old ones. I think they fit my face, they suit me. And now I'm used to them. I love them, and they will basically last forever now, if I want them to. I mean, put it this way, seeing how difficult it was to get the old teeth off, the dentist said I probably would have died with them still on. They would never have fallen out. I do prefer these new ones, but who knows? I might have another 'New me!' moment and my teeth could see another reincarnation. I just want them looking good. So, never say never, as they say.

Lessons I've learned:

- Bigger isn't always better
- Whiter isn't always better
- Find a dentist that knows when to say NO!

17

RYLAN . . .
MEET ROSS

*'Tonight, Matthew, I'm going to be . . . RYLAN.
No, Ross . . . Oh, I don't fucking know any more'*

In 1988 I was born Ross Richard Clark.

In 2012 I fully became Rylan.

In 2021, I found Ross again.

Finding the real me again was one of the most difficult processes. I'm so used to being the 'other' me, it's easy to forget who I really am at times. In many ways, creating Rylan, my professional me, was the smartest and healthiest thing I ever chose to do. It's how I actually got through all the shit in the beginning, because I was like, 'It's fine – bring it on. They're talking about Rylan.' They were not talking about Ross. Because Ross Richard Clark sits in his trackie bottoms, no makeup, no fake tan, and watches reruns of *Birds of a Feather* or *Gimme Gimme Gimme*. And Rylan? Well, Rylan is always smiling, even through the tears.

I've always been strong. I've always taken a lot of shit. As a kid, I got all the gay shit. I wasn't the tanned, dark-haired, good-looking kid that played football. I was the gay, chubby ginger one in the corner of the playground dancing with the girls: all I needed was a set of pink national health glasses and pimples for the full fucking set. So yes, I was bullied at school. Of course I was. The first three years of secondary school was hard. It was full of taunting and name-calling, and very difficult.

Then when I was probably about thirteen or fourteen, there was this playground where I lived in Stepney Green that I used to go to after school. One day I got pulled off a rope swing and some boy kicked me in the head and fractured my skull.

301

I was in hospital, and it was a horrible time. It was after that that Mum decided we should go and live in Essex. But things didn't really improve, and by Years Ten and Eleven, I'd had enough. So had my mum, because she kept telling me I had to stand up for myself: 'Don't take no more shit off of them, Ross. The kids start on you, you start back.'

One day a boy in my class said something to me as I walked past his desk; I can't even remember what it was now, but let's just say it was 'gay boy', along with the obligatory *Are You Being Served?* limp wrist gesture. Normally I would just keep walking, keep my head down, slink away, and let it be. But this time, something felt different. I felt this rage bubble up through my veins and into my fists, and without even thinking I punched him right in the face. It was as if I'd finally grown a pair of bollocks. I got suspended from school but my mum didn't care. She was so proud of me that she came and took me to a sandwich shop on Hornchurch High Street to celebrate. And then after that, to anyone who tried to be funny I had no problem in telling them, 'Yes I'm gay, now get over it you prick.'

And this, in a way, is the difference between Rylan and Ross. Because when it's Rylan I'm a brick wall. You can take the piss out of my teeth, call me a cunt, and I'll just go, 'That's fine. This is what I get paid for.' But when it's me, Ross, I don't deal with it that well. I hate bullies and I still feel like I want to punch someone sometimes.

Rylan was born when I was sixteen. By then I'd lost the puppy fat, grown a little bit of facial hair and started to put bleached blond highlights in my hair. I had also sprung up to 6' 4" and was doing some modelling work. The agency I signed up with told me that my real name wasn't memorable enough; it was too boring, so they chose Keelan instead. The only problem was that when I got my first job – for a concierge company, posing as a bell-boy delivering some flowers – the cheque for £100 was made out to a Mr K. Clark and I couldn't cash it. So I went straight into a WHSmith, flicked to the 'R' section in a book of baby names, rejected Rhydian as too posh, plain Ryan as too common, and then, like Goldilocks, happened on the perfect name: Rylan. And it just sort of stuck with anything I did workwise after that.

So then, when I went on *Signed by Katie Price*, I was Rylan. As I said, to be honest it was flawed from the start, but one thing I did get out of it was getting very close to Kate and spending time with her back then. I liked the fact that there was Kate, who I got to know behind the scenes, and then there was Jordan. I thought that if fame ever happened for me, that's how I'd deal with it. But then when I went on *The X Factor* and the shit hit the fan and Rylan was the UK's public enemy number one, I realised that I only had myself to blame. I had created him, I was the one who'd played along week in week out on national TV, trying to make something of myself. And Katie Price was one of the first people I turned to when that was all going down. I rang her and she told me to not give a flying fuck and carry on being me. She said she'd created Jordan. I'd created me. Deal with it. And that made me realise that it doesn't matter what people say about me; as long as I can laugh at myself, who gives a fuck? That's what I try to do, and most of the time it works.

So I guess you could say that Ross and Rylan are distinct identities. But it's not like Ross and Rylan are two different people. I'm still the same person, 100 per cent. My mum always calls me Ross, as do most of my family and old friends, but then sometimes they will call me Rylan when we're having a row because it winds me up.

It's almost like two different shells, with the same person inside each. You could say that Rylan is a performance. When I'm presenting a show, obviously there has to be a certain dialling up, but it's not a complete transformation. If you see me on telly, when I'm doing my job, I might unconsciously be 'playing' a character, but it's still the real me. Everyone's gotta have a little bit of a character, I think. We all do it – like when you put on your best telephone voice, or that slightly different person you become when you walk into a room full of strangers at a posh party, or when you're at work. We all do it. And, well, I just do that publicly. That's my job.

Rylan is the smiling, full-on me, but when you actually meet and get to know Rylan, well, you then meet Ross. And that's still me, but just a lot looser, not as 'turned on'. That said, when people really properly get to know me in real life, as I said, they're quite shocked at how different I am. But in a good way, obvs, not in a bad way. They will think that Rylan is someone, or *something*, they're not gonna like. Then they meet me and I've got a beer in one hand and the other down my trousers, and they're like, 'What the fuck?' And I'm like, 'What? What were you expecting?' As the bearded lady sang in *The Greatest Showman*, 'This Is Me'.

As much as Ross and Rylan are one and the same, it's funny – and this is hard to describe – but I almost feel in my body when I have to make that switch. Let's say that I will be in a car with Jamie going to an event, and when we pull up, there'll be a lot of people standing outside wanting photos with me or an autograph. Two seconds before, it's Ross that's sprawled in the back seat, looking at my phone, in a sort of 'flumph'. Then I feel myself change. I do this thing where I take a deep inhale, reset, smile, and then I step out of the

car, straighten up, and flash the teeth: 'So nice to see you!'
I can feel myself doing it.

Obviously, last year when I wasn't well with the end of my
marriage and everything, I couldn't be Rylan. I could not be
Rylan whatsoever and that's when I disappeared. Even now
that I'm better, though, there are times when it's difficult.
Especially if I go out for a meal, for example, when I'm not
working but I'm out in public. In some ways I've still got to be
Rylan. Because that's who I am. And, of course, I always *am*
Rylan, to a certain extent, but sometimes you just wanna go
out with your mates and forget all about your day job. Put it
this way: if you're a gynaecologist, the last thing you want to
do is come home, or go out for a meal, and look into someone's fanny. That's the very last fucking thing you want to do.

For me, the last thing I want to do is to go out for dinner
and have to sit there doing 400 photos with other diners and
recording video messages for people. But my job is different
and I understand that. I get it. If that was me ten years ago
that had bumped into someone, I'd think, 'This is my only
chance to get a photo, or this is my only chance to get that
video message because I know my mum loves him'. So I always
say yes. I've never said no. But sometimes I wish I could.

I will never forget when my mum was really ill in hospital
a couple of years ago. She was admitted with complications to
do with her Crohn's and then it turned out that she had sepsis.
She nearly died and was hooked up on drips and machines, she
was so thin and there were wires and cannulas everywhere.
I remember coming out of the ward after seeing her and I
was a bit upset. One of the nurses came up and said, 'Do you
mind if we have a photo?' I was in a bit of a state, but I just
said, 'Umm . . . Yeah, of course.' What I really wanted to say
was, 'Babe. This ain't the time or place and I'm really not in

a great way, like.' But I didn't. I was frightened, because I thought, 'Oh my God, what if I say no? They might fucking put something in me mum's solution!' That's not the nurse being rude or unprofessional. Some people might say it is, but I get it. People just don't think. Why would they? She didn't think that right then I was just Ross Clark, Linda Clark's son, that she was in there desperately ill and I was standing there, terrified and sad. But I'm not at the hospital for a day out, am I? I'm not there doing a meet and greet. I was there for a reason. And you know, actually it takes nothing – and it takes less time – for me to smile and say hello and be polite. And of course, that one time you said 'no', it would end up being a whole massive thing. You just have to say 'no' to one person and the next thing, you've got a reputation as being an arsehole. Or that person starts abusing you in the street, so it's not worth being rude or unkind. Kindness costs nothing. It's that simple.

It could have been so easy for me to let my feet come off the ground. So easy. There have been so many times when I could have played a card or been an arsehole, but I just couldn't do it. I couldn't change. Wouldn't want to. I will still just talk to anyone and not give a fuck. I think that's because of my mum and how she is. She always says to me, 'Don't think you're something special, Ross. Don't get too big for your boots.' As I say, she's a very normal mum and even after being on the radio or *Gogglebox*, she hasn't changed one bit. I don't honestly think that most people want to change when they get a sniff of success. Maybe they do, I don't know. But I just couldn't. That's one thing that hasn't changed over the years. I've always stayed the same person; I've just been through different shit. In that sense there isn't really any dividing line between Rylan the performer and Ross.

Last year, when everything came crashing down and I stopped work, I saw a therapist and I had a lot of time to think – about myself; about what I wanted; about who I was. My breakdown was obviously triggered by the sudden end of my marriage, but I'm realising now that there was a lot more to it. I think that something else had been building: along with all the pressures of my crazy work schedule and 'success', maybe my identity was wobbling. That dividing line between my two lives and the two versions of 'me' had become blurred. I'd become so good at being Rylan. I know how to do my job – what's right, what's wrong; what works, what doesn't. I mean, I do Rylan really fucking well. But actually, I hadn't had control for so long, because my whole life was really my job. I didn't realise how much of Ross I'd lost. And actually, the demands of being Rylan had left me, Ross, a bit starved, a bit lonely. I felt like Britney! And I realise now too that I was lonely in my marriage.

That whole decade of doing this job of being Rylan, and then coming home to live that lie, had slapped me around the arse and stabbed me in the stomach until something inside me just broke. And, like the end of my marriage, I now know I needed that to happen. As I said before, I just wish it hadn't happened as hard as it did and that I hadn't got so ill. That was completely out of my control, of course, but I don't regret saying what I said. I don't regret doing what I did, and I definitely don't regret my life changing as a result.

My natural personality is one of honesty, and one of always putting other people first. Most importantly, being true to myself is at the heart of who I am. I had to look myself in the mirror and accept that maybe I was being untrue to myself. I had been trying to pretend that everything was a bed of roses, when deep down in my heart I knew that something wasn't right.

The biggest blessing to come out of my breakdown is that I know now that I need to do a better job of looking after 'me', because I know for sure that I can't go there again. I'm finding a new 'me' now, and I know I need to take a step back from the performance of being Rylan and allow Ross Clark to have his time in the sun. Over the years there's so many things that I would say 'no' to. I was made to question myself – 'Why are you doing that? Why would you do that?' – and I let that voice control me quite a lot. So now I'm gonna always trust my own instincts. I just sit there and think, 'If I want to do it, I'll fucking do it.' I'm enjoying having more freedom at the minute. Being able to do what I want to do, and when I wanna do it is quite nice. I'm really looking after myself and enjoying being selfish for a change.

Yup, I'm channelling YOLO Ross who is happy to go with the flow. Even though things can still stress me out sometimes, it is very much a case of 'don't sweat the small stuff'. That's the new Zen me, the me that I'm nurturing now. The Ross that comes home from work, takes off his makeup, lets his hair down, and doesn't give a fuck. The Ross who forgets to put his fake tan on sometimes and is more and more comfortable in his own skin. The Ross who's had his teeth redone, still dazzling but definitely smaller, toned down a bit. The happily single Ross who is learning that it's OK to be alone, and who is comfortable being alone. And who now gets to walk around the house stark bollock naked, talking to my fake rubber plant. The joys.

For a long time, I thought that creating the superhero 'Rylan' let me be in control and powerful. But now I've worked out that it has always been Ross who pulls the strings.

Lessons I've learned:

- No matter what your success or your achievements, always keep your feet on the ground
- Remember where you came from and don't forget your roots
- Remember the 'real you' even when you're being the 'pretend you'

18

THE MODERN MAN

Fuck off mate, it's only a bit of concealer

'Personally, I think if you can try your best to look good, you should do all right in life.'

That's what I said in my *X Factor* audition. But fuck me, I look back at some of the pictures of me when I was young, and I think, 'What the fuck was I thinking?' Honestly, I looked a sight. There's one where I'd had my hair dyed blond, but it wasn't even toned properly so it was orange, and I was wearing a lemon-yellow T-shirt that said:

'BLONDES ARE MORE FUN
BELIEVE ME'

Classy. But I was only young and people did wear shit like that then. All my money went on what I looked like: my hair, treatments, spray tan, the lot; and, of course, my clothes. I used to say back then, 'If I can't eat, I can't eat.' I used to dress very much to be seen, so the look that I would always try to go for was standout gorgeous, but on a budget, so what that actually meant was an H&M or Topman special.

When I went for my *X Factor* audition, I went all out for it. I had the teeth whitened. I had my beauty girl Claire over to my mum's house and she gave me a full-body spray tan in the back garden. I had my eyebrows done, my nails, and long blond extensions put in. On the actual day of my first performance in front of the judges (Tulisa, Rita Ora, little Louis Walsh and Mr Barlow), I wore my trademark mid-wash blue skinny jeans with a black logo belt, white Converse, and I accessorised the look with a white pearl bracelet, and a white T-shirt with big bold capitals that read:

**AIN'T
THIS
LOVE?**

Again, classy. I really did wear some godawful clothes ten years ago, especially on *The X Factor*. The only outfit I loved from that experience was the Union Jack blazer I wore on week six. The theme was 'Best of British' and I wanted to do a Spice Girls megamix, because I love the Spice Girls, obviously. Also, in my dreams I was always Ginger Spice, so I'd always wanted to wear my own Rylan version of the Union Jack dress that Geri wore at the BRIT Awards in 1997. Instantly, I was told 'no'. They said they wouldn't be able to clear the music permissions, so I wasn't allowed to do it. But I stuck to my guns – I'm a stubborn fucker when I want to be (I get that from my mum) – and, lo and behold, they let me do it. The wardrobe department made me this fantastic blazer which they'd completely customised with Swarovski crystals – the glamour! I got it framed and it's in my house now. That was probably the only week on *X Factor* that I didn't care about the judges' withering comments, or the backlash, I just went out there and enjoyed every second of it.

But I look back in horror at pretty much everything else I wore on that show. At points, there was a lot of spray-tanned skin out. As I said, my job, back then, was to be the outrageous gay one. I was dressed to stand out – to be the one that everyone talked about, whether it was good or bad. And I was Wardrobe's absolute wet dream. They could put me in whatever they wanted – feather boas, gold chainmail vests or that notorious light-up boiler suit. I literally hurt myself wearing some of those outfits. I mean for the boiler suit to light up, I had to have eight battery packs gaffer-taped to my bare chest and back. My skin was ripped to shreds. I'd be prancing about, doing some elaborate dance routine and trying to sing while literally in agony – whereas others could just stand there in a nice dress, jeans, or a smart tailored suit and not move. I've never forgotten that and that is why I will never, ever be in a situation again where someone tells me what to wear. Now, I can dress exactly how I want.

And believe it or not, I'm a very normal person when it comes down to most things. I'm a man of modest tastes – well, yes, apart from my teeth. So when I had my breakthrough after *Celebrity Big Brother* and I started presenting *Bit on the Side*, as we know I splashed out on the best Harley Street Hollywood smile that money could buy. But in terms of my clothes, it's not like I suddenly went up a notch and started buying designer brands and all that bollocks. I will shop for clothes where everyone else shops: places like Zara, Topman – when it still existed – and ASOS. Though, as I said, much as I'd love a little wander round Zara or even Selfridges, I hardly ever go out actual 'shopping' shopping any more; I buy everything online. The jeans I wear all the time, whether they be blue or black, are still exactly the same ones I was buying ten years ago. They're by a brand called Collusion and they're about fifteen quid on ASOS. All my T-shirts, shirts, sweaters, the same – just regular high-street brands.

I don't care about having designer labels written all over me, but then sometimes I just want to buy myself something really posh. But I've got more picky about what I'll spend money on. I like a good accessory, whether it be jewellery, shoes or a watch, and I like a nice belt. I like a really nice pair of shoes. I like a nice pair of designer sunglasses. That's what I spend money on and I'm in a position where I can do that. I'd rather spend that money on a designer accessory than an overpriced T-shirt that I'm going to rip in a week or get covered in makeup.

Since my wedding ring's off – good fucking riddance! I threw it in a lake – I splashed out and got a really great rose gold bracelet and matching ring from Cartier. And recently I bought myself a new watch from Audemars Piguet. When I start a new job, I'll get a new pair of shoes that I'll wear for that job. I do love a pair of Chelsea boots, usually black or sometimes maybe tan or cream, and I will spend good money on a pair of boots because I wear them all the time and they last. I often wear black suede Chelsea boots by Louboutin – hark at me with my Louboutins! And I love YSL black Chelsea boots. I've bought the same pair of shoes about eight times over, the Louboutins or the YSL ones with the straps, and I've got some posh trainers too, like Dior Nikes. Thinking about it, I could give old Carrie Bradshaw a good run for her money – I've got A LOT of shoes.

And I've got A LOT of belts. I like a nice designer leather belt, because I will wear it for years. I got myself a Gucci one, and I like a Louis Vuitton or Hermès number, too. And same with my sunglasses; I've got so many pairs of designer sunglasses, because I think a pair of good glasses can make all the difference. My whole outfit will cost pennies and then I'll be walking about with a £300 pair of glasses on, but as long as I don't lose them, or have my mum walk off with them, I know I'll have them forever. But I really don't buy myself loads of stuff. If anything, I spend more on things for my house – shit that I don't actually *need*, but that I will get a notion about. Like building an actual train station and bus stop on the drive outside my house.

So, I don't have a favourite designer, but I definitely have a look I like to go for. Over the years I've learned what suits me. I've got my casual look that I like, which is just the same skinny jeans I've always worn and a T-shirt. And I suppose you could say that over the last decade in public, I've developed my 'signature look' – which basically is just a slightly sleeker version of my casjh combo – black skinny jeans, a plain white or black shirt or T-shirt and black Chelsea boots.

Then weirdly, over the last year, I've started to dress slightly differently again. I've had the urge to zhuzh myself up and be a bit more 'out there', you might say, but really only for work. Rather than just wear the same old suit, or my standard black shirt and black blazer combo, I'm now starting to wear things which are a little bit more like my old style, but updated to be more 'me'. In Turin at Eurovision, for example, I really felt like being more flamboyant. So, I got *The Great British Sewing Bee* finalist Raph Dilhan to make a load of outfits for me. I gave him a sketch of what I wanted, he came and took my measurements, we talked about the fabrics and looked at swatch samples, then he went away and ran them up. And they're beautifully sewn and finished, really gorgeous work. We make a good team and Raph's going to make some more outfits for me for various award ceremonies I've got coming up. If I'm going for a proper showy, 'out there' look, I like to get something custom-made because otherwise, to find unusual off-the-peg pieces online, I really have to dig. Normally, for my more extravagant clothes, I'll look to Japan. I'll track down some random crazy designer who's made some outrageous blazer that fucking lights up, or something like that.

One thing that's always been the same is my hair and the fact that I've always dyed it. I've never tried to hide the fact that I'm naturally a ginger, though actually it would be more accurate to say that it was a dark auburn. Whatever, I always fucking hated it. As I said, in my teens I tried to bleach it blond, so those were the orange years. But then by the time I was in 4bidden in Ibiza, I'd sort of got the hang of it a bit better and I was more of a proper sun-kissed blond with darker roots showing through. Ten years ago, for my *X Factor* audition, I had long blond extensions that I'd actually had put in two or three days beforehand for something else. When I went back to boot camp, I lopped them all off and dyed my hair black. Was Barbie . . . now Ken. Halfway through the show, I went back to platinum blond and had it cut short, and then the following week went back to black. There was so much bleaching and dyeing going on that the whole midsection of my hair fell out. It had just been bleached, coloured, then bleached again and coloured, and it had been burned off by all the chemicals. To top it all, just after *X Factor*, I noticed I was going grey. I think it was the stress of it all. I went into the *Celebrity Big Brother* house and for the whole time I was in there, my hair looked exactly the same every single day because, since I'd lost so much of it and it was so short, I couldn't style it any other way. Half the time I hid it under a hoodie or this funny white beanie hat that I bought specially for that purpose. What a catch. Now my hair is in really good condition. Today, as I'm writing, it's very natural i.e. big and pouffy, but very glossy and soft and healthy, if I do say so myself. But I think if I let my hair dye grow out now I'd probably just be completely grey.

I've also always worn makeup. I started making myself up when I was in my late teens, though it was never a full face of makeup. I didn't wear full-on mascara and bright red lipstick or anything, but the same sort of makeup as I wear now – foundation, a touch of mascara and maybe a tinted lip using a nude matte lipstick. Makeup has always been something that I had access to and an interest in exploring, but it took me years and years to properly work it out – and bear in mind that after I left school I used to work in makeup as well, on the Benefit counter in Boots. Before that, I remember the first thing that I ever used was St. Tropez bronzing powder and it was so fucking orange it was disgusting. And it was only because one of my mates at school had it and I used to borrow hers. From that shaky start, I went on to Maybelline Dream Matte Mousse, which I'm sure every single person will remember. That was THE thing. As the ads said, it was a 'mousse revolution . . . with an amazing air soft feel'. It cost a fiver and it was a whipped mousse foundation that came in eleven shades. Everyone used it, but none of the shades ever matched anyone – especially NOT me, with my pasty ginger complexion. But we all still wore it and walked around with a massive makeup line underneath our jawline.

As I've grown older, I still wear foundation, because I hate my freckles. I know, I know! I should shut up about my pasty skin and be grateful for what I've got – i.e. a healthy body and a healthy outlook – and I really am trying to love myself and be comfortable in my own skin, but I would just love no freckles and that perfect even skin tone. Freckle removal is something that I always fret about. I'm sure there's probably permanent treatments I could have done that will make it all happen one sunny day, but I just don't know where. Though, as I said, as I get older I'm learning to live with what I've got. Ten years ago, I would mask absolutely everything, whereas now, I've gone for a sort of half-translucent 'barely there' approach with my makeup.

I'll still wear bronzer and maybe a bit of contouring, of course I do. And, of course, because I'm naturally a redhead,

I dye my beard as well. And because I have that very fair redhead complexion, I never appear in public without my fake tan, and then if I'm going out on a night out, yeah, I will wear a full face of foundation on top of that. I love reading all those celebrity 'What's in Your Makeup Bag?', 'beauty-secrets-of-the-stars' articles. So, for anyone who's interested, cos no fucker's ever been arsed to ask me, my very basic everyday routine is this:

If I'm leaving the house, I get up and it's coffee, cigarette, coffee, then I get in the shower. I'll use a face exfoliator and a cleanser on my face. Shampoo and conditioner. For my hair, I use L'Oréal professional products. And for my face, I go through phases, but usually something like a Harley Street Skin Care, BeautyLab or Dermalogica product.

I'll get out the shower and put Moroccan oil through my hair, when it's still wet. I use that almost like a blow-dry cream, you could say, so that it doesn't go too big when I dry it and style it – otherwise my hair is so thick it goes really BIG. My hair's dead straight as well, so it will grow straight up on top of my head like a giant quiff if I let it, but the Moroccan oil sort of tames it down and smooths it all out. Gives it a good shine. And then I dry it, which usually then makes it all go quite quiffy and pouffy, which it is right now, which I hate, but I'll get to how I deal with that later. Then I'll put on a skin serum and a moisturiser.

Next, I do my makeup: a foundation, a powder, eyebrow gel, contour, blush, lash mascara and then lipstick. I always wear a nudie-pink neutral lipstick that doesn't look like I'm wearing lipstick – and always matte, not gloss. Then I use a wet wipe to get any makeup out of my beard, eyebrows and hairline. Finally, I will brush my teeth, which as you can imagine is quite an effort because that is a lot of tooth surface to cover. I always brush my teeth last, I don't know why. And then finally, finally, I will get a hair cream, a smoothing cream or something like that, and I run my hands through my hair with that and then just a spritz of hairspray. I don't use gel, I don't use wax, I don't use anything like that, I just use a bit of smoothing treatment to tamp down the hideous pouffiness. Then that's it, I'm done, I'm out. And I can do all of that in ten, fifteen minutes, max. And it's so easy.

Genuinely, I think people would look at me and think I'm really high maintenance and that I take hours to get ready, and I'm really not. The truth is, if I really want to be, I can be out of the shower, fully made up, ready and in the car in less than ten minutes.

I'm a very simple bloke in truth. I have my makeup artist Bernice for any telly work, cos for that you need a professional. And I get my eyebrows done, though not as often as I should. Apart from that, in terms of my everyday beauty and grooming, I prefer to do everything myself. I don't have spray tans; I fake tan my body myself. In fact I do it all myself: I colour my own hair, I colour my own beard, and I do my own hair and sort the beard out for telly.

As I said, I started out in hair colour years ago, my first ever job as a junior, so I just do it myself and use a black hair colour. I started to learn but never properly qualified or anything, but I will cut my mum's fringe, for example. It's not difficult. Of course, I should say that people shouldn't really play with things like hair colour if they don't know what they're doing. **DISCLAIMER: DO NOT TRY THIS AT HOME!** But it's not rocket science. I don't cut my own hair, though, or at least not often, just sometimes. I've got a guy called Bradley who cuts my hair. He's Bernice's friend. I'll have it cut once every five to six weeks, which I think is maybe a bit too long between trims. And I do like getting a good haircut with Bradley. It just perks you up. Also, when mine grows out it gets so thick I can spend half an hour trying to fucking dry it. When it's shorter it just feels so much lighter and nice when I wash it. But I don't care too much, I just get a trim when it gets unbearable. And I don't bother with all the beard-grooming malarkey. I just shave it and tint it, then that's it. I've never used beard oil or anything like that, though I guess I should. But I don't. Never have. I've got fragranced beard oils but it's just something I always forget to do in my ten-minute routine. Genuinely, I'm not as groomed as people think I am.

I used to get a lot of stick about wearing my foundation, but I think nowadays it's no longer a big deal for men to wear makeup. I mean, I know loads of typical straight blokes that will wear concealer, or borrow their girlfriend's bronzer, or use their wife's fake tan. There's been such a big change since I started out and there's much less stigma around men looking after themselves and wanting to look their best, even with 'additions'. But then there's always this thing with these so-called 'men's makeup' lines. That always winds me up. Jean Paul Gaultier did one and Armani, and there are now several brands such as MMUK and War Paint for Men, for example, 'designed for men by men'. It's all complete and utter bullshit. It's exactly the same product as the women's ones, only with all this butch black packaging. So, for example, there's a really good serum for the face from one of the big cosmetic brands. I get the women's version, which costs £22 for 100ml. But for just 70ml of the men's serum, exactly the same product made by the same company, it will cost you £25. Basically, if you're too embarrassed to go to the counter with a woman's product and you're duped into getting the macho man's version, you're just paying an extra £3 for it to be black and smaller.

If men feel more comfortable with that, that's absolutely fine, but it's not as if the packaging for the women's product comes in some fucking bright pink bottle, it's just a perfectly neutral-looking blue. That's where targeting really works, but people just don't realise that it's exactly the same product. And I think men do fall for it – the same way they fall for Lynx deodorant, or Bulldog moisturiser 'for men', rather than Sure or Dove or whatever.

Still, especially when it comes down to men and grooming, we're miles away now from where we were in 2012. It really does feel like a decade of change. When I was growing up, I remember people referring to aftershave as 'poof juice'. I think in the past that wearing an actual scent, rather than a dash of cologne, was maybe an exclusively 'gay' thing. But male scents are almost the norm now. Why would any man not want to smell nice? And, almost above and beyond makeup and what I wear, fragrance is MY thing. Everyone knows me for how I smell. I would not go to the shop without a fragrance on.

A lot more men are now taking a lot more care of their skin and spending time on their appearance. Take my brother, for instance. Jamie is the most stereotypical east London bloke, and he has just gone and had an Invisalign brace fitted to fix his teeth. And this is the same bloke who took the piss out of me for getting my Hollywood smile!

That transition from the real hard 'blokey' bloke and what I would call the modern twenty-first-century man is quite dramatic. You know, ten years ago, no one ever used to give a shit about eyebrows. I mean, women might pluck their brows, but I didn't know many men who really bothered with that, and none of us had heard of 'threading'. But the growth in the eyebrow industry is just crazy, they're the biggest thing now. And the bigger the better. Like a lot of these trends, I think we have the Kardashians to thank for this. I mean, I remember when people started first talking about threading eyebrows instead of plucking them. My mum's eyebrows are plucked to within an inch of their life. She's only got about four eyebrow hairs left, whereas now it's about big, bushy, hard, defined lines. I've always had my eyebrows done, though. Call me a trend-setter, but even before I went on telly, I'd have them shaped and tinted. Now I have a woman called Rebecca who comes to do my brows. I go for an HD brow, a Bang Bang – that's what I like as an eyebrow – so they're tinted, waxed, threaded, plucked. Mind you, at the minute I haven't had them done for fucking ages and I'm badly in need of a bit of a groom in that department, but I'm growing them out, that's why. I'm going to go for a bit of a fuller brow, a bit more bushy, a little bit of a Cara-Delevingne-meets-Brooke-Shields look.

But now everybody knows – blokes included – that the eyebrows are the picture frame of the face. According to Bernice, along with every other makeup artist I've worked with, the eyebrows are the single most important thing. And you only need to look on telly to see how many men now get their eyebrows seen to. It's the same with makeup and the way people do their makeup – with things like contouring and highlighting, that has also changed so much. Before, people would just put bronzer all over their face and maybe a bit of blusher, that was it. Now it's all about straight lines and angles with your contouring. The way some people use contouring makeup, it's almost like trickery.

Obviously, some of these trends come from America, and from Instagram and makeup bloggers, but in terms of fashions or attitudes towards men's makeup and grooming in particular, I think a lot of that is influenced by reality TV. With shows like *The Only Way Is Essex*, and in particular *Love Island*, we see the men taking really good care of their appearance and, for good or bad, I think that's rubbing off on all blokes. Again, call me Mr Ahead-of-the-Curve, but it is something I've always tried to do, and I've been ridiculed for it in the past. But I'm a firm believer that if you're not happy with something and you wanna change it and you're in a position to change it, then fucking change it. Fuck what everyone else thinks. If you want a tit job, get a tit job, if you can afford it. If you want your teeth done, get your teeth done, if you can afford it. It's as simple as that.

I think a load of blokes are now sitting there thinking, 'well you know it's not a bad thing if I have my teeth straightened, it's not a bad thing if I put a bit of tan on every now and again.' I honestly do think that in that sense, the modern man has finally come of age.

I've made no secret of the fact that I've had 'work' done to change my appearance. I mean, as well as the obvious things, like the new teeth, the fake tan, foundation, and the colour of my hair, I've had Botox. I've had fillers. I've had my lips done. I get facials and I have someone to sort out my eyebrows. The first thing I had done, when I was about twenty, was get lip filler and a bit of Botox, just because I'd always wanted to get it done. I've always looked at those 'tweakments' as a preventative measure rather than a cure. The way I see it, why wait to start having Botox until I'm in my forties or fifties to try and correct really deep lines, when I can start preserving what I've got now? That way, I might not get those deep frown lines, what they call your elevens, in the first place. So, why fucking not? For the time being, for me, that's it though: new teeth, tick; fillers, tick; lips, the occasional filler, tick.

But I also think you can sometimes go too far. In the past, I've gone way too far with my makeup, the first set of new teeth, maybe, the size of my lips, and some of my more lurid looks and outrageous outfits. Again, I've had a bit of a new start where all that's concerned. Every now and again, I still might have the odd facial treatment, maybe a derma-peel or a hydra-peel facial, or a microneedle treatment, but not often. I'm lucky because apart from the freckles, I have pretty good, clear skin. I get the odd spot now and again, but never a great big throbbing monstrosity. And, thank God, I never got them as a teenager, which was strange. So many of my friends had really bad acne at school, and God, that can be traumatic. But then, at the end of the day, I was ginger and gay. I didn't need the spots as well. Jesus Christ! I mean, give the boy a chance.

Now with my appearance, I feel I've found a good balance between Ross and Rylan. Today, writing this, I'm sitting here in a pair of jeans and an Abercrombie T-shirt. I've not done my hair, I've hardly got any makeup on, and that's fine. Couldn't give a fuck. But then next week when I'm at an awards ceremony, I might be in a custom-made fitted cape with a gold waisted belt. That's the difference.

There have been behavioural changes as well, in terms of my own personal take on modern masculinity. As a young boy, realising that I was gay, maybe I moulded myself to be what I *thought* a gay man was. Growing up, I would be the one with the girls, pretending to be the Spice Girls. But at the same time, I would happily have played football with the boys. I just didn't. I enjoyed singing and dancing, and I wasn't naturally very good at football. I didn't mind it, but didn't love it. Being so tall, I was better at netball and I was really good at rounders and gym. Anyway, I went to a rugby school, but it wasn't for me, so I used to literally put the ball on the ground and give it to the other team. I just thought, 'Fucking take it, then. I'm not going to wrestle you for it.' The rest of my teammates hated me: 'Clarky, what you doing that for?' I just didn't wanna play. I don't mind watching rugby, I wouldn't mind marrying a rugby player, but no. That's as far as it goes for me.

Then ten years ago, I was put in a box and I played up to the camp stereotype. And fair play to me, because ultimately that's what put me on the map. But when I look at clips of me from back then, that's really not *me*. It doesn't even sound like me. Don't get me wrong – I'll be the first up on karaoke, fucking hell, of course. Yes, I'll wear some crazy outfits. And obviously, I wear makeup. I tick a helluva lot of boxes for the old stereotype. But then there's a lot of boxes that most people do not fucking know about.

As I've said, I have to do a job, and I do it properly, but over these last ten years, when I'm at work I've worked really hard to try and be more and more who and what I genuinely am when I'm at home. Less polished, less perfect, more 'Ross'. On the whole, I think I've got the right balance. That's why people are shocked when they actually meet me for the first time. They tell me that in real life I am nothing like they thought I was going to be. As I said, I speak differently; my voice is a lot lower than people expect. I stand differently and I'm a lot more boyish than people imagine. And I get on really well with straight blokes – I mean really 'laddy' straight blokes. I never went there before, just because I thought I couldn't. But I'm more comfortable around that environment now, because I realise it's no threat. It's not like I've got to impress straight lads, or *feel* that I have to impress them. I mean, straight men in general are a lot more accepting of me personally, because within two seconds of meeting me, they know I'm not trying to fuck them. Of course, sometimes I'm up for the odd bit of flirty, dirty innuendo, but that's all part of my banter. And, well, I'll do that even when I'm not at work, because I'm just normal.

Being out and gay is a lot more normalised now, but it's not all happy, clappy, waving rainbow flags all the way. Far from it. That's where social media comes in. As I wrote about in chapter six, basically anyone can be anyone, and can say whatever the fuck they want. And that can be a good thing but also a bad thing. I hardly ever get any homophobic comments or treatment in real life, only online. I get the odd comment and I just think, 'Are you on drugs? What year do you think this is? I mean, it's 2022 and the United Kingdom we're living in, not the 1950s!'

I think the modern man in general now, whether he's single, married, gay, straight, or whatever, really doesn't give a fuck what anyone else is up to in the bedroom. He's someone who's comfortable thinking, 'I'll wear this if I bloody want to.' Absolutely, and if he wants to get his eyebrows shaped, or wear foundation, it's not some kind of failing of his masculinity. He's someone who doesn't really give a shit what someone's wearing, he just wants to enjoy himself and look after himself. Because maybe, hopefully, masculinity means something different today. And I think it took us a long while to get here. I'm just glad I can say I was ahead of the curve.

Put it this way: the blokes that used to take the piss out of me in the early days – about my teeth, grooming and the things I'd wear, the things I was interested in, my confidence, my outgoingness, the music I liked – are now doing it themselves.

I mean, I see you having a little dance to Steps there, so don't fucking start!

Rylan's makeup and beauty secrets

- **Tired and puffy eyes?** Here's my top tip: I always get haemorrhoid cream in my weekly shop. No, not for that – to put under my eyes. It's very good for tightening under the eye area and depuffing tired eyes. I'm not fussy about the brand, any of them will do: Anusol, Preparation H, Germoloids . . . And actually the one I usually get doesn't smell like you think it might. It smells really nice. It's a bit clinical and coconut-y, sort of medicinal, so you know it's actually doing something. That's a great old makeup artists' trick.

- **Eyebrows.** This one's courtesy of my friend Bryony Blake who works at *This Morning*. She said, 'Rylan, eyebrows are the picture frame of the face, and they should be sisters, not twins.' In other words, your eyebrows shouldn't look completely identical, because when they are, if something else on your face isn't entirely symmetrical, it stands out more. Good tip, thank you, Bryony.

- **Always use a good primer and a good foundation.** Put it this way, doing good makeup is like being an architect. Think of your face as a building: as long as you've got a good foundation, you can put whatever shit on top of it and it will stand up. So, you can spend 2p on a bronzer, 3p on a blusher and 1p on a lipstick – it will look good as long as you've got a good fucking foundation underneath. But use a shit foundation and it all falls off.

- **My go-to primer:** for me, it's either Mac Prep + Prime, or Hylamide HA Blur.
- **My go-to foundation:** even though it's not expensive, Max Factor's Lasting Performance is a really good everyday foundation. It gives really good colour and really good coverage for the day. And bear in mind I've used foundations that cost a hundred quid, but I still always reach for this one because I love it – I'm 109: Natural Bronze.
- **For a night-time foundation** I like Charlotte Tilbury's Airbrush Flawless. And then whatever you put on top doesn't matter. I don't mind Laura Mercier either – they do a good under-eye concealer.
- **Don't forget your neck and your ears.** One day, a LONG time ago, I noticed that my ears were really pink-y red, compared to my cheeks. So now I always put foundation on my ears. And down my neck, *naturellement*, just to make it look even and avoid the tell-tale jaw-line problem.
- **Save money on the rest.** You don't necessarily need to spend thirty quid on a mascara; a bog-standard two-quid mascara from Superdrug is going to do pretty much exactly the same job: Maybelline, Max Factor, Boots No7, any of them. I couldn't give a fuck.
- **Use a setting spray** if you're going on a big night out. It stops your makeup just slipping off halfway through the evening. And I always use a translucent foundation press powder to put over my liquid foundation just to set it.
- **The perfect nude lip.** For my 'no makeup' lipstick look, it's got to be Charlotte Tilbury Runway Royalty or Victoria Beckham Girl.

- **Makeup brushes.** I use three brushes: a stipple brush for my foundation, a powder brush for my powder, and a blusher brush for blusher. And that's it. That's all I want. Three brushes.
- **Always wet your sponge.** If you use a beauty blender for your foundation, run it under the cold tap, give it a squeeze so it's full of water, turn the water off, then squeeze all the water out. It blends better when wet. Don't ever use it dry. That's what I use sometimes for foundation instead of a brush if I want it really much heavier.
- **Nostril hair and hay fever.** I use a nose-hair trimmer thing. Or you can get that black-cherry wax. You get a ball of it on a little stick and shove it up your nose, wait, then whip it out, and it looks like a little hedgehog with all your nostril hairs on it. But I don't do that often because you're supposed to have some little hairs up your nose to stop hay fever and pollen and shit. I suffer badly from hay fever so I have to get the injection every year. Also, a little trick is to put some Vaseline inside your nose if you suffer from hay fever because it grabs the pollen before it goes up.
- **Use bronzer on your eyelids.** It makes the whites of your eyes look whiter.
- **'No makeup' mascara.** If you don't want to look like you're wearing mascara, place the mascara brush just on the outer edge of your lashes, blink once and that's it. Don't put any on the inner corner of the eye. It will still give you a defined eye but won't look like you're wearing mascara.
- **Holiday lashes.** I sometimes get my eyelashes tinted – not all the time, but it's handy if I'm going to be on

holiday with the family in Spain and I'm in and out of the pool. I've got quite long lashes so when they are tinted it looks like I'm wearing mascara.

- **Eyebrow hack.** If you run out of eyebrow gel, a lick of Vaseline does the trick.
- **Cleaning your brushes.** It's terrible, but I like a dirty makeup brush. You're supposed to clean your brushes, but I will only clean my brushes probably once a month. I love a dirty brush. For me it's like one of those frying pans that you're not supposed to wash so it builds up the perfect patina. It's disgusting. But I hate a new brush.
- **Always have a clear, transparent makeup bag.** It's so much easier. You can actually see where everything is instead of fucking rummaging through for hours to find your lipstick.

LESSONS WE'VE LEARNED . . .

Bernice Cole

Friend/Makeup artist – Team Rylan

I met Ross back in 2010, when I had been booked to do hair and makeup for a judge on a local talent show. Rylan was also a judge on the panel and once he knew I was there he obviously wanted to get in on the glam. From that first day we met, I was with him throughout his X Factor journey. In fact, his famous blond locks were actually my hair extensions that he nicked! He always had a vision, which of course I got dragged into somehow. I even helped him make his outfits for Bootcamp. I vividly remember taking a call from him once he had landed after he'd got home from Judges' Houses. I asked him how he'd got on and if he'd cried, to which he replied, 'A little bit, yeah.' Slight understatement!

As lots of friends do, due to busy lives, we drifted a little for a few years, still keeping in touch but not seeing each other like we used to. Then in 2019 I got a call asking if I could come and do Linda's hair and makeup for Celebrity Gogglebox. After the filming, I stayed and we chatted for ages. I've basically been a part of 'Team Rylan' ever since.

Obviously, as everyone knows, the past couple of years have been pretty hard for Ross and seeing one of my closest friends go through all that pain and upset was heartbreaking. In a very strange way, being there for him through that awful time has made our friendship stronger than ever. Watching him build himself back up from where he was has made me forever proud of the person he is becoming, and now I'm seeing glimmers of the boy I met back on that talent show all those years ago.

As much as I have been there for him, equally he has done the same for me. If I am ever having a tough time, he is always my voice of reason and my shoulder to cry on. It's kind of like we think so similarly, but when we are having a 'moment' we also need each other to calm the other down. We are more than friends now. We are sisters.

Our professional relationship is quite different. Ross truly is amazing at what he does, and I can guarantee on pretty much every job we do together that someone will always be singing his praises and telling me how there's no one like him to work with! I'd like to think part of that is because behind the scenes I'm constantly on his case, running around trying to get him organised and sat down for his glam, probably arguing over which fake tan to use! But he always shows up pristine, smiling and ready to go, smelling unreal as well. Working on some truly iconic shows has been an absolute blast and getting to do that with your best friend is even better. I really am a lucky girl!

Ross is always so quick to give compliments, and being around him has made me realise that being kind and friendly is so, so important. Turning up to a job and introducing yourself, always saying, 'Hi, how you doing?' sounds so small, but the number of people that don't do that! He always has time for everyone and likes to make them feel good – that's probably why so many people think so highly of him and love him so much.

The past few years have been a whirlwind of hard work, laughs, and ups and downs, but one thing is for sure – not a day goes by when I don't get to see Ross for the truly beautiful person he is, inside and out.

The lesson I feel we have learned together is that you should always be kind, no matter what. Kindness really does go such a long way. And always be you. Don't change yourself for anyone!

Finally, even after ten years, I'm afraid that the one thing we still disagree on is . . . makeup brushes. He will never convince me to keep his makeup brushes dirty, even if he is adamant you get a better application.

Sorry babe, Bernice xxx

19

RYLAN FOR PM

You never thought I'd last this long . . .
Just wait till I'm running the country

Well, they say a week is a long time in politics . . . and what a week this one has been. Today as I write this, it's Thursday, 7 July 2022, and it's funny because when I first drafted this chapter we still had a cabinet and a prime minister in Number 10 Downing Street. Now everything is up for grabs. And maybe, once people read my proposed ministerial cabinet below, maybe Rylan for PM isn't so far-fetched after all.

I've always been fascinated by politics and the goings-on in Westminster, but ever since Brexit I've really got into the mechanics of it all. And Jesus, when I genuinely think I could do a better job than the current, or should I say ex-administration, well that's a fucking worry. It's bloody ridiculous what's been going on in those murky corridors of power.

Just spend an hour watching BBC Parliament and you'll know what I'm talking about. It's such a load of bollocks, I love it! Have you ever sat there and watched it on a Wednesday? It's hil-*ar*-ious. Labour MP Dawn Butler sitting there, every two minutes telling the Tory front bench to shut up. She's my favourite. She never fails to let the old po-faced House of Commons mask slip. Jess Phillips is another one – what a trooper. How Prime Minister's Questions is not a primetime show on terrestrial TV I have no idea. I've never seen more liars in one room! It's better than any episode of *Love Island*.

Under my watch, it would be a very different story, I tell ya. But for now, that's all I'm going to reveal about life under Prime Minister Rylan. You'll just have to wait until I formally throw my hat in the political circus ring, because you may have noticed that I've always been very private about my personal political preferences. I can give opinions and sort of make things known, but you won't know if I've voted for the Green Party, or for Labour, the Tories, or the Monster Raving Loony Party – or if I haven't voted for anyone – because I've never publicly said who or what political party I support. I happily would, but obviously because I'm a BBC employee I'm not allowed to even hint at it. And I don't think that my views are obvious, or at least I hope that's how it comes across.

My *Big Brother's Bit on the Side* training was very handy in that respect. Back then I always had to be impartial when it came to talking about housemates, and I think that's now the case for everything else I do. I prefer to be impartial anyway, because it's not my job to express any bias. I think it's a distraction from the art, or the performance or whatever, when you know how an actress, a singer, a comedian, or whoever, votes. It can't help but affect how you experience their work – unless, of course, they're a political artist, like a Bruce Springsteen or a Billy Bragg, say. That's different.

You know, people always scoff when I talk about politics publicly. And I'm the first to admit that in many ways I am extremely superficial. I mean, I must be pretty fucking shallow to care about my freckles and get all the tweakments I do. But just cos I've always got to have a full face of foundation and a year-round fake tan, don't ever think that I've got nothing inside my skull, because I can talk almost anyone under the table about politics. Obviously, I'll always get the arseholes saying, 'What the fuck does he know? *X Factor* reject.' I say,

'Bollocks to that', because it's probably a lot more than most of them do.

In 2016 before the EU referendum, for example, I was due to interview Boris Johnson on *This Morning*. Then I found out that he had threatened to pull out because his advisers heard that I was standing in for Phillip Schofield that day. Apparently they thought I wasn't 'qualified enough' to ask him questions. Obviously, *This Morning* didn't tell me this, and I am sure it wasn't Boris who said it; it was probably someone on his team, and I did eventually interview him, but how do they know if I'm qualified or not?

It was exactly the same problem when I was announced as the presenter of Channel 4's *Alternative Election Night* in 2019. People were saying, 'Why the fuck is he hosting the election?' – again, apparently I wasn't 'qualified' to host the election coverage. And again, BOLLOCKS TO THAT!!! I actually like the snobbery. I love the fact that people underestimate me, because there is nothing I love more than proving people wrong. And that's exactly what I have done for the last ten years.

I may not have gone to Eton. I may have left school at sixteen with twelve GCSEs, but I've got one philosophy about that: just because some Oxbridge educated politician's got a piece of paper that tells you he can do it, well, I can do it with my eyes shut without the piece of paper. My mouth can talk me out of anything. If I was ever out of work, I could get a job. Anywhere I wanted. If I wanted to work in politics, I'd do that. I don't need another piece of paper; I know if I got the chance I could stand in Parliament and talk the opposition round to my way of thinking. That's the way I look at it. And I guarantee I would wipe the floor with any frontbencher.

All I will say about my politics, and any potential future election manifesto, is that I think it's time for party-less politics. I say let's get rid of all the parties – Labour, Conservative, Green, Lib Dem, SNP, DUP, Plaid Cymru, independents, whatever, I don't care. Let the civil servants get on with their jobs, and have a parliament working together. Voters would be represented in such a parliament by politicians from and working for each constituency; people coming together and hashing things out, not all these clashing groups marching to different drums. I actually think that a bit of challenge among the ministers might help the government mechanism give better results. If things continue as they are, I don't think it will be long. I reckon within the next ten years we will have a Prime Minister that isn't the norm, someone that hasn't had the Eton upbringing and isn't the staunch Labour stalwart either. It will just be someone normal. And you never know, maybe that person will be me.

So, here's the question: would you vote for me, babe?

RYLAN for PM

Would you vote for me, babe?

(✔Tick as appropriate)

☐ **Yes**

☐ **Absofuckinglutely**

MY FANTASY CABINET

Deputy Prime Minister – Claire from Steps
Secretary of State for Justice – Rob Rinder
Chancellor of the Exchequer – Martin Lewis
Secretary of State for Foreign, Commonwealth and Development Affairs – Sam Ryder
Minister for Women and Equalities – Victoria Beckham
Secretary of State for Levelling Up – Jess Phillips
Secretary of State for Defence – The Wealdstone Raider
Secretary of State for the Home Department – Kelly Hoppen
Secretary of State for Health and Social Care – Joe Wicks
Secretary of State for Environment, Food and Rural Affairs – Gordon Ramsay
Secretary of State for Transport – Francis Bourgeois
Secretary of State for Digital, Culture, Media and Sport – Alison Hammond
Secretary of State for Northern Ireland – Eamonn Holmes
Secretary of State for Scotland – Lulu
Secretary of State for Wales – Joanna Page as Stacey
Speaker of the House – Rustie Lee
Night Czar – Lizzie Cundy

20

THE NEXT TEN

This time in ten years I'll be . . .

And just like that . . . a decade has passed. Has it felt like ten years? Yes and no. Would I change anything? Genuinely, no. If I tried to change a thing then maybe I wouldn't be where I am today. A lot has happened, career-wise and personally. Some of it has been amazing, some devastating, but every single thing was *supposed* to happen. I know that now. I've learned so many lessons, a million probably. But I can honestly say that FINALLY, after a decade, I've realised that there is only really one basic lesson – and I know it will be the biggest one I'll ever learn: look after yourself, be happy and enjoy life. I'm not fully there yet, but I will be. I know I will.

I made the mistake of finishing my last book with the words: 'And they lived happily ever after . . .' So this time I'll just conclude my reflections on this last decade with the following: here's to the next ten! x

My bucket list for the next ten years:

There's just one thing on my list . . .

• Be happy ☐

I can't wait for the day I tick this box.

POSTSCRIPT

Ten and Counting . . .

SO much has happened since the hardback publication of TEN at the end of September 2022. About a week later, a month to the day before my seven-year wedding anniversary, was the day of my Decree Absolute. I was officially divorced. So that was that. Officially single again.

Fast forward to January 2023, it was all over the papers: 'Rylan says he's ready to date again.' I went on a date with one guy. Good looking, nice bloke – well, I thought so at first. It was going really well. Then I got a bit pissed on a night out with him, forgot where I was and, next day, a picture came out of us kissing in the street. I was so embarrassed. I thought it was all on me, so I messaged him and said I was sorry, it was a hazard of my profession, I wasn't being left alone at the time, if anyone found out I was with someone, people would try to get photos of us together. He wasn't the least bit bothered though, and we went out on more dates. It happened again – same thing: 'candid' picture of us out together. Then, long story short, I got reason to believe that the source of these pictures was closer to home.

Then I met that person, a maths professor, a *really* nice guy, someone who was totally *not* into the showbiz side of my life. We were total opposites in terms of our interests and, professionally, in completely different worlds, but that's what attracted us to each other. We dated for about ten weeks, and it was all going in the right direction. I really liked him and the feelings were mutual. But then one night, at the point where it was, like, this could potentially be a real thing, he told me he didn't think he could cope with the whole fame side of dating me, which I'm afraid would be part of the deal if we had gone full tilt into a relationship. I appreciate that, and I respect his honesty. But I was proper gutted. Because in another world, if I was working in Sainsbury's, say, or whatever – anything other than being famous and being Rylan – maybe the maths professor and I would still be together. We still talk, as mates, and I suppose that's something, at least.

And since the hardback came out, that, sadly, is my dating history so far. I've had the two opposite ends of the spectrum. And it sometimes feels like I'm never going to be able to find that balance in the middle.

However, BIG CONFESSION: there is a special someone. A man I met quite soon after my divorce and who I genuinely believe is my soulmate. When me first met, we just clicked, but we were both coming out of something long-term and the timing wasn't right. We were sort of seeing each other. But not seeing each other, if that makes sense. Anyway, we talked all the time, became very close. And then he met someone else and started dating, which was a proper kick in the gut. 'Ummm. Hello? I thought you didn't want a relationship? At least, that's what you told me!' It really threw me and I thought, 'Well, clearly, he simply didn't want a relationship with *me*.' And I went back to accepting that whatever we had was only a friend thing.

Since then, though, he's split up with the other person, and we're back in touch. Still as flirty 'friends'. But the thing is, *he's* not with anyone. *I'm* not with anyone. And we talk and message each other ALL THE TIME. I'm forever bullying him, saying, 'Come on then. When are we finally going to get it together and get married?' Now even Bernice, my makeup artist, is in on the act, messaging him, joking about when he's going to propose to me. But thing is, I'm serious. I *would* marry him, like, tomorrow. You know when you just *know*? Well, in my head and heart, I know I should end up with him. And I think he knows it too. He makes me laugh. I make him laugh. We've only got to say one word and we're in stitches. I've got my own thing going on. He's got his own thing going on. He truly don't give a fuck about my job, likes me simply for me, and I'm the same with him.

What I want to say, I suppose, is that I know he's always there for me, constantly, like a thread. When I was ill last year, he turned up one morning with a McDonald's breakfast for me. And I thought, 'Now, *that* one's a keeper.' I know he'd fit right into my life – my friends and my family would love him. His family would love me. I mean, how could they not? He's just gotta realise he ain't gonna get any better than me. Not in a big-headed way or anything, right, but he's got *the* dream man waiting for him to make the call. Seriously though, I doubt I would get better than him, and vice versa. And the more we carry on being how we are, if and when that day ever comes, that would be it. We'd be like a ready-made couple. It wouldn't feel unusual or weird in any way, or moving too fast. The hard 'getting to know each other' work's already been put in. I know I'd be happy with him. 100%. And while I don't like speaking for other people, I think he knows he'd be happy with me, too. We just GET EACH

351

OTHER. It's as simple as that. I wish we could stop fannying about and get on with it. But we live in different parts of the country, so aren't able to see each other as much as I'd like, and it feels like that endless cycle of 'just mates'.

Do I think we'll end up together somewhere down the line? In my heart of hearts, yeah, I do. I don't know how, when, or what that moment will be, but I do think one day we'll end up together, settle down and have that cuddle of a night. That's all I want. I don't know what the issue is with us both. He basically needs to get back to Essex, grow a pair of bollocks, stop fucking about and realise that he *should* be with me. He knows I'm here, and I'm ready for a relationship, and I would love it to be with him. And this is a message directly to him: at the time of publication, he might be with someone, I don't know. But one day, we'll see each other and I know the click will happen. And then we'll go, 'Right. OK, we're ready.' I think I'm ready now.

All that said, I'm happy with where I am. I'm in a good place. I'm really busy and that's a good thing. In terms of the rest of my life, work and all that, as you probably know, in early 2023, I left *Strictly It Takes Two*, which was a big decision because I absolutely fucking *love* Janette Manrara and I *love* that show. After *Big Brother* ended, it was the perfect job for me. I mean, five nights a week of live TV, working on the biggest broadcasting franchise in the UK? I was blessed. Why would I walk away from that? Well, I'd presented four series and I had a moment where I was like, 'You know what? I've been doing this job long enough now. For the last eleven years, all I've been known for is as a host on the sideshows.'

The thing is, over the past year or two, there's been a lot of telly opportunities where I thought, I would have been perfect.

And they hadn't approached me. Perhaps subconsciously, people in TV may have started to see me *only* in that role of 'side host'. And you know, without sounding like dickhead, I think I'm a *really* good live presenter. So, I suppose I felt it was time to take a bit of time away, pass the *It Takes Two* baton on to someone else, and, hopefully soon, take my step up to something that I can fully own. Not gonna lie, it was a wrench. But in my gut, I know it was the right thing for me to do. And it felt really empowering to be able to leave *on my terms*. I now know that I'm passing the baton to Fleur East and I wish her all the best of luck. She's going to have the best fucking time and I can't wait to watch the show as a viewer and see everyone that I know and love. And don't you worry, I have every intention of popping up there now and again, and going to the live shows to catch up with the whole gang on a Saturday.

Second big news update: again, as most of you will know by now, I won't be working on the ITV2 revamp of *Big Brother*. Obviously, as I said earlier, everyone knows how much I love that show, and I campaigned so hard for it to come back. And I had some meetings with the new team on the programme but, in short, they gave it to someone else.

They say everything happens for a reason. Well, maybe not getting the *Big Brother* job was the right thing to happen. Because in some ways I feel I am taken a bit more seriously with the work I do with the BBC on R2, *The One Show*, and previously on *Strictly*. And I can still be silly and funny and take the piss. I finished my *Big Brother* chapter last time saying that whatever happened, whoever gets the job, I wish them well. And that still stands: I wish you well.

My new lesson? Personally, to never get so invested in a show like that ever again. Because, ultimately, someone can click their fingers and you're not part of it anymore. I will never, ever again let myself fall that headfirst into something that isn't mine. Ever.

Meanwhile, in the middle of all that drama, in January 2023, somehow, suddenly, I owned a pair of hiking boots and was in training for a mountain expedition in the Scottish Highlands. How the fuck did that happen? Well, I was on a night out, a bit pissed, and Emma Willis's manager collared me. She said, 'Our Emma's doing the Big Red Nose Day Challenge for Comic Relief. She's climbing a mountain. Do you want to do it with her?' And I was like, 'Yeah, sure. Of course, I'll climb a mountain with Emma!' Well, I did say I was drunk – more accurately, I must have been off my face!

Next thing, I'm on a Zoom meeting with the whole of the Red Nose Day team who are thanking me for agreeing to take part in the 2023 challenge. And I'm like, 'Fuck! What have I signed up for?' Well, me, Emma and *Strictly*'s two-time glitterball winner Oti Mabuse were heading to the Highlands, tasked with attempting to summit Cairn Gorm, the sixth-highest mountain in the British Isles at 1,244.8 m (4,084 ft) above sea level.

I knew none of that at the time, though. Probably as well. Emma made it sound like it was gonna be like a little ramble up a hill. Truth is, being outside is not something I really *ever* want to do. I'm frightened of *everything* about 'the outdoors'. I'm scared of tents, the rain, snow, wind, cows, sheep, wild deer – all of it. But I couldn't let Comic Relief down. So there was no turning back.

8 February 2023, we got to the village of Braemar, right up in the north near Aberdeen, and it was hideous. We sludged our way through the foothills of the Cairngorms. Emma and

Oti and me were all really fit and well up for it, but the weather conditions were nightmarish, and we really, really felt it. One minute it was sunny, the next, we were in a snowstorm, battling against 70mph Arctic winds, snow and ice. As the sun set, we set up camp for the night and there we were, buffeted about in the freezing blizzard, trying to put up a tent. When we finally got inside, I snuggled down to find that my sleeping bag barely reached up to my waist. I had warm legs at least. Then at two o'clock in the morning, my inflatable mattress burst. So, I was literally laying shivering on the icy floor. And then my inflatable pillow sprang a leak too. I got zero sleep whatsoever. First thing the next morning, we had to pack up camp and set off for Day Two, and a further gruelling 20-mile ascent, or whatever the fuck distance it was, in rapidly descending sub-zero temperatures.

On the second night, miraculously, I did actually fall asleep. Then at three o'clock in the morning, I'm woken up by something rustling about outside our tent. I unzipped the door flap, stuck my head out in gale-force winds and there against the sky I could see like the silhouette of what I think was a deer. I was sat there, peering at it, trying to stay calm, when suddenly it fucking kicked out. This hoof was coming straight at me through the tent-flap. My heart nearly gave out. I thought, 'Oh my God, this is how I'm gonna die. I'm gonna get hoofed to death by a rampaging stag.' It was fucking horrendous. And Emma and Oti were fast asleep, blissfully oblivious to my near-death ordeal.

I can honestly say I've never more terrified or physically uncomfortable than up on that mountain. Partly because I didn't go to the toilet for like three days – there's no way I was doing *that* in the 'great outdoors'. But honestly, reaching that final goal and getting to the top of Cairn Gorm was magical. It was like, 'Oh, my God, I actually did this.' It really *was* a challenge and all three of us made it. It's something I would never have done a few years back, because nothing and no one, not even Comic Relief, could have persuaded me to go up a mountain and sleep in a tent. But you know, I'm all about trying new things now. And we also raised loads of money. I've done my karaoke marathon for Children in Need, conquered Cairn Gorm for Comic Relief. So, you know, I've done my good bit for charity now. If they ring again, I won't be answering the phone.

And then some things never change. I'm still loving my job at Radio 2 and Ka-RY-oke is going from strength to strength. Helen, Laura, and the team at Radio 2 have always got my back, and I always know where I stand with them. They're never frightened to let me have free reign, and do what I do best with minimal restrictions. I cannot thank them enough for the support that they showed me during the bad times, but also during the great times. Long may *Rylan on Saturday* continue . . .

Same goes for Eurovision. After our lovely Sam Ryder finished in second place after Ukraine's Kalush Orchestra in Turin in 2022, and the winning nation, obviously, unable to host, the UK took on hosting duties on its behalf. And Eurovision 2023 took us to Liverpool, the home of music. Being asked to be part of the BBC commentating team once more was amazing, and there was so much hype in the UK this time around Eurovision. I got to announce our act, Mae Muller, who's such a great girl, on Zoe Ball's BBC Radio 2 show. And then the promo for Eurovision started, and I got asked to be in an episode of *The Archers*. What could they possibly want with me in Ambridge? I was like, 'Really?

Like, what, *me* and Eddie Grundy down The Bull together?'
And then they explained the storyline, they were like, 'It's
a Eurovision thing. It's all part of the promotion. Do you
wanna do it?' And, again, I thought, 'You know what, why
not?' Then I find out it's quite prestigious, actually, to be in
The Archers – I mean, it's the world's longest running soap,
and people like HRH Princess Margaret, Queen Camilla, Sir
Terry Wogan and Judi Dench have famously all been 'special
guests', and so I thought, 'Shit. I'd better do a good job here!'

My storyline was that on my way to Liverpool, I stop off in
Ambridge where Linda Snell has invited me to judge the village's
Eurovision Variety Show. But my sat-nav goes on the blink, I
get lost and David and Ben Archer at Brookfield Farm come to
my rescue, offering to host me for the night . . .

I went up to BBC Birmingham to record my episode and it
was literally like stepping back in time. You can tell that the
way they record the programme hasn't changed in 70 years, the
actors standing around the mic, script in hand. Time came for
my first scene. I went into what is, in radio terms, the biggest
sound studio I've ever seen, and found myself walking across
the floor, that's completely covered in heaps of old VHS tape.
What the fuck? Turns out, apparently, it sounds like you're
walking on grass. Then I start speaking my lines: 'Oh hello,
sorry guys. I know I can't park here, but I'm a little bit lost
. . .' Then, the next thing I know, there's this woman, a mature
lady, shall we say, who I presumed was the studio assistant,
and she drops to her knees and starts crawling around on the
floor, panting and scratching my leg. And I'm looking down at
this woman, like, is she well? But everyone else was so casual
with it, carrying on with their lines, like this is completely
normal behaviour. Then I realized she's the dog – the sound
lady, I mean, playing a sheepdog. But no one had told me. I

thought the sound people added all the sound effects at post production! Fucking crazy.

As an acting debut, I was kinda thrown in at the deep end, but the Ambridge lot took me to their hearts, and I had a real blast. It's an honour to be able to say that I was in an episode of *The Archers* and the fact that my name has been added to their 'Wall of Fame' alongside the Queen, well, that's pretty cool.

Shortly afterwards, when me, Scott Mills, Hannah Waddingham and musician Julia Sanina, the Ukrainian host, launched Eurovision in Liverpool, I actually got to meet Queen Camilla and King Charles. They came to pay a visit behind the scenes of the arena and to turn on the stage. We were having a chat, as you do, with the King and Queen, when Queen Camilla said to me, 'I've heard you're doing *The Archers*.' She's a fan and still listens to it. I was like, 'Yeah, I've recorded my episode,' and not to be outdone, she said, 'You know, I've been on it too?'

King Charles was hilarious. He said, 'You've done Eurovision for quite a while now, haven't you?

How's this year going to be different?' And I said, 'Well, I can't be rolling around Liverpool 'til four in the morning, staggering in and out of clubs with different men every night, because people know who I am here.' And he laughed. I saw him again recently when I went to Buckingham Palace with The Prince's Trust. He said, 'Well, did you behave yourself in Liverpool?' I had to tell the truth . . . 'No,' I said.

So, we're up there, we've launched the whole razzmatazz, and then I started doing the interviews with all the acts, which for me is a real bonus, because I get to know all the artists really well before the live shows start. As always, I became best friends with the Irish lot, the boys from Wild Youth who took me out to an Irish pub. I was in there til three in the morning, dancing on the bar, pouring Guinness for everyone, my ONE big night out pre-Eurovision. It was so different, not like my normal Eurovision experience, because for me that normally means going abroad, doing a job that I absolutely love, being able to enjoy being Mr. Anonymous and generally having the time of my life. Well, you've read about my Eurovision exploits earlier, but in being Liverpool, obviously, *everyone* knows who I am. The whole world had descended on Liverpool and every single place I went, even coming out of my hotel, was like a minor mobbing. I felt like Beyonce!

In addition, in Liverpool, not only was I presenting for the BBC, but I was also working for the EBU (The European Broadcasting Union), doing all the master interviews for the Eurovision acts. So, that meant I was up there with my EBU hat on for an extra week without Scott. And it was completely surreal and meant I was sort of in this fabulous Eurovision bubble for two-and-a-half weeks, basically locked up in my hotel. Luckily though, I had some great people staying in my hotel, Käärijä from Finland, a strong favourite with his catchy 'Cha Cha Cha'; Marco Mengoni from Italy with the emotional 'Due Vite'; and Australian prog-rockers, Voyager, with the banging 'Promise'. All of us got on brilliantly.

Then when I say Eurovision week hit, it hit like a tornado. It was chaos as per usual, relentless. For the first time ever, the semi-finals were shown on BBC One. We all had to be really careful with how we dealt with the commentary, and me on my best behaviour, because firstly, we were on home turf; and secondly, because I was also working for the EBU, I couldn't be seen to be having favourites. Obviously, though, every year I do. Well, for me, 2023 was always going to be Sweden's year with Loreen, one of my favourite artists ever, who won the competition back in 2012 and was back with her entry 'Tattoo'. Oh, and to add to the madness, not only was I working for both the BBC and the

EBU, I was also hosting an extra episode of *The One Show* on the Saturday evening. So, on the night of the final, until 7.50pm, I was on air with Alex Jones, dressed in my full Grand Final finery, tight leather trousers and shimmery, sheer white top, complete with my new seven-inch black platform heels that I'd got signed the night before by Christian Louboutin himself (because he's a Eurovision fan and had come up there to watch the show.) I had exactly ten minutes to run from *The One Show* studio, through the Exhibition Centre, through Liverpool Arena, and up the stairs to the very top level to join Scott in our commentary box. I made it at 7.59pm, sat down, and started work.

And what a show, what a final. Much as I desperately wanted Mae to do well with 'I Wrote a Song', I was thrilled for Loreen. To be there for her triumph was incredible. But I really felt for Mae. I know she found it quite difficult because there was so much pressure following on from Sam Ryder's second place in Turin, but I'm so proud of how she performed. She's an absolute trooper and I know she's going to have a fantastic career.

And for me, I feel like the 2023 show changed the United Kingdom's view of Eurovision. The way that the BBC threw themselves into the ring, pulled out all the stops and staged a final on such a grand scale, it felt like it took over the whole nation. And I think it made viewers kind of wake up and realise that Eurovision really is quite a thing. I'm so glad that people got to see why we love it so much. And now our job is to keep that momentum going for next year in Sweden. Those Swedes live, breath and eat Eurovision, it's the spiritual home. Plus 2024 is the 50th anniversary of ABBA winning with 'Waterloo'. I've always wanted to do a Eurovision in Sweden, so that'll be quite a buzz.

So, what's next? I've got so many exciting new things in the works. It's been stupid busy. I've done a Grand Tour in Italy with Rob Rinder. I've done a show called *Sex Rated*, which is either going to be the end of my career, or will be quite enjoyable, I don't know. And I've also filmed and hosted Amazon's very first reality show in Greece. There's a lot in the pipeline. And still a little bit of fuel in the engine as well. I don't know where I'm going to be or what I'll be doing in a year's time, but it's very nice to be able to sit here now and do an update for this paperback because, while to make it to ten years in this business was staggering, to make it to eleven, feels even better. So, here's to years twelve, thirteen, fourteen, fifteen, sixteen, seventeen, eighteen, and nineteen . . . And hopefully one more at twenty. What's gonna happen in the rest of this next decade? Who knows, but I'm up for it. I can't wait to live it to the fullest.

I've still not quite managed to tick the box below, but I've got time. And I'm getting closer every day.

- Be happy ☐

THE INNER CIRCLE

Claire, still my sister, love her to bits. She's about to release her new album and I'm so happy for her. She's worked so hard on it, and I can't imagine her not being in my life.

Linda. What can I say about Mum? Linda is still Linda. She will always be Linda. Still checking in every day, nagging me about out the bins, coming in here with her fish, filling up my fridge with her stinking bags of whelks and what have you. Never, ever fucking leaves me alone. She'll be here in a minute, I'm sure. Long live Linda.

Nads. Since writing *Ten*, Nads has now moved out of management and is working at a digital company. I love him so much and miss him every single day, but he'll always be my best friend. And I'm so proud of him for following what he wants to do. He's happy, he's healthy, but I'm sure we'll end up back together very soon. I still chat to him all the time. He's another one, don't fucking leave me alone.

Jayne, my sister-in-law is fantastic. She's living her life with my brother. Her and Jamie have enjoyed a nice few holidays since the book first came out. Basically, they could be recording *Wish You Were Here*. And the kids, Harvey and Olivia, are all good. Still bleeding me dry, as usual.

Ruth, always and forever my TV mum. I know she's been through it looking after Eamonn as he's not been too well. But they're still the dream couple. Recently, I went over to see the pair of them and check out Eamonn's new chair lift, and well, needless to say, there is nothing like a Ruth and Eamon cuddle.

And then my **Bernice**, B, makeup maestro, my friend, my rock, what can I say? My partner in crime. The adventures we've had over the past year have been amazing and I couldn't do it with anyone else by my side.

ACKNOWLEDGEMENTS

I'll keep this brief as, surely, you're bored by now . . .

To Mummy:
Thank you for being there for me last year, I'm so sorry for what I put you through – no mother should ever have to see their child in that state. I wouldn't be here if it wasn't for you and I don't really have the words to say how much I love you. Thanks, Mum.
P.S. Text me when you're coming round just in case, yeah . . .

To my family:
I have to say the same as what I said to Mummy. Jamie, Jayne, Harvey, Olivia: thanks for being the best anyone could ask for. I'm sorry for what I put you guys through, but we got there. And to the rest of my family who supported my mum, I love you x

To my extended family:
Bernice, Nads, Holly, Claire, Ruth and Eamonn. You truly are genuine friends – we lose some along the way, but you guys are unfortunately stuck with me. I wouldn't want it any other way.

To my team:
Along with Holly and Nads, thank you to everyone on my amazing team at YMU. Minnie and Jess, welcome to the team, and you guys have been great helping me prep the book and everything that goes with it. The odd day off wouldn't go amiss . . . jokes. Amanda, thanks so much for all your help with the book. You're amazing at your job and I'm pleased we finally did this together. To the rest of my team – social, digital, brand – thanks for everything you do for me.

To the Seven Dials massive:
Vicky, well, thanks so much for putting up with me and my lateness . . . now you've read the book you understand why haha. You've been amazing, along with Francesca, Helena, Jen, Sarah, Nat, Claire and everyone else at Orion. Thanks for trusting in me and *Ten*. Rose, you diamond. I found this so much harder than my first book but you was there to pick up the pieces with me. Thanks for being a lovely woman, and I forgive you for breaking my dining room chair.

To Cinch:
You can be certain you've absolutely cinched it *whistle* . . . and we did. Since I joined the Cinch family, you have exploded. From TV to football, and festivals to radio, you're literally everywhere. And the team is always such a pleasure to work with. So I wanted to take this opportunity to also say a massive thank you to everyone at Team Cinch. Last year you gave me the time to heal and I know it pushed your schedules back, yet you still did it. Not many companies would have done that, but you did. So, to Avril, Nic, JoJo and everyone else at Cinch – thanks for being the best.

To those who have supported me:
If it wasn't for you guys buying the book, following me, being there to cheer me on, none of the last ten years would have happened; you mean so much to me and thank you for always being there. I'll try not to let you guys down.

To the people lost along the way:
Thanks for the memories.

Ross x

CREDITS

Seven Dials would like to thank everyone at Orion who worked on the publication of *Ten*.

Agent
Amanda Harris

Publisher
Vicky Eribo

Editor
Rose Davidson

Copy-editor
Amber Burlinson

Proofreader
Chris Stone

Editorial Management
Sarah Fortune
Tierney Witty
Jane Hughes
Charlie Panayiotou

Tamara Morriss
Claire Boyle

Audio
Paul Stark
Jake Alderson
Georgina Cutler

Contracts
Anne Goddard
Ellie Bowker

Design
Nick Shah
Joanna Ridley
Helen Ewing

Picture Research
Natalie Dawkins
Emily Taylor

Finance
Nick Gibson
Jasdip Nandra
Sue Baker
Tom Costello

Inventory
Jo Jacobs
Dan Stevens

Marketing
Helena Fouracre

Production
Sarah Cook
Katie Horrocks

Publicity
Francesca Pearce

Sales
Jen Wilson
Victoria Laws
Esther Waters
Group Sales teams across
    Digital, Field Sales,
    International and
    Non-Trade

Operations
Group Sales Operations team

Rights
Rebecca Folland

IMAGE CREDITS

Section 1

Page 1, Above and Page 2, Above – Fremantle / Simco Ltd

Page 3, Above – Getty Images / Tim Whitby / WireImage

Page 3, Centre – Getty Images / Mike Marsland / WireImage

Page 4, Above – Ken McKay / Shutterstock

Page 5, Above – Getty Images / Gareth Cattermole

Page 7, Above – Endemol Shine UK Limited

Page 7, Below – Courtesy of STV Studios / Matt Frost

Page 8, Above – Ken McKay / ITV / Shutterstock

Section 2

Page 1, Above – James Shaw / Shutterstock

Page 2, Above – Courtesy of Primal Media

Page 3, Above – Fremantle / Thames

Page 5, Above – Ray Burmiston / BBC Studios

Page 6, Top left – Mark Bourdillon / Love Productions

Page 6, Centre left – BBC Pictures

Page 6, Centre right – Dave J Hogan / Getty Images